The Japan That Never Was

THE JAPAN THAT NEVER WAS

Explaining the Rise and Decline of a Misunderstood Country

Dick Beason
Dennis Patterson

State University of New York Press

Published by
State University of New York Press, Albany

For information, address State University of New York Press
90 State Street, Suite 700, Albany, NY 12207

Production by Judith Block
Marketing by Anne Valentine

Library of Congress Cataloging-in-Publication Data

Beason, Dick, 1958–
    The Japan that never was : explaining the rise and decline of a misunderstood
country / Dick Beason, Dennis Patterson
        p.   cm.
    Includes bibliographical references and index.
    ISBN 0-7914-6039-8 (alk. paper).
    1. Japan—Economic policy—1945–1989.   2. Japan—Economic policy—
1989–   3. Japan—Politics and government—1945–1989.   4. Japan—
Politics and government—1989–   5. Industrial policy—Japan.   6. Structural
adjustment (Economic policy)—Japan.   I. Patterson, Dennis Patrick, 1953–
II. Title.

HC462.9.B375 2004
338.952—dc21   2003052607

10 9 8 7 6 5 4 3 2 1

CONTENTS

TABLES AND FIGURES

ACKNOWLEDGMENTS

The idea for this book began when we were students at the Inter-University (Stanford) Center for Advanced Japanese Language Studies in Tokyo. It was the fall of 1986 and a very exciting time to be living in Japan. We were both graduate students at the time, Beason in Economics at the University of Michigan and Patterson in Political Science at the University of California, Los Angeles, and we were looking for a way to understand Japan's postwar political-economic trajectory. It was the beginning of the economic bubble period and a time when many said that Japan had developed a political-economic model that allocated resources more effectively than in Western market economies and practiced democratic politics in a way that avoided the inefficient, parochial focus that is characteristic of other advanced nations. Japan, in the words of one proponent of this point of view, was a developmental state and differed substantively from the nations of the West.

We never accepted this label and all that it implied about Japan and, as a result, set off from our days as students in Japan to develop an alterative explanation that would possess two qualities in particular. First, our alternative explanation would have to subsume Japan's entire postwar trajectory and not be characterized by the temporal limits that one witnesses so often in the literature on postwar Japan. In other words, what explained the high growth period would also have to account of the current period of little or no growth and what explained the Liberal Democratic Party's electoral predominance should also explain its decline. Our explanation then would have to avoid the problem of saying that the troublesome developments of recent years in Japan are the result of something being fundamentally different in its political-economic system. Second, while focused on a specifically Japanese problem, our explanation must be informed by the concepts and methods of our respective disciplines, mainstream Political Science and neoclassical economics.

The result of this effort is the current volume, and, as in any effort of this type, we encountered a number of intellectual debts along the way that must be acknowledged. For Patterson, the bulk of these debts go back to graduate school days at UCLA where two professors were most influential. Hans Baerwald was an encouraging mentor who introduced the world of

Japanese politics and inculcated an appreciation of the details of Japanese politics. John Petrocik was an invaluable advisor who encouraged the analysis of Japanese politics in a way that informed our understanding of politics in other electoral democracies. Brad Richardson has been a friend and advisor who spent long hours, in both the United States and in Japan, discussing the details of Japanese politics. For Beason the same must be said of Gary Saxonhouse of the University of Michigan.

Parts of the work presented in this volume have appeared elsewhere. Parts of Chapter 3 were originally published as "Growth, Economies of Scale, and Targeting in Japan, 1955–1990." This article was co-authored by Dick Beason and David Weinstein in *The Review of Economics and Statistics,* copyright © by the President and Fellows of Harvard College and the Massachusetts Institute of Technology. Parts of Chapter 7 had their origins in two previously published articles. One part derived from the previously published article, "Electoral Interest and Economic Policy: The Political Origins of Financial Aid to Small Business in Japan." The information on this article is as follows: Dennis Patterson, *Comparative Political Studies* (27;) pp. 425–447, copyright © 1994 by Sage Publications, Reprinted by Permission of Sage Publications. Another part of this chapter originally appeared in the July, 2001 issue of *World Politics* as "Politics, Pressure, and Economic Policy: Explaining Japan's Use of Fiscal Stimulus Policies." Finally, parts of chapter 8 were derived from the doctoral dissertation that Patterson completed at the University of California, Los Angeles in 1995.

Many individuals and institutions supported us as we prepared various parts of this volume. The International Division of the Ministry of International Trade and Industry provided us with an office and access to library materials and many important resident officials as well as officials in the Ministry of Finance. This occurred during the summer of 1998, and we are grateful for the Ministry's generous support. We would also like to thank the Japan Studies Association of Canada which offered us many opportunities to present chapters from this volume while they were in various stages of development. The Japan Foundation of Toronto provided us with a very stimulating forum to present the basic argument of the book, and we would like to extend our thanks to that institution for its generous support. Michael Donnelley of the University of Toronto has commented on parts of the manuscript at various times, and we are grateful for his insights. The title of this book came from a suggestion made by John Hazewinklel when he was directing JCMU programs at Michigan State University. We are grateful to him for his suggestion.

Throughout the writing of this book, we decided to meet in places that were equidistant between our homes in Michigan and Alberta. This led to us gathering in such unexpected places as Bozeman MT, Bismark ND, and Winnepeg Manitoba, as well as the number of times we met in Japan to complete the chapters in this book. As a result, we were often absent from our homes for somewhat long periods. In light of this, we would like to thank our wives, Shelby and Mariko, and our families for putting up with these not infrequent absences. This volume would not have been possible without their support and understanding.

I. THE MISUNDERSTOOD COUNTRY

Chapter 1

THE JAPAN THAT NEVER WAS

Thanks to MITI, Japan came to possess more knowledge and more practical experience of how to phase out old industries and phase in new ones than any other nation in the world.

—Chalmers Johnson (1982)

Japan has complacently continued to protect its structurally corrupt and gangster ridden companies and has made only gestures toward holding anyone responsible.

—Chalmers Johnson (1998)

All of Japan's domestic policies serve the goal of building its industrial strength.

—Clyde Prestowitz (1988)

The arteries of Japan's economy are presently so clogged that all the standard stimulus measures have little effect except in massive doses that tend to further distort the economy . . . Unfortunately, there is no sign that Japan's leaders are preparing to grapple with this problem or even that they recognize its nature.

—Clyde Prestowitz (1998)

As the postwar period progressed, the political-economic system of Japan received an increasing amount of scholarly attention from both Japan specialists and nonspecialists alike.[1] Initially, the motivation behind this growing intellectual attractiveness was the desire to explain Japan's postwar success, that is, its remarkably high levels of economic growth combined with perhaps the most stable and productive politics in the democratic world. Japan's importance as an object of scholarly investigation has not diminished in recent years, but the issues that have drawn scholars to this interesting and important country have changed utterly. This is because the decade of the 1990s has been witness to many troubles in Japan. Indeed, it was in this decade that the nation, which once served as an economic model for many of the world's developing nations, produced year after year of little or no economic growth with small hope of the future being any different. It was also in this decade that Japan's political system, which many said was able to design and implement enlightened economic policies and avoid the parochial focus normally associated with democratic politics, collapsed under the weight of its own corruption and ineffectiveness. As a result, recent scholarly treatments of Japan have revolved around attempts to reconcile what appear to be very different countries.

Such efforts are in no way uniform and can be distinguished, among other things, in terms of the principal concepts and methods employed by investigators as well as the level of analysis that scholars have targeted as the principal cause of Japan's problems in the last decade.[2] Despite such differences, most attempts to reconcile Japan's past success with its current troubles are similar in that they proceed from the idea that it is the same political-economic arrangements that once brought the country high levels of economic growth and enviable amounts political stability that are now at the heart of its problems. Along these lines, some scholars argued that Japan's political-economic system "soured" while others asserted that "key Japanese political and economic institutions that were once crucibles of creative adjustment now inhibited flexibility, dynamism, and movement in new directions."[3]

When scholars refer to political-economic arrangements that brought Japan high growth and political stability throughout most of the postwar period, they are pointing to a wide variety of institutional features that are said to be specific to Japan. Perhaps the most important of these institutional features is Japan's "elite" and "powerful" bureaucracy. This is because, as many have argued, it was members of Japan's economic ministries who designed and implemented that country's industrial policy and helped see to it that resources were allocated to strategic industrial sectors, which arguably would not have grown as fast as they did without such direction and assistance. Other oft-cited political-economic arrangements involve those that were designed into the structure of Japan's business-government relations. Most important among these are Japan's bank-centered system of corporate finance, implemented through financial *keiretsu* and various forms of government guidance, and its system of labor relations characterized by enterprise unionism (labor peace), lifetime employment, and seniority-based promotions.

To be sure, the Japanese political-economic system is characterized by institutions and practices that are in many ways specific to Japan, and, as a result, current attempts to reconcile that country's past success with its ongoing problems are not incorrect in how they described it in its economic and political life.[4] Nonetheless, scholarship that attempts to reconcile Japan's past success with its current problems is lacking in our view and, thus, reflective of an intellectual problem that needs to be addressed. The intellectual problem we refer to here involves not simply how we can explain Japan's political and economic troubles in the 1990s and beyond but, rather, whether or not we can say that, in attempting to come to terms with Japan's current crisis, we have truly understood the postwar "miracle" itself, specifically, the political-economic system that has been deemed responsible for its past success.

When we say that attempts to reconcile Japan's successful past with its current crisis are lacking, we are not arguing that they possess no correspondence to Japan's postwar trajectory because most recent scholarly efforts have a certain straightforward and intuitive appeal. This appeal can be understood as follows. To rebuild itself in the wake of the Pacific War, it was necessary that economic sectors with the potential for growth get a sufficient share of economic resources that were particularly scarce in the early postwar period. Through a strategically oriented industrial policy that was implemented by "elite" and "powerful" bureaucrats in Japan's economic ministries,[5] and through other venues of government-business cooperation, the Japanese government designed and implemented policies that made sure this happened. The result, as scholars over the last two decades have asserted, was the highest levels of economic growth in the developed world. However, as the postwar period progressed and economic targets were reached, this development strategy resulted in resources being locked into certain sectors, keeping them from being mobile in the face of changing economic circumstances. It was this situation that led scholars to conclude that what worked well in the past now contributes to Japan's current problems.

There is little to dispute that, during the period of high growth, Japan looked like a very different country than it was in the last decade. As a result, it is not unreasonable to think that, in the last several years, something has gone wrong with Japan's political-economic system. On the other hand, if we step back and probe the assumptions that underpin this assessment of Japan's postwar trajectory, certain problems should be apparent. Specifically, it is curious how the same "elite" and "powerful" bureaucrats, who ostensibly played a central role in Japan's postwar economic "miracle," have been unable, at a very minimum, to keep the current crisis from continuing as long as it has. In like manner, we must also ask how is it that Japan's bank-centered system of corporate finance, which directed capital to those sectors with the potential for growth in the past, and supposedly in a more effective way than would have been the case with Anglo-American-type arrangements, allowed so many nonperforming loans to be made? And, finally, if lifetime employment and other special features of the postwar Japanese labor system were part of an elite strategy to employ human resources in a way that ensured their positive contribution to the country's essential economic interests, then why haven't these same elites simply redesigned Japan's labor-market institutions so that they could continue to contribute to economic outcomes as they had in the past?

The truth is that, if the Japanese political-economic system was organized and operated in the way that most recent attempts to reconcile Japan's past success with its current problems have contended, it should never have encountered the problems with which it is now consumed. We have referred to this as the problem of "the Japan that never was" and note that it is not an intellectual problem that stems from a lack of quality scholarship on the postwar Japanese economic and political systems. Rather, this intellectual problem rests with how it has become almost a revealed truth that Japan's special political-economic features were in large part responsible for the postwar "miracle."

To be sure, there are disagreements over how important each one of Japan's special political-economic institutions was with respect to its postwar economic resurgence, but there is virtually no disagreement that their impact on postwar economic outcomes was on balance positive. Unfortunately, such a conclusion was justified more by Japan's dramatic postwar trajectory than by empirical research that demonstrated how the implied causal mechanisms actually worked. Consequently, it is our view that this nearly universal acceptance of the positive impact of Japan's special political-economic features—at least until recently when some scholars have questioned their beneficence—prevented scholars from seeing that certain long-term political and economic trends suggested in subtle but unambiguous ways that the crisis of the 1990s was long in the making.

In light of this, our purpose in this book is to develop and test an alternative explanation for Japan's postwar political-economic trajectory, one that avoids this intellectual dilemma. We begin this effort by noting that, to avoid this problem of "the Japan that never was," it is necessary that we proceed from the notion that Japan's current political and economic crisis is not the result of a generally well-functioning political-economic system that suddenly failed to respond to exogenous demands in a way that produced the miraculous results that defined Japan in the past. Rather, Japan's postwar trajectory is the result of a political-economic system that is functioning today in essentially the same way that it functioned in the past. This is because the course that Japan followed throughout the postwar period is the result of, first, politicians setting the direction and content of national economic policy in response to the changing electoral imperatives they faced throughout the postwar period and, second, actors in the private sector making business decisions in response to the economic incentives they faced throughout the postwar period.

When we say that Japan's politicians have been the driving force in the country's economic policy-making process, we are not contending that they have molded every aspect of every economic program the government enacted in the postwar period. Rather, we are saying that they are like elected officials in other parliamentary systems who use the available tools of economic policy to serve their political interests. For the Liberal Democratic Party, which singularly ruled Japan for most of the postwar period, this process began with providing benefits to the party's support groups, giving economic policy its well-known pro-farmer, pro-rural area, and pro-business orientation. As the postwar period progressed, the complexion of the Liberal Democratic Party's support base changed in a way that led to its Diet majority beginning to hemorrhage away. To maintain its electoral predominance, the LDP needed to use economic policy not only to keep its traditional supporters satisfied but also to attract new supporters into the party's fold. This led to an increasing public goods emphasis in economic policy in the 1970s and beyond.

Focusing on Japan's politicians and the electoral imperatives they face is nothing new in studies of politics and policy making in the postwar period. In fact, as we show in our discussion of the literature (chapter 2) that informs the various analyses we perform in this book, elected officials were at the center of most studies of postwar Japanese politics until Chalmers Johnson's influential work on the Ministry of International Trade and Industry encouraged scholars to focus more attention on Japan's bureaucracy. While very few Japan specialists accepted Johnson's "developmental state" idea as a completely accurate description of how Japan worked,[6] many directed their attention to specific agencies of the bureaucracy and their role in the policy-making process in specific economic sectors. This led to a shift in the agenda of Japanese studies, which resulted in a body of scholarship that taught us much about the interaction between bureaucrats and actors in Japan's private sector but was not very helpful for explaining Japan's overall postwar political-economic trajectory. It is only by focusing on Japan's elected officials and private actors that we can avoid "the Japan that never was" problem and explain how essentially the same behavior led to high growth and political stability at one time but ongoing political-economic stagnation more recently.

Perhaps the best illustration of the intellectual payoffs that our emphasis on electoral politics provides is witnessed in our analysis of industrial policy in postwar Japan. While most treatments of this important topic conclude that industrial policy was at least partially responsible for Japan's postwar economic miracle, the same scholars who have touted the virtues of the Japanese approach to economic management—even if only for the early decades of the postwar period—have also concluded that economic policy in Japan has been biased in favor of the country's many inefficient sectors, such as agriculture and small business, for political reasons. Moreover, much recent scholarship that has focused on policy making in specific economic sectors has shown that the process has in fact functioned quite differently from the way that it was described in the original "developmental state" model, and, perhaps more important, that it was not conducted in a way that allowed it to be economically effective.[7] In light of this, the question that must be asked is why one should believe that industrial policy in particular— and economic policy more generally—had the miraculous impact on the Japanese economy that so many have said, and continue to say, it did.

In chapter 3, we offer a thorough empirical analysis of industrial policy that identifies which economic sectors received the different types of industrial policy support the Japanese government provided and in what relative amounts. The result of this effort shows that Japan's industrial policies have been far less effective than most Japan specialists have acknowledged. The reason for this, as our electoral politics perspective suggests, is that the direction and content of economic policy was determined by Japan's governing politicians in light of how those tools could be employed to deal with the changing electoral imperatives they faced throughout the postwar period. This is because Japan's inefficient economic sectors (e.g., mining and textiles) received the bulk of the government's largesse and that, even when infant industries did receive government support, the impact of this support on their productivity was negligible at best.

The results we provide in this chapter suggest strongly that the positive impact of Japanese industrial policy has been overstated and that the positive influence attributed to other arguably unique Japanese political-economic institutions has also been exaggerated. In chapter 4 we show how this is true for Japan's bank-centered financial system and the country's labor market institutions. It is well known that the financial system and labor relations in Japan are characterized by certain distinctive institutional arrangements. We do not argue with the way these features of postwar Japan have been described per se but rather emphasize that their positive impact on economic outcomes has been nearly taken for granted. In this chapter, we revisit these institutions and explain how Japan's bank-centered financial system and such practices as lifetime employment, enterprise unionism, and just in time inventory management are best understood as the expected responses of Japanese firms to the economic incentives they faced early in the postwar period. Moreover, we show in this chapter how high growth essentially masked the negative consequences associated with these institutions, leading many scholars to conclude that their overall economic impact was positive.

If such features of the Japanese political-economic system are expected and did not carry the positive impact that so many have said they did, we are left with the question of why Japan performed economically as well as it did, especially in the earlier years of the postwar period. We address this issue in chapter 5 and note that our approach proceeds from the idea that Japan's postwar economic trajectory does not require any type of special explanation. In fact, as we show in this chapter, scholarship that is based on such an assertion very often mischaracterizes the standard growth model of neoclassical economics and ignores such essential growth-accounting issues as the roles played by increasing economic inputs and total factor productivity in Japan's postwar economic outcomes. In this chapter, we demonstrate how the neoclassical model more than adequately accounts for Japan's postwar economic trajectory. Indeed, our effort in this chapter involves revealing how it is only through the standard growth model and the economic theory that underpins it that we can adequately explain how the Japanese economy went from high growth to structural adjustment.

Our focus in part II on economic outcomes is followed by an extended treatment of electoral politics, particularly as it pertains to the making of economic policy in the postwar period. The problems we address in the third part of the book proceed from the idea that Japan's political system, while characterized by features that are specific to that country, nonetheless operates much like other parliamentary systems in the democratic world. As we discuss more fully in chapter 6, this means that elected officials use the tools of economic policy to serve their electoral interests, and this universal characteristic of electoral politics in democratic countries gave Japanese economic policy in the postwar period its pro-farmer, pro-small business, and pro-rural area bias.

This is a description of economic policy making in postwar Japan that, on its face, will generate few disagreements, but its implications are controversial in how they require us to explain changes that occurred in overall patterns of economic policy making throughout the postwar period. In chapter 7, we address this issue by showing how it was the evolving electoral imperatives faced principally by Japan's ruling Liberal Democratic Party that best explains how the overall direction and content of economic policy changed throughout the postwar period. In this chapter, we discuss the different ways that electoral change impacts on a ruling party's support levels. In some cases, a ruling party's core supporters remain loyal but demographic change reduces their presence in the electorate. In such cases, a ruling party must respond by attracting new supporters while keeping core groups loyal. At other times, core supporters, for one or more reasons, fall away from their benefactor party. In these cases, a ruling party must redouble its efforts to keep core supporters loyal.

Throughout the postwar period, Japan's LDP faced both kinds of political change, and it responded to these exigencies in exactly the expected manner. For example, in recent years, the Japanese government turned increasingly to the announcement and implementation of fiscal stimulus packages to revive the country's stagnant economy. These policies were, at least initially, strongly opposed by bureaucrats, especially those in the Ministry of Finance, who argued that they not only worked counter to sound fiscal policy but also were counterproductive to seeing Japan through its current period of structural adjustment. In spite of this, more than a dozen packages were announced over a fifteen-year period which, as we are able to show clearly, is best understood as politically motivated attempts by incumbent governments to generate electoral support at critical political junctures. Conceiving of this particular economic policy effort in this way also helps us to understand that the fairly long period of government ineffectiveness in the face of the current crisis was the result not so much of recalcitrant bureaucrats but, rather, an electorally weakened LDP, governing in coalition and unable to afford any policy initiative that threatened to reduce its support base any further.

Showing that the LDP used the tools of economic policy throughout the postwar period to serve its electoral interests forces us to address the question of why it ultimately lost its status as Japan's predominant party. We address this question in chapter 8 and show that the LDP's continued decline can be traced to two principal factors. The first is that, as the ruling party was forced to use economic policy to attract new supporters, its economic policies worked at cross purposes and ultimately undermined its efforts to maintain its ruling status. Second, as the ruling party's majority hemorrhaged away, the costs of maintaining itself in power increased. This circumstance naturally rewarded individuals in the party who could bring more political money to the electoral process, creating increased incentives for corruption. This problem of corruption has been ever present in Japanese politics, but the Japanese public has tended to be rather tolerant of this kind of malfeasance. This generally tolerant attitude toward political wrongdoing was encouraged by the LDP's ability to provide benefits to its members' districts in the form of, among things, pork-barrel projects, which required an ever expanding economic pie. Unfortunately, when Japan's economic bubble burst, and especially when the dramatic decline in asset values began to show up in the real economy, the LDP's ability to use economic policy to sustain its majority was seriously compromised.

By showing how important postwar outcomes were the result of public and private actors responding to the economic incentives they faced, we offer what we hope is not only a better explanation for Japan's postwar political-economic trajectory but also a more effective way to understand the political-economic challenges that Japan currently faces. This is the question to which we direct our attention in the final chapter of this book, and we call this ninth chapter "The Past in Japan's Political-Economic Future." We selected this as the title of our final chapter because of our contention that understanding how the public and private sectors have responded to Japan's structural adjustment thus far, and how actors in these two sectors are likely to behave as time goes on, requires that we understand correctly how Japan's public and private actors behaved throughout the postwar period. This is perhaps the most important reason why it is necessary to avoid the intellectual problem of "the Japan that never was" because, as we have emphasized here, this intellectual problem is not about comprehending the challenges that Japan currently faces as much as it is about not fully understanding how its political-economic system was organized and operated in the past.

In light of Japan's postwar economic evolution, the explanation that one provides for the current period of structural adjustment must be developed in light of the political and economic constraints Japan's leadership faces in its attempts to design and promulgate meaningful political and economic reform. Many scholars have been clear as to the policies that need to be enacted if the end of the current structural reform is to be hastened. What is often missed in the recent literature, however, is how difficult it would be for Japan's elected officials to depart in any notable way from what they have been doing since the economic bubble first burst. Like their behavior throughout the earlier decades of the postwar period, the response of Japan's politicians to the current crisis is exactly what we would have expected given the political conditions they have been facing in the last ten years. These conditions have rendered any policy action that departs radically from what we have witnessed partner to very high political costs. Consequently, unless political conditions change in some dramatic way, the response of Japanese officialdom to the current crisis is unlikely to veer much from its current course.

Chapter 2

HOW DIFFERENT IS DIFFERENT?

Bureaucrats, Politicians, and Economic Policy Making in Postwar Japan

Power in Japan is held 90% by bureaucrats and only 10% by politicians.

—Miyamoto Masao
Bureaucrat, Ministry of Health and Welfare

The bureaucracy drafts all the laws. All the legislature does is to use its powers of investigation which for about half the year keeps most of the senior officials cooped up in the Diet.

—Sahashi Shigeru, Former Vice Minister
Ministry of International Trade and Industry

I am in charge of everything.

—Takana Kakuei,
Former Prime Minister of Japan

Politicians are pitchers, bureaucrats their catchers. A good pitcher decides himself if he will throw a fastball or a curve, but a weak pitcher throws the pitches as his catcher signals them.

—Nakasone Yasuhiro
Former Prime Minister of Japan

The 1990s was a decade of surprises for Japan scholars. This is true because the country that was often said to embody a different kind of capitalism proved to be no more immune to the structural adjustment difficulties associated with mature economies than any other advanced nation. This is also true because Japan's political system, which so many said possessed an institutional logic that enabled it to advance national economic development goals like no other nation, appeared to be plagued by the problems of political stasis that often characterize democratic politics elsewhere in the developed world. Because of this, the events of the 1990s brought to light the idea that there may be something lacking in how we have understood the way that Japan is organized and has operated in its political and economic life throughout the postwar period. This does not mean that Japan scholars failed to offer insights into why that country's economic engine stalled in the 1990s and why the political supports that helped sustain the system of high growth for so long collapsed. Rather, it tells us that our picture of how Japan's political-economic dynamics worked throughout the postwar period has been incomplete, and this in turn has kept us from understanding why its postwar trajectory followed the dramatic course it did.

While there may be many reasons that the 1990s caught the community of Japan scholars off guard, perhaps the most important rests with how the agenda of Japanese studies changed in the last two and a half decades. As mentioned above, in the 1980s and 1990s, Japan scholars became increasingly attracted to intellectual problems that, when addressed, resulted in an increasingly thorough mapping of the economic policy-making process but not a broader theoretical understanding that could explain why Japan's postwar political-economic dynamics involved high levels of economic growth and relative political stability for most of the postwar period only to vanish in the wake of the bursting of the economic bubble. This shift in the agenda of Japanese studies occurred because of the influence of what is known to all in Japanese studies as Revisionism.

When we say that Revisionism was influential, we are not arguing that revisionist ideas were universally accepted nor that the manner in which individual promoters of that view described Japan's political-economic system went unchallenged. Indeed, most Japan specialists in economics and political science never entirely accepted the view of Japan advanced by revisionism's most vocal proponents.[1] What we are saying instead is that Revisionism was most important in how it encouraged Japan scholars to think of the politics of economic policy making in Japan as a process whose essential working mechanisms are located within the agencies and bureaus that combine to form the Japanese state. As a result, areas of research that involved analyzing the policy-making process by mapping the internal and external interactions of bureaucratic actors in specific economic sectors became endowed with elevated levels of intellectual significance.

For more than three decades after the close of the Pacific War, nearly all scholarly writing in English on the postwar Japanese economy and political system was based on certain assumptions. These assumptions recognized that Japan's political evolution was influenced by cultural traditions and historical circumstances that are fairly specific to Japan and that, as a result, its postwar political system possessed qualities that differentiate it from those of other democratic nations. In spite of these differences, it was also assumed that, in its political life, Japan is a democratic country with a parliamentary system that is not unlike other parliamentary systems in Europe. Similar assumptions guided scholarship on the Japanese economy earlier in the postwar period. Specifically, while most scholars at this time recognized that Japan's economy has certain institutional features and behavioral properties that distinguish it from economies elsewhere in the developed world, they also assumed that Japan is essentially a capitalist country with a market economy that is not entirely unlike the market economies of other advanced nations. These assumptions can be summed up in the statement that, while Japan in the postwar period is politically and economically different, it is different, small *d*.

There have been individual scholars who did not wholly subscribe to this different, small *d*, view of Japan, and there were scholars in this tradition who helped mold this particular view of Japan from within. These dissenting views produced changes at the margins of this different, small *d* thinking from time to time, but they never formed an organized alternative to the view that Japan is essentially a democratic and capitalist nation.[2] In this way, Japan scholars adhering to this different, small *d* understanding held a near intellectual monopoly that lasted until the 1980s when this view of postwar Japan was directly challenged by several individuals who promoted a very different way of thinking about that country.

As stated above, this challenge is known as Revisionism, and its founder is former University of California, San Diego, Political Scientist, Chalmers Johnson. To be sure, there are other individuals who had been writing what were essentially revisionist views of Japan prior to the 1980s,[3] but it is Johnson who organized these ideas into a single, forcefully executed argument that Japan is politically and economically different from its counterparts in the West. Evidence of Johnson's very different view of Japan can be found in his earlier academic work on that nation's quasi-public corporations,[4] but his revisionist challenge received its fullest expression in his analysis of Japan's Ministry of International Trade and Industry.[5] By reconstructing the institutional history of this important government agency and by discussing the various reports it issued and the policies it recommended, Johnson sets out what he claims are those political-economic features of the Japanese state that distinguish it from its counterparts in the West.

There are other individuals who promoted Johnson's revisionist view of Japan, but they have generally not been professional social scientists. While there are certainly more, the most important involve a triumverate of two journalists and one policy advisor. The individual from the policy world is Clyde Prestowitz who, after five years as a special counselor to the Secretary of Commerce in the Reagan administration, became founder and president of

the Economic Strategy Institute in Washington, D.C.[6] The first of two journalists is James Fallows who was affiliated with *The Atlantic Monthly* when
he completed his most notable writing on Japan,[7] while the second journalist
is Karel van Wolferen who has lived in Japan for many years as East Asia
correspondent for the Dutch newspaper *NRC Handelsblad*.[8]

While the views of postwar Japan propounded by these and other Revisionists are in no way carbon copies of each other, they all share certain
common characteristics.[9] The most important of these concerns the assumptions that these individuals brought to their respective attempts to explain
why Japan experienced such remarkable postwar economic success, assumptions that go to the heart of how the Japanese political-economic system is
put together and operates. Contrary to other Japan scholars who contributed
to the literature earlier in the postwar period, revisionists have assumed that
Japan was not simply different, but different capital *D*. This means that they
assumed that Japan is not really democratic in the way that other parliamentary systems are democratic and not really capitalist in the way that other
market economies are capitalist.[10]

Revisionists assume that Japan is less democratic than the parliamentary systems of Europe not because of what it lacks in its political structures.
Johnson and other Revisionists acknowledge that the institutional prerequi-
sites of democracy including free elections, political parties, constitutionally
protected rights of individuals and the press, all exist in Japan more or less
as they do elsewhere in the developed world. Rather, the inability of Japan's
polity to transcend the limits imposed by its authoritarian past and function
as other democratic nations ostensibly function is due much more to what the
Japanese political system does possess. Most important is Japan's "elite"
bureaucracy that Revisionists have asserted actually rules the country in spite
of the fact that the Japanese constitution explicitly makes the National Diet
the highest organ of state power. To use Johnson's words, in Japan, "bureaucrats rule while politicians reign," which means that, unlike other parliamentary systems, public opinion and the will of the people do not have much
impact on policy outcomes. It is for this reason that Chalmers Johnson and
the small number of his committed acolytes accept the assertion that Japan
is more a "soft authoritarian" nation than it is a democracy.

The idea that politics and policy making in postwar Japan are dominated
by a class of unelected "elite" bureaucrats represents a dramatic departure from
how Japan scholars handled the issue of political power and policy making
prior to the rise of Revisionism. To reveal just how much Revisionism departed
from prevailing views, we must remember that, when we ask the question, who
possesses and exercises political power in a country, we are asking which
public and possibly private actors, either singularly or in some combination,

determine the direction and content of that nation's policy. This is a difficult question to answer precisely for any democratic country because it requires that one trace out all potential sources of policy influence, calibrate the relative impact of each influence on each policy area, and then sum up these weighted influences over all policy outputs.

While American political scientists have studied the United States much more than any other country, the debates over who possesses and exercises political power in Japan, particularly as this relates to the making of economic policy, are similar to those that divided scholars studying the American political system. With the rise of Revisionism, Japan scholars became divided over whether policy making there is essentially pluralist with the balance of political power held by elected politicians or whether it is more authoritarian and elitist where the balance of political power is held by bureaucrats, particularly those in the country's economic ministries like the former Ministry of International Trade and Industry and the Ministry of Finance.

Nonetheless, there have been a number of studies that essentially continued the tradition of placing parties and politicians at the center of the political process as Japan specialists did earlier in the postwar period.[11] While not ignoring Japan's bureaucracy, such studies proceeded from the notion, either explicitly or implicitly, that parties and politicians determined the direction and content of national policy, specifically, economic policy. By making political parties and politicians the target of their scholarly attention, these Japan specialists were in a sense helping return the agenda of Japanese studies to what defined it earlier in the postwar period. This is important for our purposes because, by focusing on broader postwar political trends, they helped us provide a way to understand why the 1990s brought such dramatic changes to Japan's economy and political system. As stated above, to show why this is the case, it is helpful to trace out how the scholarly debate over the locus of political power in postwar Japan helped define the agenda of Japanese studies and, thus, encouraged a certain line of research on Japan's political-economic system.

POLITICAL POWER IN POSTWAR JAPAN: A RETURN TO THE PAST

There are many features of Japanese politics that arguably make it distinctive, but perhaps most notable is the pattern of single-party predominance that defined election outcomes throughout most of the postwar period. While Japan entered the postwar period with many active political parties,[12] from the Fall of 1955, one party, the Liberal Democratic Party, emerged as the predominant force in the nation's electoral politics. It is for this reason that the numerous studies of Japanese politics that appeared in the early decades of the postwar period tended to focus on how the nation's politics were dominated by this single political party.[13]

When one examines this early literature, one immediately notices that scholars who wrote about politics and policy in Japan prior to the ascendance of Revisionism recognized the central role played by the National Diet in the policy-making process. This was largely because they understood its constitutional position as "the highest organ of state power and . . . the sole law-making organ of the State."[14] These scholars did not in any way stop at the Diet and leave policy making entirely to Japan's politicians because they recognized that the process involved more influences than the above-quoted chapter and article of Japan's constitution suggests. Such scholars noted that policy outcomes in Japan were influenced by all of the country's affected private interests as well its country's civilian bureaucracy. Nonetheless, acknowledging the influence of other actors was not in any way meant to suggest that the National Diet was located anywhere but at the apex of decision-making power.

This point of view is aptly illustrated by the work of Hans Baerwald, a member of the Government Section of the Allied Occupation of Japan and, for most of his academic career, a professor of Political Science at the University of California, Los Angeles.[15] Baerwald dedicated much of his career to studying the politics of Japan's National Diet, and he wrote the first complete study of that ever interesting political institution.[16] In that volume, Baerwald explained that Japan's politicians are important in the policy process and that the Diet's influence, given its constitutional mandates, is "not to be denigrated lightly" because "[n]o legislative bill, whether it be entirely new, an amendment to existing law, a treaty, or a resolution, becomes the law of the land until it has been approved by both houses."[17] On the other hand, Baerwald, like other scholars writing earlier in the postwar period, did not take the position that Diet politicians were the only important policy actors in the Japanese government. He was very clear that, while the Diet and the politicians who controlled it were allocated the supreme level of political power by Japan's constitution, Japan also had a civilian bureaucracy that was staffed with the nation's educated elites and, for a number of reasons, had influence on the policy-making process.

Japan's bureaucrats were influential because of the education and government experience they possessed. Even today, Japanese bureaucrats tend to be the nation's educated elites, graduating principally from Japan's top universities. Consequently, when the Pacific War ended and the Occupation began, members of the bureaucracy undoubtedly had accumulated much government experience and substantial policy expertise. The expertise and experience advantages that bureaucrats possessed were enhanced at the time for two other reasons. First, politicians were severely constrained during the war years by the militarist government, and, second, when such constraints were removed by the Occupation, many of the most experienced politicians were purged by the Allied Occupation because of their involvement in the war.[18] Because of this, scholars writing earlier in the postwar period argued that, as the LDP's tenure as the nation's ruling party continued, its members gained government experience and acquired policy expertise that helped the party gain increased power over the bureaucracy.[19]

THE REVISIONIST CHALLENGE

This understanding of power and policy making in Japan represented the prevailing view until about the mid-1980s when, as stated above, the revisionist view of political power in Japan made its way into the scholarly discourse and, within a very short period of time, challenged the different, small *d* view. Revisionism took what was understood as a complicated, multi-actor bargaining process with the Diet and turned it into an authoritarian process whereby the direction and content of national policy was determined by a class of nonelected bureaucrats regardless of what their elected counterparts thought or did. As stated above, Chalmers Johnson was not the first Japan watcher to assert that, in Japan, bureaucrats are more powerful than politicians, but it was his 1982 book on the Ministry of International Trade and Industry that organized such ideas into a distinct revisionist challenge. Why Japan's bureaucrats are more powerful than elected officials can be found in the second chapter of his book on MITI entitled, "The Economic Bureaucracy." Paradoxically, while the understanding of Japanese politics that Johnson advanced is unambiguous, the argument he offered in support of such a view is anything but.

There are many reasons Revisionists contend that bureaucrats are Japan's most powerful political actors and, thus, dominate the process by which economic policy is made and implemented. While somewhat forced, we have attempted to simplify matters by reducing these to three reasons that are essential for understanding why Johnson and other promoters of the revisionist view see bureaucrats as Japan's most powerful political actors. The first of these reasons is rooted in the allegedly ongoing influence of Japanese history and culture, specifically, the notion that Japan's political past is one of authoritarianism where elected officials were hardly the dominant class of political actor. The argument is that, despite the political reforms that the

Allied Occupation imposed on Japan, bureaucratic strength and politician weakness has continued throughout the postwar period. Again, this is because there have been certain ongoing historical and cultural influences that continued to empower bureaucrats and enfeeble their elected counterparts.

We refer to this first reason as a historical-cultural continuity argument and note that part of it is quite amorphous and requires that one see Japanese politics as possessing an almost transcendental quality, that is, a quality that provides members of Japan's bureaucracy with the highest levels of respect and deference accorded to any political actor in the nation. This respect and deference endows members of Japan's bureaucracy with a very high social status that has its roots in the fact that Japan's modern governmental apparatus was conceived and assembled largely by former samurai. As Chalmers Johnson has asserted in his discussion of the sources of bureaucratic power in Japan and its persistence throughout the postwar period, "Japanese do not normally question the authority of the government because they respect its 'samurai sword.' "[20]

This enormous respect and deference ostensibly accorded to Japan's bureaucrats also derives from another more objective source, one that concerns the education and examination patterns characteristic of a bureaucratic career in Japan. It is well known that a college education is necessary to join one of Japan's government agencies at the national level, and it is also well known that many of Japan's governmental agencies accept only top graduates from a very small number of elite universities.[21] This is particularly true of such important agencies as the Ministries of Finance, the former International Trade and Industry, and Foreign Affairs. Moreover, to join such a group of august college graduates requires that individuals pass the most competitive exams administered in the country, and, in some ways, the strict educational path of the Japanese bureaucrat stands in stark contrast to the making of a typical elected official. This does not mean that nonbureaucratic or "pure" politicians are not college graduates. Most Diet members are college graduates and often from Japan's top universities. It means, rather, that the educational patterns that define a bureaucrat are not necessarily those followed by an elected official who comes up through local politics to obtain a seat in the National Diet.

The second reason Revisionists argue that bureaucrats are the dominant political actor in Japan concerns the conditions that prevailed during the Allied Occupation of Japan and, specifically, how these conditions helped increase bureaucratic power at the expense of Japan's politicians. One aspect of this involves the fact that, unlike occupied Germany where the Allied Powers ruled the country directly, the Occupation of Japan was conducted through certain extant agencies of the Japanese government. This does not include all politicians and bureaucrats who were serving in the government when hostilities in the Pacific War ceased because, as mentioned above, MacArthur and the Allied Occupation purged from government service those individuals deemed to have had any involvement with the war. Purged individuals included all police and military personnel and many elected officials who were serving in wartime governments, but many, if not all, bureaucrats in the economic ministries were left untouched.

Another aspect of this involves the socioeconomic conditions that prevailed in the first years of the postwar period. As is well known, the war effort stretched Japan's human and material resources to the point of complete exhaustion, and the waning months of the conflict heaped an untold amount of destruction on Japan. When the Occupation started, the bulk of Japan's citizens were without food and shelter and the means of acquiring either of these material necessities. Such desperate conditions demanded decisive policy action, which Revisionists have argued fell mostly on the shoulders of bureaucrats in those agencies that were retained by the Occupation to assist in ruling the country. Moreover, since politicians were weakened by the purges and divided by intense partisan bickering that was common in the first few years of the Occupation, the policy imperatives faced by the country during that time had the effect of empowering bureaucrats at the expense of their elected counterparts.

The third reason that Revisionists advance a dominant-bureaucracy view of political power in postwar Japan concerns how certain actions taken by bureaucrats in the Occupation and post-Occupation periods helped advance their power and diminish that of Japan's elected Diet members. One part of this is a continuation of the second reason that, as Japan's administrative agencies began to grapple with the country's enormous economic problems in the early postwar years, they effectively acquired more political power. In the first decade of the postwar period, many laws were passed and numerous procedures were established to administer such things as the allocation of scarce credit and foreign exchange for the rebuilding of Japan's industrial capacity. In support of such efforts, members of Japan's bureaucratic elites drafted numerous reports and plans and established many regulations and administrative rules that made their involvement in the day-to-day operation of the nation's economy a reality. These actions then allowed Japan's bureaucrats to establish their power and administrative capabilities at the expense of Japan's elected politicians, especially in the area of economic policy making.

The other part of this reason recognizes that, while the behavior of bureaucrats worked to increase their effective political power, it also had the impact of keeping the Diet from developing into a national legislature with political power similar to that found in other democratic nations. Part of the problem supposedly rested with LDP politicians themselves, specifically the divisive tendencies of ruling party factions, the lack of cooperation among the opposition parties, and the argument that Japan's politicians are ever consumed with parochial matters and, thus, unable to rule Japan in an effective manner. This is not to be underestimated, but even if politicians in Japan could have overcome their divisive tendencies and parochial orientation, Revisionists assert that they still would not have been able to overcome the power of the bureaucracy. This is because the ruling party in Japan was effectively colonized by former bureaucrats who left their posts in one of Japan's important ministries and got elected to the Diet. Chalmers Johnson made this point clearly when he concluded that the "influence of former bureaucrats in the Diet has tended to perpetuate and actually strengthen the prewar pattern of bureaucratic dominance."[22]

PLURALISTIC POLICY MAKING: MULTIPLE ACTORS IN MANY ECONOMIC SECTORS

As stated above, while most Japan specialists trained in economics and political science agreed that Japan's bureaucracy is comparatively powerful, they never accepted the revisionist argument that bureaucrats are indisputably the country's most powerful political actors. For this to be true, one would have to believe that the Occupation's democratic reforms were not all that meaningful and that the formal powers granted to the Diet by the postwar constitution simply did not amount to anything. These are difficult things to accept if, at the same time, one also accepts that Japan is a democracy even with special characteristics that make it more or less distinct. This is why many Japan specialists had trouble taking the revisionist view at face value. Nonetheless, the revisionist view was provocative enough to encourage the same Japan specialists to try to determine just what role bureaucrats played in the policy-making process by investigating that process in greater detail in specific economic sectors.

As mentioned above, the result was a shift in the research agenda of Japanese studies away from politicians, political parties, and the Diet to those agencies and bureaucrats responsible for economic policy in certain economic sectors and, moreover, to the private actors who were the targets of economic policy in those sectors. Numerous studies were conducted which, in detailed analyses of economic policy making, revealed quite clearly that the revisionist perspective involved a greatly oversimplified view of the process through which economic policy is actually designed and implemented in postwar Japan. Johnson and other proponents of the revisionist perspective took note of this work and eventually came to the view that Japan's politicians had slowly encroached on the policy autonomy of the bureaucracy as the postwar period progressed.[23] While there are some Japan scholars who echo this theme of declining bureaucratic power,[24] the research that Revisionism encouraged showed that the problem with the "developmental state" view of Japan went far beyond the growing power of Japanese politicians.

The dominant-bureaucracy view of Japanese politics was undermined as Japan scholars uncovered more and more details of how the policy-making process actually worked in specific economic sectors. While many aspects of this process in Japan were shown not to fit the revisionist perspective, most important was how this research revealed that policy making in Japan is more complicated than Johnson's model of bureaucratic dominance suggested. This involved numerous features of economic policy making in Japan, but we can reduce these features to those that rest with Japan's bureaucracy and those that rest with other influential public and private actors.

In the literature on the Japanese bureaucracy, and the developmental state more generally, the bureaucracy of Japan has been presented as a kind of institutional monolith.[25] This does not mean that scholars ignored the inter- and intraministerial disagreements that existed within the Japanese bureaucracy, because adherents to the developmental state view of Japan recognized that sectoral conflicts do in fact exist. Rather, it means that Revisionists and other promoters of the developmental state view relegated whatever ministerial disagreements existed by arguing that Japan's bureaucratic leaders overcame their divisions because of how their collective agreement on national economic goals allowed them effectively to speak in unison and to act in concert.

From the distinctive perspective of the visions and reports that have been prepared and published by Japan's numerous ministries throughout the postwar period, this view is not entirely unjustified. However, when considered in light of how bureaucrats in the subunits of Japan's ministries have actually carried out their duties in specific areas of economic policy making, a different picture emerges. That sectoral competition exists within Japan's bureaucracy and has posed operational problems on Japan's bureaucrats, particularly in those areas where jurisdictional boundaries were not clear, is not really new.[26] Nonetheless, research carried out in the last two decades has shown in much greater detail just how the Japanese bureaucracy is often consumed by sectoral conflicts that sometimes impede its ability to monitor the economic sectors over which its many agencies and their bureaus have jurisdiction. In this way, more recent research has revealed just how extensive sectoral conflict is and to what extent such conflict has inhibited the bureaucracy from acting with the authority it has been said to possess.

Japan's bureaucracy has always been polycentric, but research conducted in the last two decades revealed that this posed more and more of an operational problem for bureaucrats as the postwar period progressed.[27] Part of this was due to the fact that, as economic growth continued and production raced past prewar levels, the single goal of catching up with the West economically, a goal that helped unify the agencies of the Japanese government in the past, allowed the bureaucracy's centrifugal tendencies to resurface. Consequently, while attendant to higher levels of prosperity and satisfaction with the material aspects of life among the average Japanese, Japan's emergence as a postwar economic power led to the unraveling of the national policy consensus that helped smooth over the divisions that existed within the national bureaucracy.[28] In his study of high-technology policy, Scott Callon (1995) places the breakdown in the mid-1970s, arguing that "the emergence of Japan as an economic and technological power has seriously complicated the process of formulating industrial policy," and, more than this, "made it more difficult to achieve both cooperation and functionality."[29]

Another part of this had to do with factors that were largely exogenous to the bureaucracy. These factors were twofold and involved the introduction of new production technologies into the marketplace and the setting of new policy directions by the Liberal Democratic Party. Concerning the former, the introduction of new technology facilitated interministerial rivalry, especially when the new technology involved the crossing of jurisdictional boundaries. This was witnessed in the growing conflicts that occurred between the former Ministry of International Trade and Industry and the former Ministry of Posts and Telecommunications in such areas as fiber optics and digital technology and among MITI, the Ministry of Education, and the Science and Technology Agency over the role of each in promoting the country's growing need for basic over applied scientific research.[30] Concerning the latter, at different times throughout the postwar period, the Liberal Democratic Party intervened in the policy-making process and affected its direction and content, sometimes in dramatic ways. There are numerous studies of such LDP intervention that emphasize different aspects of Japanese politics in their respective attempts to explain the policy shifts that resulted from the LDP's intervention.[31] What is important, however, is that the intervention of the LDP to promote certain policies encouraged competition among agencies of the government both to mold the policy changes in a way that coincided with their respective agencies' visions and to benefit themselves from the increased resources such policy changes often involved.

Overall, these exogenous factors militated against Japan's bureaucrats acting in concert thereby undermining their collective ability to provide the policy leadership that at least partially characterized the bureaucracy in the area of economic development early in the postwar period. In light of this, recent scholarship on policy making in Japan revealed that the process was far more pluralistic than the dominant-bureaucracy model had suggested, and, while a good part of this was due to divisions that existed within Japan's bureaucracy, another part rested with the degree to which other actors, particularly those in the private sector, influenced the process of determining the direction and content of economic policy.[32] Influential private actors have included corporations in certain industries and the industry associations and other interest groups that represent them. Recent research has shown that the extent and level of involvement of such private actors varied depending on the area that was examined. This is because firms in different economic sectors varied in terms of their size, number, and diversity, and, as a result of this, economic sectors varied in terms of the manner in which their respective firms were organized and, thus, able to press the central government to advance their interests.

For example, in a study of Japan's basic materials industries, Mark Tilton (1996) found that industry associations were the principal private actors influencing the substance of policy and the way it was implemented in that economic sector, while, in his extensive study of the allocation of industrial finance, Kent Calder (1993) found that private firms, especially Japan's banks, were perhaps the most influential private actors. The broader conclusion from these and similar studies is that different economic sectors in Japan tend to be characterized by different sets of prominent private actors, which in turn affects how policy outcomes are actually derived in those sectors.

While the significance of such findings is not to be underestimated, it is important to note that individual researchers did not treat the interactions of the private and public actors in the specific sectors they examined in the same way. Indeed, treatments of economic policy making and its essential actors often emphasized very different factors that were specific to the sector being examined and the research orientation of the scholar conducting the study. For example, in his study of Japan's energy industry, Richard Samuels, on the one hand, emphasized the influence of private actors on the process as the result of their response to the market incentives they faced.[33] In the area of financial markets, James Horne, on the other hand, found that the influence of public actors most often varied with the extent to which Japan's politicians saw the particular policy initiative as being electorally strategic.[34] In the same policy area, Kent Calder reached a somewhat different conclusion, arguing that private actor influence is explained by the manner in which the state's essential economic actors are organized.[35]

THE RETURN TO PARTIES: POSTWAR TRENDS VERSUS PRINCIPAL-AGENT THEORY

It would be unfair to say, on the one hand, that this research ignored the role played by Japan's elected officials because politician involvement was an integral part of what made economic policy making in postwar Japan pluralistic. It would, on the other hand, be inaccurate to say that this research made the politicians who controlled the Diet the lead actors in the process. In spite of this, there have been a number of other studies of Japanese politics that appeared in the last two decades that revived the idea that the elected officials who controlled the Diet are at the apex of power and, thus, at the center of the economic policy-making process. While these studies are similar in terms of where politicians were placed in the process, they differed in terms of how the policy-making power of politicians was explained. One version mentioned briefly above is perhaps best referred to as the incremental power view because it saw Japan's elected officials becoming more powerful as the postwar period progressed. It is important to note here that scholars who promoted this view did not relegate the constitutionally derived powers granted to the Diet and, thus, the politicians in the party(s) that controlled it. They simply argued that certain postwar developments helped Japan's politicians exercise the authority they possessed more effectively over their bureaucratic counterparts.

While different scholars emphasized different factors, all agreed that most of the influential postwar trends could be divided into those that helped politicians and those that hurt bureaucrats. The former refers to the irrefutable fact that, as the LDP's tenure as the nation's ruling party increased, its members were the beneficiaries of the governing experience and policy expertise that this long tenure as ruling party provided. This increasing policy expertise of LDP politicians had an institutional expression that is known as *zoku*, or policy tribes in Japanese, which refer to organized cliques of politicians with expertise in certain policy areas in their relationships with other public and private experts. The latter, as has been discussed above, refers to the increasing sectoral conflicts that characterized the bureaucracy and, as a result, provided opportunities for politicians to intervene and help resolve.[36]

A second version of this return to the centrality of politicians in the policy process proceeds from the notion that politicians have not become more powerful as the postwar period progressed because they were always powerful and, thus, the central players in Japan's policy drama. The proponents of this view have argued that scholars adhering to the incremental power view have mistaken politicians becoming more visibly active in the policy process for their having become more powerful. Proponents of this view argue that postwar changes gave the LDP more incentives to be active in the making of economic policy but that nothing changed to give the party more power to act in its electoral interests. While this view of politician power can be attached to a number of Japan specialists, it received its clearest expression in the controversial volume, *Japan's Political Marketplace,* by J. Mark Ramseyer and Frances Rosenbluth.[37]

While provocative because of how it challenged the incremental power view, the controversy of this volume rests more with how its authors analyzed Japanese politics rather than the content of the conclusions they presented. Ramseyer and Rosenbluth assumed that the power of Japanese politicians had not changed because their essential role in the political process had not changed. Using the rational decision model, particularly that aspect derived from principal-agent theory, Ramseyer and Rosenbluth argued that Japan's politicians are the policy process' principals, which means that they are the actors who determine the direction and content of policy. Bureaucrats, on the other hand, are the process' agents, which means that they are the actors who essentially implement the policy that is determined by the principals, albeit with varying levels of discretion.[38] The implication of this view is that the policy behavior of bureaucrats is essentially their efforts to carry out ruling party desires, either those tasks that are directly delegated to them or those that are undertaken more or less independently but in anticipation of ruling party preferences. What this means is that bureaucrats have discretion but not power, and this discretion exists only within the limits of the agency slack that defines a particular policy area.

That many Japan specialists would respond negatively to Ramseyer and Rosenbluth's application of the rational choice framework to Japan was not unexpected.[39] The theoretical developments that helped give this framework the growing prominence it has enjoyed in political science came largely from studies of American politics. Gerald Curtis captured this class of criticisms when he asserted that principal-agent theory "does not travel well" because "Japan's different institutional structures and history created a different logic of political action than in the United States."[40] Moreover, the rational choice framework has not been without controversy in studies of American politics.[41] Nonetheless, the negative reaction of many Japan specialists to applying the rational choice perspective to Japan is curious for a number of reasons.

This first is simply that the application of the rational choice framework to political-economic contexts outside of the United States with significant intellectual payoffs is hardly a new trend. Robert Bates's study of the political economy of sub-Saharan Africa as well as Samuel Popkin's study of the peasantry of Vietnam are but two of many such influential studies.[42] The second reason for this concerns the substance of the argument made by

Ramseyer and Rosenbluth about why politicians are the more powerful political actor in Japan. Politicians who control the National Diet are, and have always been, more powerful than Japan's bureaucrats. This is because whatever policy action bureaucrats may deem appropriate, it must be acceptable to politicians. For policy actions to have the force of law and get implemented, they must be sanctioned by elected officials who control the National Diet. Even if bureaucrats initiate some policy through administrative action, politicians can simply enact legislation that counters it if that is their collective desire.[43]

POLITICIANS VERSUS BUREAUCRATS: DIFFERENT INTERESTS, DIFFERENT ROLES

What is perhaps most curious about the debate over rational choice and Japanese politics is that the view of political power advanced by Ramseyer and Rosenbluth is the one that is most consistent with the view of political power in Japan promoted by their nonrevisionist critics. Specifically, while conceived and executed differently, the way that Ramseyer and Rosenbluth understood politics and policy making to work in postwar Japan is not inconsistent with the view of this subject revealed in studies that appeared earlier in the postwar period. Indeed, while their concepts and analytic methods are reflective of recent developments in economics and political science, the substantive argument of Ramseyer and Rosenbluth is in many ways represents a return to the earlier postwar period where, as mentioned above, discussions of Japanese politics emphasized the central role played by the country's elected officials.

While the view propounded by Ramseyer and Rosenbluth is not a carbon copy of work completed on party politics early in the postwar period, it is similar in a couple of important ways. First, like Japan specialists writing earlier in the postwar period, it recognizes the importance of formal authority in the process of determining the direction and content of national policy. In other words, the power granted to politicians by the postwar constitution is taken seriously and not relegated to the realm of insignificance as is characteristic of revisionist writing. Second, and perhaps more important for our purpose of explaining Japan's postwar political-economic trajectory, Ramseyer and Rosenbluth used the elegant logic and analytic power of principal-agent theory to set out the different roles that bureaucrats and politicians play in the economic policy-making process.

These different roles derive from the different positions that each holds in the political system and, as a result, the different interests that are naturally attendant to their respective positions. As mentioned above, the role played by Japan's elected politicians is that of principal while the role played by bureaucrats is that of agent. In the context of making economic policy, the principal sets out the broad outlines of the policy, that is, its direction and content, while the agents are left with the details of implementation.[44] Japan's politicians have generally determined the direction and content of national policy in Japan simply because they can and because it is in their interest to do so. Again, this is because the postwar constitution requires that all laws be passed by the Diet, and that institution is controlled by politicians.

Some scholars and journalists have rejected this idea of Japan's politicians being principals in the policy process because of their lack of information relative to bureaucrats. It is true that individuals employed in Japan's ministries have extensive knowledge of their respective policy areas, but to say that this necessarily gives them more political power misunderstands the politician-bureaucrat relationship in two ways. First, it mistakes knowledge of policy details, which politicians generally lack relative to bureaucrats everywhere in the world, with politicians not knowing what they want and need to accomplish while serving in elective office. Elected officials, be they Japanese, Dutch, or American, all live with the imperatives of the electoral process, and this requires that those who are in the governing position remain focused on the policy process in certain ways at all times. Second, this argument glosses over what actually happens to be the one source of bureaucrats' ability to act in the policy process, namely agency slack.

In the Japanese case, agency slack refers to the gap that exists between what LDP politicians expect bureaucrats to do and what Japan's bureaucrats actually do. On the one hand, this gap may become particularly wide when the interests of politicians direct their attention to things other than the detail work of specific policies that is generally the provenance of bureaucrats. On the other hand, this gap will become very narrow when the interests of politicians behoove them to focus on how bureaucrats put together and implement specific details of programs of concern. In light of this, the most important factor determining how elected officials will treat bureaucrats in their duties as agents of the policy process turns on how a particular policy relates to the electoral interests of Japan's ruling politicians. This is the essence of democratic politics, and it is the issue to which we turn in part III of the book. Before delving into this important topic, we first examine the form that economic, specifically industrial, policy took in Japan and explore how policy making in this area corresponded to the principal patterns that defined economic outcomes in the postwar period.

II. POLITICAL ECONOMICS IN A CAPITALIST JAPAN

Chapter 3

THE PROBLEM OF
JAPANESE INDUSTRIAL POLICY

Japan is a good example of a state in which the development orientation predominates [where] the government gives greatest precedence to industrial policy, that is, to a concern with the structure of domestic industry and with promoting the structure that enhances that nation's international competitiveness.

—Chalmers Johnson (1982)

In developing national strategies, the Japanese goal is to focus on those industries with high income elasticities of demand, high rates of growth in productivity, and high value added per employee.

—Lester Thurow (1992)

Perhaps the greatest danger in industrial policy is not that aid is given to the wrong industries—although this is a danger. The greatest danger is that the policy goes on for too long. Protectionism and aid must be ended once an industry is close to meeting world prices. Otherwise, it will simply be a permanent crutch. This is the heart of Japan's pre-1973 problems.

—Richard Katz (1998)

Most studies of Japanese industrial policy convey the impression that it is coherent, effective, and far-sighted. The problem with these studies is that they tend to focus only on Japan's success stories—steel, automobiles, electrical power generation, and shipbuilding—and not the less successful—petrochemicals, wholesale and retail distribution, aerospace, and large commercial jet aircraft. Occasionally, a few examples are cited, but even when they are, one gets the impression that the analysts have searched long and hard to ferret out the aberrant cases and that the exceptions merely underscore the general rule.

—Daniel Okimoto (1989)

In the preceding chapters, we stated that the direction and content of economic policy in postwar Japan can be understood only by focusing on the political imperatives faced by politicians, particularly those in the Liberal

Democratic Party. If this is in fact the best way to approach policy making in postwar Japan, then this process should be characterized by certain patterns. Specifically, the design and implementation of economic policy should have occurred in a way that allows us to trace out the influence associated with politicians, and we should also be able to connect economic outcomes in the postwar period directly to the policy preferences of Japan's elected officials. Our focus in this second section of the book is the latter issue, that is postwar economic outcomes and how our electoral politics perspective offers the best explanation for the patterns they manifested throughout the postwar period. In this process, it is undoubtedly necessary that we clearly identify the economic outcomes that were the result of a politician-directed policy-making process, but it is also necessary that we show that there have been other outcomes that were the result of private actors responding to the economic incentives they faced.

Accomplishing this leads us to three issues in particular, Japanese industrial policy, Japanese management practices and labor relations, and the current period of structural adjustment and its relationship to the period of high growth. Each of these issues in its own way has contributed to "the Japan that never was" problem that we are attempting to address in this volume. Specifically, assessments of Japanese industrial policy—which, with few exceptions, are positive even if only for a specific period of time or for certain economic sectors—are based on limited case work, involve discussions of misunderstood concepts, and are generally not the product of carefully designed empirical analyses that calibrate the impact of specific industrial policy tools on productivity trends in Japanese industry. Similarly, treatments of Japanese management practices and labor relations tend to be case-based and do not adequately discuss such topics as corporate governance and how the economic incentives faced by firms and workers in the early postwar years affected developments in these two interrelated areas. Finally, while there are many useful studies of the current period of structural adjustment, these studies have generally been guided by the assumption that the high-growth period was something special, that is, not the product of market forces working in well understood ways with the bubble economy and its inevitable collapse as predictable outcomes.

We begin our examination of these important topics with Japanese industrial policy, perhaps the most misunderstood issue in studies of the Japanese political-economic system in the postwar period. Unlike other treatments of industrial policy, however, we make no assumptions about nationalist sentiment, public consensus, or other common goals on the part of the Japanese government and populace that most scholarship has treated as part of the driving force behind Japanese industrial policy. Again, our guiding assumption is that, in the process of making industrial policy, relevant public and private actors have been goal oriented and sought to achieve their respective objectives in light of the constraints and opportunities they faced at the time. While this may not be an entirely neutral approach, it coincides with our purpose of providing an exact mapping of how industrial policy worked in postwar Japan with an eye toward calibrating its impact on overall industrial productivity. Moreover, the analysis we offer here is broadly empirical in that it identifies exactly what economic sectors got what level of industrial policy support and what impact this government attention had on these sectors' overall postwar performance. Our analysis will show that industrial policy did not produce the miraculous results that so many said it did and that this is true for the reasons already articulated, specifically, that it was essentially a politically-directed process.

In many ways, our findings contradict much of what has been written because even scholars who have long been critics of Japanese industrial policy, or became critical of government intervention over time, generally acknowledge that industrial policy worked in the past and, thus, contributed to the period of rapid growth that Japan experienced in the early decades of the postwar period.[1] Why so many scholars have come to such a conclusion about industrial policy is curious, because most of the evidence gathered in the casework that has been conducted on this topic pointed to a different conclusion. What we mean by this is not that the research we reviewed above revealed that Japanese industrial policy overall was not economically effective. Such a conclusion would not be tenable given the case-based, sector-specific nature of the research. Rather, our point is that the research conducted on this topic showed clearly that the process worked very differently from the way it had originally been characterized. Taking this problem in combination with the conceptual and analytic problems that also characterize much of the literature on this important topic, what we have is a positive conclusion based strictly on economic outcomes rather than the policy mechanisms that were supposedly behind it.

THE PROBLEM OF INDUSTRIAL POLICY

Industrial policy has been a controversial issue in not simply because most assessments of its effectiveness rested on the assumption that government intervention in Japan worked in concert with market forces, but also because it generated a discourse that considered the Japanese model superior to Western capitalism and, for some countries, something to be emulated.[2] In recent years, the controversy over Japanese industrial policy changed as scholars evaluating it in a positive way attempted to square Japan's long-argued systemic strengths with its current period of economic stagnation. The response from analysts who never wavered in their support of the Japanese approach to economic management is typified by the writing of Chalmers Johnson and other Revisionists.[3] It will be remembered that Johnson argued that, whatever crisis Japan faces at the present time, it is a bureaucratically instituted and managed crisis to accomplish a restructuring of the economy so that the Japanese state can more effectively get on with its principal business of promoting economic growth.[4] Similar assessments were expressed by Fingleton (1995) and Fallows (1994) who acknowledged that Japan's current economic problems are real but added that the "system" will respond as it always has and soon get back on track and "overtake the United States."[5]

Scholars who have been critical of the Johnson, "developmental state" view of Japanese industrial policy responded to the current crisis in a somewhat different manner. One response came from those we refer to as substantive critics, that is, those who find Japanese industrial policy to be a source of the country's inability to manage the current structural adjustment better than it has. These include University of Washingotn economist, Kozo Yamamura (1982 and 1990), who warned of the potential danger of the Japanese government continuing its intervention in the economy, its positive impact on economic outcomes early on notwithstanding. It also includes Richard Katz (1998), who offers in many ways a very accurate assessment of the troubles Japan currently faces but who has also clearly noted that "ideas and strategies that worked so brilliantly in an era of industrial takeoff have outlived their usefulness [leading to the situation where] past strengths became the source of weakness."[6]

Another response came from what we call analytic critics whose work has been more critical of the positive assessments generally associated with Japanese-style industrial policy. We refer here to those scholars, like Samuels (1987) and Richardson (1997) who have shown economic policy making to be more pluralistic and involving many more conflicts than the original, developmental state model suggested. Among other things, these analytic critics challenged the way proponents made their case that industrial policy was at least partially responsible for Japan's postwar economic miracle. For example, Daniel Okimoto criticized the tendency of advocates of Japanese industrial policy to overestimate Japan's success stories while at the same time understating the failures that occurred. In spite of this, Okimoto like many other analytic critics notes that industrial policy implemented through the Ministry of International Trade and Industry involved a "track record over the postwar period that inspires confidence."[7]

It is certainly true that the literature on industrial policy is characterized by a variety of opinions on how that important process worked and the impact it had on postwar Japan's economic growth. Nonetheless, a closer examination of writing on Japanese industrial policy reveals certain common features. The first of these involves the manner in which industrial policy has generally been treated, specifically, the fact that discussions of Japanese industrial policy have included a recitation of certain facts. Some of these have been very specific and referred to laws that were passed and gave power to the Ministry of International Trade and Industry to achieve certain economic goals. They have also included references to specific actions taken by MITI bureaucrats, such as promoting cartels in certain economic sectors or rationing foreign exchange to pay for the importation of needed technology. Other facts that have been cited are much less specific. Indeed, they have sometimes been quite amorphous. The reference here is to how analysts have mentioned the historical conditions that Japan faced both in the Meiji and postwar periods and how these conditions led to the formation of a nationalist ideology around the imperative of economic development and industrial prowess.[8]

This recitation of facts implies that analysts of Japanese industrial policy have assumed that political actors behaved exactly in the way that government policy statements have suggested. As discussed above, however, studies of policy making in different sectors of the Japanese economy found that the behavior of bureaucrats did not match the way it was characterized in the developmental state model and that the making of economic policy was strongly influenced by the behavior of private actors and the impact of market forces. In light of this, one must naturally ask how industrial policy could have carried the positive impacts that so many have suggested it did. Moreover, we must also ask, if industrial policies were implemented in the past in a way that helped contribute to the postwar economic miracle, then why has economic policy making been so dysfunctional in the last several years?

In light of these questions, the problem of industrial policy that must be addressed is twofold. The first part concerns the idea that work on economic policy making in specific sectors has been narrowly focused, that is, directed to the way that process worked only in selected areas. This is not to criticize this work in any way but rather to point out that it has not been focused widely enough to capture the full impact of the Japanese government's intervention efforts and, thus, to permit conclusions about the overall economic impact of Japanese industrial policy. The other issue to be addressed concerns scholarship on industrial policy which concluded that its overall impact has in fact been positive. Such optimistic assessments of industrial policy have been rendered without the use of a systematic framework that assesses the impact of industrial policy in an empirically sound manner. In the industrial policy literature, there is really insufficient evidence to conclude that, without industrial policy, Japan's postwar industrial development would not have occurred in the way that it did or as quickly as it did.[9] To render such a conclusion requires an analysis that focuses on measurable criteria, a task to which we turn next.

EVALUATING INDUSTRIAL POLICY

The argument that industrial policy had a significant and positive impact on the direction and speed of Japan's postwar economic development is based on the idea that the government (bureaucracy) targeted certain industries as critical for Japan's economic rebirth and then directed government support to those industries. The support the government extended included such things as trade protection, subsidies, low-interest loans, and tax breaks, and the economic sectors included in this targeted group were often clearly identified in the "visions" and White Papers produced by MITI throughout the postwar period. Discussions in the literature note that targeted industries included such well-known success stories as automobiles, electronics, and shipbuilding but also the equally well known failures such as petrochemicals and aircraft. While most treatments of industrial policy acknowledge that there were failures, they nonetheless conclude that the internationally competitive sectors owed at least part of their success to government industrial policy efforts.[10]

The reaction of neoclassical economists to these claims is best described as skeptical, something that is true for two reasons in particular. First, economists generally approach government intervention from a regulation perspective. This means that they see government intervention as an effort to minimize distortions rather than an attempt to alter economic incentives for the purpose of redirecting productive effort. Since most neoclassical economists did not view Japan as being different enough to justify a departure from this established economic view, they simply remained skeptical about arguments asserting the positive impact of Japanese industrial policy.[11] Supporters of industrial policy anticipated this skepticism and not only argued that Japan's approach was market conforming rather than market distorting they also pointed to Japan's postwar economic success as evidence of this.[12] In spite of these counterclaims, economists were generally unmoved by the challenge that Japan ostensibly represented.

A second reason for skepticism had to do with the manner in which advocates made the case for the effectiveness of Japanese industrial policy. Generally, supporters of the Japanese approach reviewed the manner in which the Japanese government intervened in the economy, discussing in detail the content of the visions, reports, and so on that were prepared by bureaucrats and that told how Japan would catch up economically with the West. Industrial policy proponents then used Japan's high levels of economic growth as evidence for their positive assessments, noting that growth remained relatively robust even after two oil shocks. In addition to this, proponents argued that the manner in which the structure of the Japanese economy rapidly evolved in the face of such shocks was evidence that industrial policy played an important, positive role in the process.

There are several problems with this type of supporting argument. First, by holding up Japan's economic progress as evidence of industrial policy effectiveness, proponents effectively used a *post hoc ergo propter hoc* framework. Indeed, support for Japanese industrial policy was advanced more by assertion than by empirical analysis because positive assessments of Japanese industrial policy lacked an overarching framework that addressed in a systematic way the central problem posed by industrial policy in Japan. Specifically, the literature lacked an appropriately designed and executed empirical test that showed whether the structural changes and high levels of growth that occurred in the Japanese economy were actually due, at least partly, to government policy efforts. Accomplishing this required attention to a number of conceptual and measurement issues that were not adequately dealt with in the literature. We have divided these issues into three categories.

Targeted Industries

The first problem concerns the rather straightforward issue of how to define a targeted industry. The standard view is that the Japanese government picked both winning industries, those that were ostensibly allocated the lion's share of support, and losing industries, those that were then to be eased out of existence. The bureaucracy, particularly MITI, is supposed to have carried out detailed analyses of long-term trends in technological evolution and comparative advantage which then allowed it to identify those industries that were most likely to succeed in the future. These were industries characterized by such things as increasing returns to scale, the potential for international competitiveness, and higher value added per employee, which means that their promotion today would arguably give rise to large payoffs tomorrow. Together with this effort to promote winning industries was the identification of industries in secular decline as well as those industries with decreasing returns. With this kind of information, a policy mix could be established that would promote the former set of industries while easing the latter out of existence.[13]

The problem with this description turns on how one actually identifies which industries were targeted for growth and which industries were to be eased out of existence. Most discussions of Japanese industrial policy offer no independent way to isolate those sectors that were targeted for support from those that were not. The fact is that, in the early decades of the postwar period, nearly every economic sector in Japan received some form of government assistance. Clearly, it is not intellectually reputable to assume all sectors were then targeted. Central to a scientifically valid analysis of industrial policy is the implicit and correct assumption that, to be effective, industrial policy must represent a reallocation of *scarce* resources toward the targeted sectors. This means that one must identify the relative sums that were extended to industries, showing that certain economic sectors received government support that other sectors did not.

The literature on industrial policy has dealt with this problem in one of two ways. The first is simply to use government statements as the way to identify targeted industries. This method, however, requires that official statements of policy be equated with empirical reality. Given our knowledge that nearly every economic sector received something from the Japanese government, this method does not tell us which industries received the greater share of government assistance.[14] This problem was not lost on some industrial policy analysts, because they reacted with the employment of a second method to identify targeted industries in Japan. Unfortunately, the second method employed did not really solve the problem either because it involved identifying targeted industries through what was essentially a tautology. This approach is perhaps best represented in Katz (1998) who simply asserts that industries with firms that became highly successful exporters were essentially the targeted industries while those that did not were the residual "protected" industries designated to be eased out of existence. In other words, industry targeting is something that is simply true by definition and not accomplished through the application of objectively derived empirical referents.

Misunderstood Concepts: Value Added, Wrong Prices, and Comparative Advantage

While the lack of a valid empirical definition of targeted industries is perhaps the central weakness of arguments in favor of Japanese industrial policy, there are other conceptual problems in the literature that must be addressed if we are to evaluate Japan's industrial policies in an empirically sound manner. One problem stems from the argument that Japanese policy makers intervened and altered economic incentives and disincentives so as to achieve a desired industrial mix. The desirable mix of industries was one that would involve rapid economic growth and international competitiveness so that Japan would at a minimum be economically equal to other advanced nations. Economists have long warned of the inefficiencies associated with such efforts because government allocations of scarce resources inevitably raise costs in those sectors that are not favored by government allocation efforts. In spite of this, some promoters of Japanese-style industrial policy, like James Fallows (1994), have taken this point to criticize the thinking of neoclassical economists by arguing that Japan succeeded by "getting prices wrong."

What Fallows meant by this is that policy makers sought to alter the incentive structure away from the structural mix that would result from a completely laissez-faire policy approach. Fallows and other critics of neoclassical economics assert that the study of economics is how market forces achieve the "right prices" and how deviations from this norm represent suboptimal allocations. While it is true that much of welfare economics and microeconomic theory deals with the issue of how free and unfettered markets can achieve optimal allocations, it is more generally true that economics is the study of incentives. This means that no mainstream economist would be surprised to find that government intervention designed to affect incentives could result in allocations that differ from the market solution. Most of regulation economics is dedicated to the study of how various regulations affect incentives and give rise to various allocations. To assert that economists fail to understand this implies a complete misunderstanding of the field.

A more correct criticism would be that mainstream economics generally does not accept the notion that government intervention to "get the prices wrong" can result in an allocation that is superior to the market solution in a welfare sense. It must be recalled that an optimal allocation in mainstream economics is one that improves the welfare of at least one individual without making any other individual worse off. Clearly, however, economists recognize that, if this criterion for welfare maximization is dropped, government intervention that "gets the prices wrong" in order to achieve a different allocation of resources is entirely possible. It is simply the case that economists see such decisions as residing in the political realm, and, as such, they remain skeptical that government efforts to manipulate comparative advantage can result in more rapid economic growth or productivity growth than might otherwise occur.

Another conceptual problem in the literature concerns the use of the economic concept of value added. Many proponents of Japanese industrial policy argued that the Japanese government picked winners by focusing on high-value-added industries.[15] The problem with this argument is that the targeting of high value-added industries is considered to be synonymous with the promotion of high technology and industries that, if promoted success-fully, will make the country more internationally competitive. Unfortunately, value added is a very specific economic concept that is calculated by dividing the amount of value added in an industry (total sales minus the cost of inputs) by the number of workers employed in that industry. As such, high-value-added per worker is not equivalent to being a high-technology industry. In resource-poor Japan, the semiconductor industry may indeed represent a high-value-added industry, but, in the resource-rich United States, such industries as tobacco, as Paul Krugman (1996) trenchantly noted, has a much higher valued-added per worker than the production of computer chips.

A final conceptual problem with discussions of Japanese industrial policy concerns what has become known as strategic trade policy. Borrowing from recent developments in trade theory,[16] proponents of strategic trade argue that certain industries, because they are characterized by imperfectly competitive markets due to such things as increasing returns to scale, economic rents, or external economies, may not necessarily conform to the trade theory maxim of comparative advantage. Many promoters of Japanese industrial policy ar-gued that high technology is one such industry and that it was industrial policy in the form of protection and other government benefits that allowed this industry not simply to develop but rather to flourish and not just in Japan but also in world markets as well.[17]

One problem with this argument is that it ignores the costs that are incurred when scarce resources are purposively reallocated through govern-ment policy efforts.[18] While this is an important point that is not to be taken lightly, more important for our purposes here is how this view of Japanese industrial policy reflects a profound misunderstanding of the concept of com-parative advantage. A nation's comparative advantage comes from its relative factor endowments, and a nation having a relative abundance of one or more factors gives it a comparative advantage in producing goods and services associated with those factors. A simple illustration is the United States' rela-tive abundance of land giving it a comparative advantage in the production of agricultural products that require large expanses of fertile soil.

Some promoters of Japanese-style industrial policy have argued that semiconductors and other high technology products are not the result of a nation's relative factor endowments (nature) but rather the result of advantage created through government policy (nurture).[19] These analysts argue that, since Japan is a resource-poor nation, its production of semiconductors must have been the result of the Japanese government nurturing that industry through industrial policy. This argument is wanting for the not very astounding reason that simple observation reveals that two key factors are necessary to produce semiconductors. These are intellectual resources and modest manufacturing costs, both of which Japan had in relative abundance. On the high end, Japan has the intellectual resources necessary to make advances in semiconductor technology, and, on the low end, it has an abundant pool of otherwise underutilized unskilled female labor is available to keep production costs down. Further observation reveals the existence of the same combination in the other key semiconductor centers like Taiwan or Korea. Indeed, the Silicon Valley in California is well endowed with well-trained engineers and low cost immigrant labor.

An Empirical Framework: Policy Tools and Productivity

Whether or not Japanese industrial policy was responsible for accelerating rates of economic growth and encouraging structural shifts in the postwar Japanese economy is ultimately an empirical question. This means that an analysis of industrial policy must begin with a clear identification of the tools that were utilized by the government. Once the tools of industrial policy are identified, they must be measured in a way that permits one to trace how much of each tool was received by each economic sector. Only in this way can one be certain that those economic sectors that were in fact treated favorably by the government have been identified. Finally, this also means calibrating the economic impacts that were associated with Japan's economic sectors receiving the types and amounts of industrial policy support they did so that the relationship between government attention and economic performance can be carefully established.

These are very straightforward requirements that any reliable analysis of industrial policy should embrace, but, unfortunately, the literature on industrial policy in Japan lacks a broadly gauged empirical framework that adheres to these analytic standards. This is not to say that there are no empirical studies of Japanese industrial policy because there are a few that have begun to address the problem in the way we discussed above. For example, Vestal (1989) studied the impact of government support on trade in technology and found that government policy was beneficial to importers of technology.[20] In a larger study, Vestal (1993) also found that the effectiveness of Japanese industrial policies was witnessed in how they helped reduce unemployment pressures and ease the social strife attendant to the restructuring that occurred in the Japanese economy throughout the postwar period.

Such studies, however, do not provide a satisfactory answer to the principal intellectual problem posed by Japanese industrial policy. Specifically, they do not tell us whether or not government intervention in the economy, and getting the prices wrong if you will, resulted in more rapid economic growth and productivity growth in the favored economic sectors and, as a result, enhanced Japan's competitive position vis-à-vis her trading partners. If, on the one hand, this could be shown, then arguments in favor of strategic trade policies (Krugman, 1990; Brandon and Spencer, 1983) and other government efforts to create comparative advantage would rest on a more solid intellectual foundation. If, on the other hand, we do not find this to be the case, then arguments in favor of emulating a Japanese-style industrial policy will have proven to be empty.

We should note here that by conducting an empirical analysis specifically for industrial policy, we are treating this specific area of economic policy making as distinct from others. In other words, the analysis we outline in this chapter is designed to determine whether or not industrial policy has been immune to the political influences that help set the overall direction and content of economic policy in postwar Japan. We should also note here that we have no expectation that industrial policy will be different from any other area of economic policy making. Indeed, we expect that the political influences that guided the overall distribution of government resources throughout the postwar period will also be operative with respect to the tools of industrial policy we examine below. To show that this is the case, we use the analysis of Beason and Weinstein (1996), who tested empirically the impact of industrial policy from 1955 to 1990, a span of time that includes the high-growth period as well as the post–oil-shock period when Japan's economy matured and economic growth began to slow.

In this analysis, the "null hypothesis" is that the actual mix of benefits the Japanese government dispersed will have been so broadly distributed so as not to be meaningful as a purposive allocation of scarce resources.[21] This means that such a broad distribution of government resources could be partner to three possible results. On the positive side, the outcome of this process might be enhanced rates of economic growth in those industries that received the larger relative shares of government resources. On the neutral side, government largesse may have been so widely distributed among economic sectors that no discernible influence can be detected. Finally, on the negative side, it may be that resources were actually allocated largely to declining rather than emerging industries, leading to the finding that government support is negatively correlated with growth, economies of scale, and competitiveness.

This leads us to the more important issue of determining whether or not industrial policy accelerated the development of Japan's internationally competitive, leading-edge industries. If the government's transfer of resources worked in this way, then the benefits an industry received should be related to the productivity growth that occurred in that industry. To determine how industrial policy affected the productivity of firms in Japan's various economic sectors, we must identify and measure the various tools that the Japanese government used to accomplish this. In the empirical analysis that follows, we focus on four industrial policy tools, subsidies and grants, tax relief, trade protection, and subsidized loans. This list is exhaustive when one considers that it includes all the quantitative tools specifically dealt with in the White Papers and public pronouncements of the bureaucracy (MITI) throughout the postwar period.

Of course, many industrial policy analysts have argued that "administrative guidance" or signaling has been another effective tool of Japan's industrial policy. We agree that this is entirely possible but note that "administrative guidance" is a slippery, residual concept that involves special measurement problems. For this reason, we leave it out of the analysis that follows but make two additional points. First, we would be surprised to find that administrative guidance worked differently than the four policy tools we examine below since that would require one to conclude that its patterns of support were orthogonal to all other Japanese government industrial policy efforts. Second, the best empirical study of the impact of administrative guidance, found in Weinstein (1995), upheld this no-impact view by showing that the influence of administrative guidance in the postwar period was just the opposite of what assessments have asserted.

To these criticisms we must add the idea of how difficult it is to believe that statements from bureaucrats would carry more weight with private actors than the way government intervention actually reallocated resources. We do not dispute that government bureaucrats might have espoused well-meaning visions in various White Papers that were meant to signal to Japanese firms the direction in which they wanted to see the economy go. What we do dispute is that such visions could possibly counteract influences attendant to the actual allocation of resources that was determined by policy makers, most often for political reasons. We also doubt that, in the absence of significant government-directed resource shifts, firms would act contrary to the market signals they received. Simply put, signals from the government in the form of statements, visions, and the like would be meaningless unless supported by notable shifts of scarce resources that actually altered the economic incentives firms faced.

INDUSTRIAL POLICY: AN EMPIRICAL ASSESSMENT

The empirical analysis of Japanese industrial policy we provide here begins with a mapping of the postwar Japanese economy in terms of economic growth rates. Table 3.1 contains data on Japan's thirteen mining and industrial sectors in descending order by their postwar rates of economic growth.[22] Between 1955 and 1990, each sector registered a positive rate of growth, even Japan's most notably unproductive sectors like textiles, mining, and food processing, but, as is well known, economic growth was not consistently high across the entire postwar period. For this reason, the growth data presented in the table have been divided into two periods. The first period begins in 1955 and ends with the first oil shock in 1973. This was the period of Japan's economic resurgence, and, as expected, rates of growth during this period were much higher across all thirteen mining and industrial sectors. The second period is the post–oil-shock period, and, as expected, the data in the table reveal that growth was much slower in this period. The data also show that growth in Japan's three most uncompetitive sectors at this time was either negligible or negative in the post–oil-shock period.

Having presented the growth rates that define each economic sector, our next task is to estimate the extent to which the four industrial policy tools we identified above contributed to that sector's growth rate. Table 3.2 presents correlation coefficients between the amount of a particular industrial policy tool that an economic sector received from the government and that sector's rate of economic growth. As the data in the table indicate, coefficients were calculated for all four industrial policy tools that were identified above, and they are presented for the entire 1955 to 1990 period as well as for the pre–oil-shock and post–oil-shock subperiods.

Table 3.1 Rates of Growth of Japanese Industries

Industry	1955–1990	1955–1973	1974–1990
Electrical Machinery	12.17	17.94	6.06
General Machinery	11.39	17.35	5.07
Transportation Equipment	10.76	16.93	4.42
Fabricated Metal	10.07	16.75	3.94
Petroleum/Coal	9.78	15.47	3.88
Precision Instruments	9.33	14.93	3.77
Ceramics/Stone/Glass	8.66	14.89	3.39
Pulp and Paper	7.66	13.16	2.80
Chemicals	7.64	12.32	2.72
Basic Metals	7.17	11.13	2.05
Processed Food	6.29	8.56	0.82
Mining	3.83	7.48	0.19
Textiles	2.73	7.27	–0.23

Source: Compiled by the authors from Beason and Weinstein (1996).

Table 3.2 Industrial Policy and Economic Growth

Industry Policy	Correlation Coefficients
1955–1990	
JDB Loans	–0.31
Subsidies	–0.13
Tariffs	–0.31
Tax Relief	–0.33
1955–1973	
JDB Loans	–0.48
˙Subsidies	–0.05
Tariffs	–0.11
Tax Relief	–0.47
1974–1990	
JDB Loans	–0.07
Subsidies	–0.34
Tariffs	–0.14
Tax Relief	–0.77

Source: Beason and Weinstein (1996).

The first industrial policy tool we examine is low-interest loans from the Japan Development Bank (JDB). This tool is measured by dividing the sum of real JDB loans by the total loans extended to that sector. Low interest loans are measured in this way in order to capture the share of borrowing in an industrial sector that was obtained at a subsidized rate. For the three-and-one-half-decade period covered by the data, subsidized loans were negatively correlated with economic growth. We must remember that, as a government institution, the Japan Development Bank has been held up as perhaps the most important financial arm of industrial policy.[23] Because of this, we would expect its lending, particularly that extended at subsidized rates of interest, to be positively related to growth especially in the pre–oil-shock period when capital from Japan's private banks was generally less available. The results in the table, however, show just the opposite relationship. JDB loans were far more negatively correlated with growth in the early postwar period, suggesting that its loans were biased in favor of declining industries just when they were reputedly being directed to those industries with high growth potential.

We note that the JDB was far from being the only source of government-subsidized financing during the postwar period. Indeed, there was a plethora of specialized government and quasi-government financial institutions that played important roles, but, because the Japan Development Bank was the largest of such institutions, other financial institutions tended to play subsidiary roles, leaving the JDB as the most significant player in the government's subsidized financing plans. Moreover, because of its position as the dominant provider of government-subsidized finance, we can think of JDB-lending activities as a proxy for the lending activities of other institutions that provided government-subsidized financing. In light of these factors, the negative relationship between JDB loans and sector-specific economic growth rates becomes quite striking.

A very similar pattern is witnessed in the relationship that exists between direct government subsidies and sectoral growth. Subsidies, defined as net government transfers to industries, were measured as a percentage of their respective outputs. While the impact of direct government subsidies was negative for the 1955–1990 period, it was more strongly negative for the post–oil-shock period. This is just the opposite of what we would have expected given the way that industrial policy is said to have worked. In the post–oil-shock period, Japan's private banks were awash with funds and, thus, better able to satisfy their borrowers' financial needs compared to the early postwar period.[24] Because of this, one might have expected the Japanese government to use subsidies in the post–oil-shock period to encourage investment in industries that have significant future growth potential, like high technology, but that are also defined by risk levels that keep them from receiving the private bank financing that they need. While the post–oil-shock period is the time when Japan's presence in high technology became well known, the data in Table 3.2 suggest that such developments had little or nothing to do with government subsidies. This is because the data show that subsidies were not directed to Japan's high-growth firms in the second postwar subperiod, otherwise the size of the negative correlation coefficients would have been larger in the earlier 1955–1973 period.

The relationship that exists between sectoral growth and low-interest loans/direct government subsidies suggests that government efforts were biased in favor of declining industries, and the relationship that exists between sectoral growth and the remaining two industrial policy tools in our analysis conforms to this pattern as well. The first of the remaining tools is trade protection, which is measured in terms of effective rates of protection, where the nation's overall rate of protection was subtracted from the rates characteristic of Japan's various economic sectors. This calculation resulted in positive values for those sectors that received a greater than average amount of trade protection and negative values for those that did not. The fourth and final tool, tax relief, was measured in a similar manner. Taxes received from a particular sector were divided by the taxable component of corporate earnings, and, from these values, overall effective tax rates were calculated for the years covered by the series.

As with low interest loans from the Japan Development Bank and direct government subsidies, trade protection and tax relief were negatively correlated with growth, both for the entire postwar period as well as for the pre–oil-shock and post–oil-shock subperiods. Taken together, these results tell us that, if the Japanese government, particularly bureaucrats in such agencies as the Ministry of International Trade and Industry, had in fact meant to target the nation's high-growth sectors for special government help, their efforts were not very effective. Contrary to the standard industrial policy argument of the government targeting high-growth industries, the lion's share of government support, be it subsidy, loan, tax relief, or tariff, went to those economic sectors with declining industries. If this were not the case, then correlations between the tools of industrial policy and economic growth in Japan's thirteen mining and manufacturing sectors would have been positive, even if small.

Knowing that government assistance to an economic sector was negatively correlated with growth certainly creates doubts about the effectiveness of Japanese industrial policy, but it does not tell us exactly why the impact of government attention was negatively correlated with growth. From the data provided thus far, it appears more accurate to say that declining industries were targeted, but to answer this question more fully, it is necessary to determine the relative amounts of industrial policy support each economic sector received. To accomplish this, the thirteen mining and manufacturing sectors listed above were ranked in descending order by their respective rates of economic growth. These were ranked against the amount of each industrial policy tool these sectors received, and the results are presented in Table 3.3.

The data in the table are very clear in their suggestion that the slowest-growing sectors were among the most favored in terms of government support. Indeed, the two most favored sectors were mining and textiles. The former was the most favored sector in terms of tax relief, low interest loans, and direct government subsidies. Mining was ranked last in terms of trade protection, but this makes sense when one considers that resource-poor Japan could not afford to extend trade protection to its extraction industries given its dependence on imported raw materials. Textiles was among the most favored economic sectors in terms of tax relief, trade protection, and government subsidies. Indeed, the level of government attention this sector received was perhaps second only to mining.

This is an important finding especially when one considers the amount of time that has been devoted in the literature to how the Japanese government intervened to assist in the development of those economic sectors defined as being of strategic importance. Semiconductors is a case in point both because of arguments that Japan's productive strength in this area was due to

Table 3.3 Industrial Policy Support and Sectoral Growth

	Average Growth	Cheap Loans	Gov't. Subsidies	Tariffs	Tax Relief
Electrical Machinery	12.2	8	9	8	8
General Machinery	11.4	12	4	11	8
Transport Equipment	10.8	7	11	4	8
Fabricated Metal	10.1	10	6	12	7
Oil and Coal	9.8	2	13	7	3
Precision Instruments	9.3	13	10	6	8
Ceramics, Stone, and Glass	8.7	5	8	9	3
Pulp and Paper	7.7	6	5	10	13
Chemicals	7.6	3	7	5	3
Basic Metals	7.2	4	2	3	6
Processed Food	6.3	9	12	1	12
Mining	3.8	1	1	13	1
Textiles	2.7	11	3	2	2

Source: Compiled by the authors from Beason and Weinstein (1996).

government policies and because of parallel assertions that government assistance provided Japan with an unfair advantage that nearly destroyed the U.S. semiconductor industry.[25] Unfortunately, we can see from the data in Table 3.3 that the electrical machinery sector in Japan received such small amounts of government support that it would be more accurate to argue that government policies may have in fact raised its capital costs by directing so many more scarce resources to other sectors.

Finally, while declining sectors appeared to be advantaged at the expense of growing sectors, the patterns in the table do not lead us to conclude unequivocally that Japan's industrial policy was a deliberate effort to grow what are essentially sunset industries. This is because the application of industrial policy tools across the nation's various mining and manufacturing sectors appears to be far from systematic. In other words, it appears to be the case that a sector receiving a large share of one policy tool often received much lower shares of other tools. For example, petroleum and coal received large shares of low-interest loans and tax relief but virtually no direct subsidies and a lower than average share of trade protection. To be sure, there is most likely a distinct political-economic logic operating in such allocation patterns that is discernible on further investigation. For our purposes here, however, it is sufficient to note that these transfers of government resources do match quite clearly the changing political imperatives faced by the Liberal Democratic Party throughout the postwar period. As we discuss in more detail in Section III, when the ruling party's majority began to erode, it was forced to shuffle around its available resources to maintain the loyalty of its core supporters while, at the same time, endeavoring to attract new supporters.

The next task in the empirical analysis involves determining the impact of industrial policy on productivity in the thirteen economic sectors that were identified above. As mentioned above, positive assessments of Japanese industrial policy contend that government efforts not only raised levels of growth but also encouraged structural shifts in the Japanese economy. These structural shifts involved directing investment into industries with increasing returns to scale and, thus, increasing productivity levels of Japanese firms. To determine if industrial policy actually worked in this way, it is first necessary to define Japan's industrial sectors in terms of scale parameters, that is, whether or not a sector is defined by increasing returns to scale.

Calculating the necessary scale parameters is a complicated process that involves estimating outputs and factor shares for those the various economic sectors under consideration. When economists have made such calculations for Japan's industrial sectors, the hypothesis of constant returns to scale in most of those sectors could not be rejected.[26] What this means is that, although many have asserted that Japanese industrial policy involved targeting of industries with increasing returns to scale, the empirical work conducted on this problem suggests strongly that such industries may not actually exist in Japan, and, if they do, they are not nearly as prevalent as proponents of Japanese industrial policy have asserted. Moreover, if we ignore the problem of not being able to reject the null hypothesis of constant returns to scale, the relationship between industry scale parameters and the four industrial policy tools we examined above is not quite the way that proponents of Japanese-style industrial policy have asserted.

Relying on the empirical work completed in Beason and Weinstein (1996), industry-scale parameters take the form of decimals where a value greater than one indicates an industry with increasing returns to scale, and a value less than one, the opposite. The results of correlating these scale parameters with the four industrial policy tools we discussed above are presented in Table 3.4. The correlation coefficients in the table tell us that, to the extent there were industries with increasing returns to scale, these qualities bore no relation to the level of government assistance they received. In fact, the strongest relationship in the table rests with the scale parameters and tax relief.

Table 3.4 Industry Scale and Industrial Policy

Industry Policy	Correlation
1955–1990	
JDB Loans	–0.29
Subsidies	–0.14
Tariffs	–0.27
Tax Relief	–0.34
1955–1973	
JDB Loans	–0.31
Subsidies	0.08
Tariffs	0.02
Tax Relief	–0.28
1974–1990	
JDB Loans	–0.26
Subsidies	0.10
Tariffs	–0.39
Tax Relief	–0.76

Source: Beason and Weinstein (1996).

Unfortunately, the relationship is in the opposite direction, which means that industries exhibiting some economies of scale had to pay a relatively higher tax bill. This result conforms to the deep pockets theory of public finance, but it hardly supports the idea that Japanese industrial policy selected out industries with increasing returns to scale for enhanced government attention.

Moving now to the issue of productivity and government support, we must first recognize that there are cumbersome methodological issues involved in confronting such a problem empirically. While advocates of Japanese-style industrial policy, such as Johnson, Tyson, and Zysman (1990), use concepts like "competitiveness" in their positive assessments of the Japanese government's behavior, they develop no operational definition of what "competitiveness" actually is.[27] In order to test whether industrial policy enhances "competitiveness," it is first necessary to define and measure the concept. From the microeconomic literature, we might argue that two firms that initially have the same productivity characteristics are equally competitive. If one firm thereafter experiences more rapid productivity growth than the other firm, we might say that it has become "more competitive." While this concept is reasonably well defined at the firm or industry level, it has no real meaning at the international level, which means that arguments about industrial policy enhancing a nation's international "competitiveness" are genuinely devoid of intellectual content. Nonetheless, defining "competitiveness" in terms of productivity provides a venue for testing the impact of Japanese industrial policy.

Beason and Weinstein (1996) began this process with the estimation of total factor productivity growth for different postwar subperiods for the thirteen mining and manufacturing sectors listed above (Table 3.5). Next, a positive relationship between productivity growth and the tools of industrial policy was judged to be evidence that the competitiveness of the industry had been enhanced by the Japanese government's intervention efforts. Measures of the four industrial policy variables that were discussed above are somewhat more involved than in the data presented above. First, since the impact data that were used in this analysis are time series, all industrial policy variables are presented at one- and five-year lags.[28] Second, the analysis utilizes three different measures of trade protection to get at the different ways the Japanese government shielded industry from international competition. The first measure, "Tariff 1," is the difference between the sectoral tariff rate and the average tariff rate for a particular year. The second measure of trade protection, "Tariff 2," is the effective rate of tariff protection in a particular sector which is included to capture the potential impact of overall tariff protection. Finally, a "Quota" variable is included to capture the impact of this kind of nontariff barrier.[29]

The results of this analysis, presented in Table 3.5, are striking in their clarity. In fact, they are consistent with the results presented above on the relationship between industrial policy and levels of economic growth and industrial policy and industry scales. More specifically, over any subperiod and with several alternative specifications, the results presented in the table indicate that the tools of industrial policy failed to enhance productivity growth and therefore the competitiveness of Japanese industry on the whole. The one caveat we must add here is that subsidized loans appear to have had a small positive impact on productivity growth. While this seems to support the interpretations of Japanese industrial policy that we have been criticizing, Beason and Weinstein (1996) investigated this further and found that these results were driven by one case, Japan's mining industry. JDB loans to the mining sector represented 16 percent of all loans to that sector, but, given that this was one of Japan's declining sectors, our criticism of views asserting the positive impact of industrial policy is supported by this finding. Indeed, when the mining sector is removed from the data set, the result is that the tools of industrial policy have no positive impact on productivity growth or competitiveness for any of the industrial sectors that were examined.

Using the quantifiable tools of industrial policy, Beason and Weinstein (1996) were not able to reject the null hypothesis that Japanese industrial policy in the postwar period was neutral with respect to sector growth rates, econo-

Table 3.5 Impact of Targeting on Productivity Growth

Industrial Policy Tool	1960– 1990	1960– 1973	1974– 1990	1970– 1990
Tax (t-1)	−.00409	−.00005	−.00401	−.00382
Tax (t-5)	0.00003	.00459	−.00016	−.00086
JDB (t-1)	.00396	−.00163	−.00296	.00230
JDB (t-5)	.00032	−.00246	.00168	.00133
Tariff (t-1)	−.00088	.00088	−.00438	−.00023
Tariff (t-5)	−.00004	.00031	−.00019	−.00035
Subsidies (t-1)	.00295	.00208	.00193	.00589
Subsidies (t-5)	.00104	.00129	−.00131	.00048
Tariff 2 (t-1)	.00075	−.00156	.00441	.00092
Tariff 2 (t-5)	.00000	.0000	−.00001	−.00002
Quotas (t-1)				.08802
Quotas (t-5)				.00653
R^2	0.067	0.070	0.101	0.046

Source: Prepared by the authors from Beason and Weinstein (1996).

mies of scale, or productivity growth (competitiveness). Indeed, if anything, their findings suggest a negative relationship between industrial policy targeting and the measurements of economic success. Any positive benefit of signaling, which cannot be measured empirically, would have to have been completely orthogonal to the actual allocation of scarce public resources. We believe that the burden of proof for those who wish to believe in any positive benefits associated with government signaling rests fully with such proponents.

By way of conclusion, it is worthwhile to note that the Japanese economy managed to function quite effectively throughout most of the postwar period despite the clear failure of industrial policy targeting. This leads us to a very different conclusion about the relationship between government intervention and the high levels of economic growth that so many said made Japan structurally distinct among advanced nations. The key issue here is not that industrial policy was generally unconnected to Japan's postwar economic success but rather that Japan's high rates of economic growth were able to mask the negative influences of government policy. In light of this, we must also ask if institutions that have often been credited with Japanese economic success might actually have been neutral or even negative in their impact but that such impacts were masked by otherwise robust growth. We address this topic in the next chapter.

Chapter 4

MANAGEMENT PRACTICES AND LABOR RELATIONS

A Japanese System or Economic Incentives?

Japanese business organization at its highest levels has been another major reason for the country's economic success. This aspect of Japan's economy in particular is little understood in the West.

—Edwin Reicschauer and Marius Jansen (1995)

Some of these changes [in employment] happen through the labor market processes of retirement, entry into the labor force, and voluntary movement of individuals seeking to better themselves. Yet it seems implausible that in an economy in which a large segment of the labor force sees itself, and is seen by its employer, as having entered into a "lifetime contract," shifts of the magnitude involved could have happened by those processes alone.

—Ronald Dore (1986)

Permanent employment can be best understood by keeping two basic concepts in mind: first, the form is something akin to a family, where all employees are members of the firm; second, a psychological contract exists between employer and employee, which implies mutual loyalty.

—Steve Reed (1993)

Like Industrial policy, there are other features of Japan's postwar political-economic system that have attracted an increasing amount of attention from scholars in the last two decades, both Japan specialist and nonspecialist alike. Perhaps the most notable concerns management practices and labor relations in Japanese firms, specifically how different Japan is with respect to these business essentials and what economic impacts can be attributed to them. Scholars have approached these important issues from a variety of perspectives, and the resultant literature is hardly uniform in explaining why management practices and labor relations manifest certain patterns that are arguably specific to Japan. Nonetheless, most treatments of these interrelated topics are similar in three important ways.

First, analyses of these important economic issues all proceed from the idea that management practices and labor relations are substantially different in postwar Japan than they are in other developed nations. Second, scholarly treatments of management practices and labor relations construe Japan's distinctive patterns as components of a larger, purposive political-economic design that cannot be explained simply by economic actors responding to the incentives they faced throughout the postwar period. Third, all writing on these topics agrees that Japan's labor and management differences have been at least partly responsible for the postwar economic miracle. Indeed, as Kyoto University economist, Koike Kazuo, stated, "There is a consensus that human resource development and labor-management relations have contributed crucially to the performance of the Japanese economy."[1]

These areas of broad agreement do not mean that there have been no differences of opinion in the writing that exists on management practices and labor relations in postwar Japan. To be sure, the literature on these important topics involves disputes over why Japan evolved its distinctive patterns in the first place and whether its distinctive patterns are differences of degree or substance. Moreover, a significant debate emerged early in the postbubble period over whether or not Japan's current troubles meant that its specific patterns of labor-management relations had outlived their usefulness.[2] Rather, what is important here is that they represent another example of "the Japan that never was" problem being brought into focus by the political-economic developments of the 1990s. In the past, treatments of these important economic issues took it as a given that Japan's unique institutions were more the result of careful design than of market forces. They also universally agreed that Japan's special features were sources of economic strength throughout most of the postwar period. In the current period of structural adjustment, however, these same treatments also note that, because of the economic and financial problems that Japan currently faces, there are efforts on the part of Japanese firms to alter long-established labor and management practices.

These current assessments understand that Japanese firms have been trying to reduce scale because of the debts they acquired over the last two decades. The current debt problem occurred partly because firms overinvested in plant and equipment using borrowed funds from their principal private lenders and partly because this problem was aggravated by the collapse of asset values after the bursting of the economic bubble. Consequently, it is quite true that the cost problems Japanese firms face are more serious today than at any time in the postwar period and that this problem has forced Japanese firms to contemplate changes that were unthinkable during the period of high growth. This is important because it tells us that the intellectual problem we face with respect to Japanese labor and management practices is not that their negative impact in recent years has been misdiagnosed but rather that we do not have a satisfying understanding of their emergence in the first place and their overall economic impact.

In our view, the problem is that, by asserting that Japan's patterns of management and labor were positive in the past and negative in the current period of structural adjustment, assessments of these business essentials have not captured the connection that exists between their genesis and their essential economic functions. Stated another way, treatments of management practices and labor market institutions have understated the relationship that necessarily exists between why certain labor and management practices have become specific to postwar Japan and what economic roles they were created to perform.[3] This has occurred in the literature because most analysts have treated Japanese-style management and labor market institutions as a unique part of the Japanese political-economic system that resulted from cooperation between government and business to affect the nation's economic recovery earlier in the postwar period.

Our purpose in this chapter is to show that assessing the economic impacts of Japanese management practices and labor market institutions, both in the period of high growth and in the current period of structural adjustment, requires an explanation of why those management and labor patterns emerged in postwar Japan in the first place. In our effort to address this question, we show that management practices and labor relations in postwar Japan are manifold patterns that derive from a single source, namely large Japanese firms responding to the economic incentives they faced in their efforts to acquire and train human capital early in the postwar period. As with other aspects of Japan's postwar economic development, the role of private actors responding to the economic incentives they faced (market forces) has not been fully exploited. To develop this explanation more fully, we begin with a brief discussion of the management practices and labor relations patterns that have come to define firm behavior in postwar Japan.

LABOR RELATIONS AND MANAGEMENT PRACTICES IN POSTWAR JAPAN

Scholars have typically characterized the Japanese labor market as being comprised of three pillars of support: labor peace, lifetime employment, and the seniority wage system. The first of these pillars, labor peace, refers to the fact that labor relations in Japanese firms have come to be defined by a much lower incidence of production-threatening labor actions and by a relatively high degree of cooperation between labor and management. This labor peace that characterizes relations between employees and management in Japan is often correctly attributed to the prominence of enterprise unions, that is, workers being organized at the level of the firm rather than at the industry level in the form of trade unions.

By being organized at the level of the firm, such essential activities as wage bargaining and labor disputes take place on a firm-by-firm basis where management negotiates with an enterprise-based union that generally covers all employees in that firm except management above a certain line-responsibility level. Being organized at the level of the firm means that the livelihood of the enterprise union's members is intrinsically tied to the well-being of the firm. Bargaining games in such an organizational context are conducted with the recognition that maximization of joint gain will give the best results for the membership of the enterprise union. In other words, given that benefits accruing to the enterprise union and its membership are inextricably tied to the health of the firm, maximization of the present value of the firm will offer the most benefits for the firm's employees. By tying the economic interests of company employees to the overall economic vitality of the firm, enterprise unionism naturally promotes the cooperation that one witnesses in Japanese companies between labor and management.

Being organized in this way does not mean that enterprise unions are satellite groups that are wholly controlled by the firms within which they operate. They are independent organizations that do indeed strive to defend the interests of their respective memberships. Nonetheless, being organized in the manner described above has given Japan a greater amount of labor peace than is typically witnessed elsewhere in the developed world.[4] Again, this is because any type of industrial action that reduces output has the consequence of lowering firm revenues and, thus, shrinking the amount of benefits that can be distributed to the firm's workers. Consequently, job actions in Japan are typically characterized by lunchtime strikes and protests because these types of actions do not reduce production as those that truly harm Japanese firms have become increasingly rare.[5] Moreover, enterprise unions work with management to resolve disputes that invariably arise with attempts to increase the productivity of firms through the introduction of new production technologies. By promoting cooperation in such potentially disruptive situations, enterprise unionism does more than simply promote labor peace. It helps Japanese firms employ technologically advanced and efficient production processes while at the same time avoiding the labor disputes that are often attendant to such actions.

This type of labor organization stands in direct contrast to the manner in which industry-based trade unions organize labor in such countries as the United States and Great Britain. Generally, in a typical trade union, membership is spread across several firms in an industry, and sometimes membership can extend across a variety of industries, regardless of how those industries are related to each other. Under such organizational conditions, it may be possible to maximize gain for a majority of union members while harming some subset of the firms within which those members are employed. In other words, the benefits accruing to the union membership are typically divided across many firms in a single or in several industries and this in turn keeps membership benefits from being tied to the health and vitality of a single firm, particularly a single firm that employs the members of that union.

The second pillar of the Japanese labor market is the more familiar practice of Japanese firms guaranteeing their employees a job for life—what is known as permanent or lifetime employment.[6] The basic idea is that a certain percentage of employees hired by Japan's large firms are extended an implicit agreement that the company will not lay them off for economic reasons throughout their tenure with the firm. This provides such employees with a kind of guarantee that they will have a job with that large firm until they retire, something that occurs typically at age 55.[7] In return for this implicit company guarantee that they will not be laid off for economic reasons, employees agree not to change jobs and dedicate themselves to the company while they are in its employ.

Lifetime employment has often been held up as a feature of the postwar Japanese political-economic system that renders it unique among advanced nations. While the manner in which lifetime employment came to be practiced in the postwar period is arguably specific to Japan, a closer examination of the extent to which it is actually practiced there reveals that it is perhaps a less prevalent and unique feature than such opinions have suggested.[8]

First, lifetime employment is hardly a universal practice in Japan. As stated above, given that it covers only certain employees in large Japanese firms, typically only 25 percent to 30 percent of the Japanese labor force is covered by lifetime employment.[9] Second, the phrase *lifetime employment* implies that workers covered by such a system are never terminated before retirement. In fact, throughout the high-growth period, a small number of employees had been fired every year, even in Japan's large firms.[10] Moreover, the fact that only a small number of employees were terminated throughout the postwar period was also an artifact of the fact that the Japanese economy recorded such high levels of growth that companies did not experience strong pressures to lay off employees for economic reasons. Finally, the literature on labor relations in Japan has suggested that lifetime employment, if not unique to Japan, is one of the nation's postwar hallmarks. The truth of the matter is that employment patterns comparable to Japan's lifetime employment system have not been all that uncommon. For example, Freeman (1987) has shown that lifetime employment has been prevalent not only in many European countries but also that it is not uncommon in many large American firms.

The third pillar of the Japanese labor market is what is known as the seniority system for wages. This is a straightforward practice that begins with the recognition that individual employees enter Japanese companies at different levels. More specifically, some employees enter at the worker (or blue-collar) level while others enter at the executive or managerial level, and the level at which an employee enters a company is determined by that employee's level of education, job-related skills, and sometimes performance on competitive examinations. Those with the best education and skills and, where applicable, the highest scores on competitive examinations are the ones most likely to be placed on the management track, leading ultimately to a top executive position in that company.[11] Despite these entry-level differences, virtually all company employees can expect the same pattern of compensation increments in that pay levels are determined by seniority, that is, the employee's age and the length of time he or she has been with the company. Typically, the wages of new employees are low, indeed lower than their productivity levels, but they increase in a regular manner as their tenure with the company increases.[12] This has led to Japan's age-wage profile being defined by a steeper slope than most other advanced countries.[13]

In addition to the organizational form that labor market institutions have taken in postwar Japan and the manner in which Japanese firms have evolved relations between management and labor, the literature on the postwar Japanese political-economic system involves a large component devoted to management practices in large Japanese firms. The literature on Japanese-style management, especially writing in the popular business press, has identified several practices that were said to make up the Japanese approach to firm management. Practices like quality-control circles, just-in-time inventory management, long-term strategic planning, and consensus-type/bottom-up decision making have been widely discussed as contributing to Japanese-style management.[14] To be sure, there are many aspects to what has become known as Japanese-style management that have received different levels of emphasis in the literature. For the purposes of the analysis that follows, however, we divide these aspects into three categories.

The first aspect of Japanese-style management that we identify here refers to the generic behavior of Japanese firms and how it is reputedly different from the behavior of business firms as provided in microeconomic theory. For a host of reasons that range from the continued influence of Japanese feudalism and the dictates of Japanese culture (Abegglen, 1958, 1970) to the distinctive management-ownership structure that defines corporate Japan (Aoki, 1984, 1987; Dore 1986), it has been said that Japanese companies are guided by long-term strategic thinking in their market behavior. This means that Japanese companies are able to focus on growth in sales and market share over long-time horizons rather than short-term profits, as symbolized in quarterly earnings statements that is said to define American corporate behavior in particular. The practical importance of developing "a managerial culture which makes market shares rather than profits the index through the contemplation of which managers can massage or flagellate their egos" is not only to help firms expand into new industries but also, and perhaps more important, to assist in the "development of international competitiveness in the innovative frontier industries where aggressive pricing, low profits but high volumes can take firms more rapidly along the learning curve to a low-cost, high returns position."[15]

The second aspect of Japanese-style management that we identify here relates to what we refer here to as the external cooperative behavior of Japanese firms. By external cooperation, we are specifically referring to the manner in which Japanese firms interact with the Japanese government as well as with other firms both in upstream supplier relations and across producers of the same final products. The basic argument is that, in both cases, firm behavior in Japan is much more cooperative than antagonistic, and this in turn provides Japanese companies with advantages that are not available to firms in other developed nations.[16] This does not mean that there is no conflict between private businesses and the Japanese government or that interfirm behavior involves no competition, especially among firms that produce the same final products.[17] Rather, it means that, while there are disagreements with government policies and directives, public-private interactions are carried out in a generally cooperative and productive manner.[18] It also means that, while there is conflict among firms in Japan, there is sufficient cooperation to allow producers of the same final products to form what are in effect cartels that benefit members greatly and to collaborate in upstream-downstream supplier relationships in the form of beneficial *keiretsu* groupings.[19]

In contrast to the external cooperative behavior of Japanese firms, the third aspect of Japanese-style management concerns what we refer to as intrafirm cooperation. In general, the idea here is that employees of Japanese firms see themselves as members of the same company family and, thus, endeavor to cooperate at all levels of employment for the benefit of the firm. This aspect of Japanese management leads to strong feelings of company solidarity and loyalty, and it also manifests itself in the low levels of employee turnover one typically witnesses in large Japanese firms. This internal co-operation aspect of Japanese-style management is obviously related to the three pillars of the Japanese system of labor relations that we described above, but it is also the principal reason that certain management practices have come to define the behavior of Japanese firms. Such manifestations of Japanese management as quality control circles, worker input into management decisions, and just-in-time inventory management require high levels of employee cooperation.

Having briefly described those aspects of labor relations and management practices that ostensibly make Japan distinct, our next task is to examine more thoroughly the manner in which these business behavior essentials manifest themselves with two goals in mind. The first is to explain why Japan's patterns of corporate management and labor relations have acquired the distinctiveness they have in the postwar period. Our emphasis with respect to this goal will be on how the economic incentives (constraints and opportunities) faced by Japanese firms in the aftermath of the Pacific War encouraged the patterns that we have witnessed in Japanese management practices and labor relations. After explaining the origins of Japan's patterns, we turn to our second goal, assessing the economic function they were created to perform. As we stated above, if we do not have a clear understanding of the economic roles played by these labor-management institutions, we will not be able to explain fully their impact on both Japan's postwar economic miracle and the ability of the Japanese government to eliminate their inefficient aspects and move more quickly through the current period of structural adjustment.

Before turning our attention to these two goals, we look first more closely at the context that encouraged firms and workers to behave in a way that led to the management and labor patterns that we have witnessed in postwar Japan. The context we refer to concerns the constraints and opportunities Japanese firms have encountered in their efforts to acquire and train human capital.

ECONOMIC INCENTIVES AND THE PROBLEM OF HUMAN CAPITAL

To understand why management practices and labor relations in postwar Japan have involved patterns that are specific to that country, we must understand how Japanese firms acquire and train human capital and the economic incentives they have faced in Japan's labor market in this essential behavior. More specifically, what we need to know is that the acquisition and, perhaps more important, the training of human capital in corporate Japan is highly firm-specific. There are many factors that help account for this in postwar Japan, and the extent to which it exists is difficult to overestimate. In an example of how companies' imprints on their respective employees are nearly indelible, Ronald Dore pointed out that even ten years after the merger that produced Japan Steel, "everyone is said to be still aware of who is a Yawata man and who a Fuji man."[20]

Why the training of human capital became so firm-specific in postwar Japan has to do with the supply of and demand for labor in the early years of the postwar period and the manner in which Japan's education system came to prepare workers for the labor market. When Japan's industrialization began to take off in the 1950s and 1960s, the demand for workers with a certain set of applicable skills naturally increased. Unfortunately, the Japanese system of education was poorly equipped to provide the kind of training that was desired by Japanese firms at the time. Despite the government's best attempts to westernize the Japanese education system during the Meiji period, schooling was still highly influenced by Oriental tradition, which means that it was based on mastery of the Eastern classics and the study of Chinese literature, writing, and poetry. Indeed, to this day, *kokubun,* the method of reading that allows Japanese speakers to understand Chinese classics, is still taught in many schools. While this kind of schooling was good at creating scholars in Asian classics, it did little to provide a technically sophisticated workforce that would be most productive for Japan's rapidly evolving industrial sector.

This weakness of the modern Japanese education system was reinforced during the period immediately preceding the Pacific War not only because the education system's Orientalist emphasis was reinforced by the military's attempt to imbue the curriculum with notions of nationalism, patriotism, and other values to serve the war effort, but also because, at the same time, all vestiges of Western influence were purged from the curriculum. At the time, instead of producing citizens with useful, marketable skills, education became part of the government's propaganda apparatus, which necessitated that the types of skills needed for an evolving industrial economy would have to be provided elsewhere. This meant that Japanese firms themselves had to educate their own workforces through extensive in-firm training. These circumstances persisted even after the Pacific War when the imperial university system was replaced by the current national university system and a number of educational reforms were forced on Japan's postwar civilian authorities by the Occupation. This is because, despite many reforms to education in Japan, certain traditional aspects of Japan's educational system remained unchanged.

Many of the reforms put forth by the Civil Information and Education (CS&I) Section of the Occupation removed from Japanese education the authoritarian and propagandistic elements imposed by the military, but they had the unintended consequence of reinforcing Japanese education's generalist orientation. Among those many reforms implemented at the primary and secondary levels was the institution of curricular changes that emphasized the education of democratic citizens, which made education at those levels even less technical and rigorous than they already were. At the postsecondary level, the Occupation authorities reorganized all existing higher-educational institutions into four-year schools modeled on the U.S. college/university system. Like the results witnessed at the primary and secondary levels, these higher-education changes also had the unintended impact of reinforcing the generalist tendencies of Japanese education. As Kazuo Kawai noted, as a result of the Occupation's education reforms, "the vocational courses are no longer practical enough to be of much use; the academic courses tend to be watered down by the presence of too many disinterested or incapable students; and electives offer the temptation to too many pupils to choose the easiest possible course."[21]

It is true that many Occupation reforms in the area of education were reversed by Japan's civilian authorities when the Peace Treaty with Japan was promulgated. And while many of the reforms that were reversed by the government—such as the recentralization of administrative control over education in general—were hardly unimportant, they still did not involve changes that would help Japan's education system produce the kind of skilled employees that Japanese companies needed. The fact is that, as Japanese companies expanded during the period of high growth, the education system was not able to keep up with the rapidly expanding demand for skilled workers that high growth required. At the same time, Japan was rapidly transforming itself from a rural, agrarian society into an urban, industrial nation that further strained the education system's ability to supply all the specific skills required by industry.

We must be clear here that we are not asserting that the postwar education system in Japan produced workers who were illiterate and without any industry-applicable skills. In fact, graduates of Japanese secondary and postsecondary education institutions were highly literate and possessive of comparatively strong math skills. What they did not get, however, was the specific technical skills that would be directly applicable to jobs in industry. For this reason, the Occupation and post-Occupation periods, just like the wartime period, witnessed Japanese firms providing the bulk of the job-specific training to their respective workforces. The technical content of the training given to a firm's employees certainly varied with the career path of the particular employee, but, in all instances, the training was tailor-made to the firm's requirements, meaning that even general training had a highly firm-specific character.

These characteristics of Japan's education system help us understand why the principal responsibility for training employees has fallen on firms, but we are still left with the question of why the content of that training is so firm-specific. After all, since companies like Toyota and Nissan both make cars and other companies like Ricoh and Canon both make copiers, why should they be governed by training systems that are so firm-specific. The answer to this question rests with the idea that, beyond providing companies with skilled workers, firm-specific training serves the broader economic interests of Japanese companies. To show what these interests are, we must first examine more thoroughly the nature of the training that Japan's large firms provide to members of their respective workforces. For the majority of Japanese firms, this involves two types of training, specifically skill training and functional rotation.

By skill training, we are referring to the fact that the firm itself imparts the technical skills necessary for employees to perform the specific functions that the firm needs. The reason for this is as we stated above: education in Japan, but especially higher education, is quite general. By the end of secondary education in Japan, most students have acquired general skills typically associated with a liberal university education elsewhere in the developed world. Literacy and written communication skills are generally high, and mathematics and science education is equivalent to that of a North American university education in many respects. In university, while students "specialize," the education remains general and little new knowledge is imparted.[22] For firms evaluating college graduates as potential employees, university education in Japan functions mostly as a screening device in that students who graduate from top-ranked universities are considered highly intelligent and trainable by firms. The knowledge potential employees acquired while in college, on the other hand, is generally not regarded very highly by firms.

In practice, this means that when a firm needs say, engineers, it has little confidence that an engineering major at a mainstream Japanese university will fill the bill. The top firms may be equally inclined to hire a literature or general science major and then train him or her as an engineer, that is, in the specific nuts and bolts engineering skills that are required for that employee to function effectively within that particular firm. This may seem to contradict the commonly accepted notion that Japanese corporations—and society as well—are dominated by engineers, but, as Kinmonth (1990) has shown, relatively few "engineers" in Japan are bona-fide engineers in the Western sense. Indeed, many are simply technicians who may have studied unrelated fields in university and acquired the requisite engineering skills on the job. Instead, Japanese firms, especially the larger ones, simply hire the best and brightest from various fields from the top universities, and then train them as they see fit within the firm. Thus, when a large Japanese firm needs specialized engineering or other staff, it simply provides the requisite training in-house.

This relates to the second characteristic of the firm-specific training imparted to employees of Japanese companies, functional rotation. An employee's firm-specific training involves not only the specific technical skills company executives see as being necessary for employees to perform adequately at their jobs, it also involves being certain that the company's workforce has a certain breadth of firm knowledge. This means being familiar with company operations beyond the limited employment opportunities that tend to define the experience of the typical American blue-collar worker. For this reason, large firms in Japan typically rotate workers around the company itself and its various divisions so that they learn how to perform competently in many different firm operations.

Having described the human capital acquisition and training conditions Japanese firms faced in the wartime and early postwar periods, it is our next task to show how these conditions led to the patterns that defined management practices and labor relations in postwar Japan. Because of the predictable economic functions these institutions performed in postwar Japan, we begin this effort with a discussion of labor relations in light of why our economic incentives perspective, based on the conditions related to firms' efforts to acquire and train members of their respective workforces in the early postwar period, offers a better understanding of why labor relations manifested themselves in the three ways they did.

JAPANESE LABOR RELATIONS: THREE PILLARS OR ONE COLUMN?

As we have stated briefly above, descriptions of the three pillars of the Japanese system of labor relations in the literature are roughly correct. However, saying that labor relations in Japan involve notable levels of labor peace, lifetime employment, and seniority wages is not the same as concluding that current scholarly assessments of labor relations in Japan involve no unresolved intellectual issues. This is because the way that scholars have attempted to account for the origins of these three aspects of labor relations in Japan have involved two problematic themes, one that is generally consistent across all treatments of this important subject and another that varies across the explanations propounded by different analysts.

The theme that is generally consistent across all treatments of labor relations in postwar Japan concerns how lifetime employment, labor peace, and seniority wages are beyond the mere operation of market forces and, thus, treated as manifestations of a larger political-economic design intended to provide Japanese firms with a comparative advantage in terms of how they are run. The problem here is that, taken together, these three pillars give labor relations in postwar Japan a unique flavor, but assessments of their origins and economic functions imply that they are separate, stand-alone phenomena. In other words, while each pillar contributes to the overall system of labor relations one finds in postwar Japan, lifetime employment, labor peace, and seniority wages are treated as phenomena that can exist apart from each other.

The problematic theme that varies across scholarly treatments of labor relations in Japan concerns the different factors that Japan specialists have emphasized as the principal cause of that Japanese system's origins. For example, James Abegglen (1973), who wrote one of the first extensive treatises on corporate Japan, sees these three pillars as being rooted in Japan's traditional culture. Others like Lester Thurow (1992) see Japan's labor market institutions as a function of a nationalistic response to Japan's precarious place in the world economy. Revisionists like Chalmers Johnson (1982), Eamon Fingleton (1995), and Clyde Prestowitz (1988) agree with the nationalistic orientation emphasized by Thurow but add that Japan's pattern of labor relations is the conscious design of the nation's bureaucracy to create comparative advantage in the area of labor relations.

The view of the origin, design, and economic function of these Japanese labor market institutions, that we advance in this chapter, proceeds differently. First, we do not take these labor market institutions as a given because of the nature of Japanese society or culture. The influence of Japanese culture and society appears to be an inadequate explanation simply because the patterns defined by the three pillars of Japanese labor relations have varied more than culture and society have in modern Japan. For example, Taira (1970) and Koike (1987) have shown that these pillars of Japanese labor relations are essentially a postwar phenomenon. Prior to the postwar period, as Saxonhouse's research on cotton spinning in the Meiji era has shown, the norm was high turnover, which would have made such labor practices quite contrary to the dictates of Japanese culture. Moreover, we do not understand Japan's patterns of labor relations as a function of economic nationalism in Japan that has led the government to encourage their development for the nation's comparative advantage. We see this view as inadequate as well because, if these three pillars were the design of nationalistic economic bureaucrats, then why have these same economic bureaucrats not responded sooner and more thoroughly to the current crisis by encouraging a more flexible labor market response than we have witnessed to date.

The key to understanding the origins and economic function of these three aspects of labor relations in postwar Japan rests with the economic incentives faced by Japanese firms in their efforts to acquire and train members of their respective workforces early in the postwar period. As we noted above, the response of Japanese firms was conditioned specifically by the fact that the nation's education system tends to produce generalists that then have to undergo extensive firm-specific training to acquire the skills necessary to be effective at company operations. As a result of this, firms evolved a set of labor practices that would protect the investments they made in the training of their employees. Naturally, this meant that firms had to provide employees with certain benefits that they otherwise might not receive. Stated more directly, Japanese firms direct a substantial portion of corporate resources to their workforces for ongoing training and skill development. This is a well-known aspect of firm behavior in Japan, but what is less well known is how this investment in the development of human capital also required that firms think very carefully about how they would protect such investments in their workforces. Indeed, it would be highly unproductive for firms to invest substantial sums in the training of their respective workforces only to lose the most skilled employees to a competing firm that lured them away with a better package of wages and perquisites.

To solve this problem, large Japanese firms evolved certain labor practices that provided the employees they trained with incentives to stay with that firm over the long term. The first of these involved firms making a concession to Japanese labor on the issue of job security, and the result of this concession was the lifetime employment system. Workers in Japan had been pressing for greater job security since the late Meiji and Taisho periods.[23] While corporate leaders in prewar Japan considered making some concessions in this area, they had little incentive to give in completely on the issue until the demand for skilled workers increased dramatically with Japan's postwar economic resurgence. The demand for skilled workers increased significantly as Japan entered the period of high growth, raising the importance of ensuring a low turnover rate for workers that it trained. By granting to workers an implicit guarantee that they would not be fired for economic reasons, Japanese firms took a significant step toward ensuring a long tenure for the employees they invested so much to train.

In the context of firm-specific training and a growing demand for skilled workers that we discussed above, lifetime employment appears to make a reasonable amount of economic sense. In spite of this, there are still aspects to the practice of extending employees an implicit guarantee that they will be employed by that firm until retirement that appear to violate the dictates of economic reasoning. Specifically, two additional questions of economic justification are raised by this practice. First, in spite of the need to protect their human capital investments, why would firms still want to forgo the opportunity to reduce the size of their respective workforces by guaranteeing jobs to certain employees even if economic need dictated such an action? On the other side of the coin, why would workers agree to forgo the opportunity to test the labor market by seeing that the skills they acquired could result in higher wages and more generous benefits by joining another firm? The answer to these questions rests, first, with the extent to which lifetime employment is actually practiced in postwar Japan and, second, with the fact that other labor market institutions must be pared with lifetime employment to make it economically feasible.

From the firm side of the equation, it would seem that a labor-relations arrangement that locked the firm into possessing a labor force that it could not terminate would not make much economic sense. The fact is, however, that the features of Japan's system of lifetime employment are such that it is not nearly as inflexible as the phrase itself suggests. As mentioned above, lifetime employment applies only to a certain percentage of workers in Japan's labor force. This means that all large firms in Japan have a certain number of employees who are not extended the lifetime employment guarantee, and, if economic downturns become severe enough, a firm will opt to let its temporary employees go before considering any change to its permanent labor force.

Firms also have other options available by which they can retain permanent employees in periods of economic downturn. As we also mentioned above, all permanent employees experience a substantial amount of functional rotation as part of their firm-specific training. This employee experience serves a useful economic purpose for firm executives during periods of extensive production cuts. As Ronald Dore aptly observes, because occupational consciousness is low in Japanese firms, when there is no skilled work to be done in a particular worker's area, that worker would not object should he "temporarily be asked to weed the flower beds beside the factory gates, or be sent off for two or three months to augment the external sales force."[24]

We must also remember that, throughout the postwar period, "lifetime employment" has been coupled with a significant amount of bonus compensation. This means that workers in large firms have typically received between 25 percent and 40 percent of their total annual compensation in the form of biannual bonus payments. While in buoyant economic times workers tend to count on such payments as a predetermined multiple of a month's pay, these bonuses actually become quite flexible during economic downturns. This has allowed firms to reduce the wage bill simply by reducing total compensation, rather than resorting to layoffs. Of course, the current economic crisis has stretched this option to the limit, so that headcount reductions have become increasingly attractive to many firms.

In spite of these options, there are nonetheless times when economic conditions dictate that upper-level executives of a firm must contemplate the very difficult issue of reducing its workforce to lower costs. If a firm, at such times, merely sets out and simply terminates the number of permanent employees it feels necessary, then the lifetime employment system itself would be devoid of meaning. For this and other reasons, large Japanese firms have sanctioned the development of enterprise unions. The most important point to remember here is that enterprise unionism is not simply a second pillar that corporate Japan with government approval added to the system of labor relations in postwar Japan. It is a logical institutional development without which the lifetime employment system could not function.

Japanese firms need to encourage the long-term tenure of their respective employees in order to protect their human capital investments. On the other hand, business conditions sometimes require that company executives take action that hurts the interests of company employees. Having its employees organized at the level of the firm, however, ensures that employees' economic well-being becomes closely associated with that of the firm. Under such conditions, firm employees are more willing to make sacrifices in the form of such things as cutting overtime, paid work time, and bonuses since such sacrifices will serve their long-term economic interests as well. Again, it cannot be stressed enough that integral to making such an arrangement work is the fact that employees can rest assured that, except under the most extreme conditions, their jobs are generally safe since they have that implicit guarantee that the company will do everything it can to avoid laying off permanent employees.

Enterprise unionism is also an expected institutional development from the perspective of a firm's workers. The concomitant to being willing to sacrifice for the good of the firm is the fact that enterprise unionism gives workers a stronger voice in firm decisions, especially decisions that directly affect their economic interests. For example, if business conditions dictate that a firm must contemplate layoffs, such a process always begins with the holding of discussions with leaders of the enterprise union in that firm. Enterprise unions typically resist layoffs at all costs and, thus, make cost-cutting counterproposals that save members' jobs. Even if some reduction in the workforce becomes necessary and cannot be handled through retirements, transfers, and hiring reductions, the firm's executives will also encourage the enterprise union to participate if not take the lead by recommending which employees will be terminated.

While these institutional arrangements serve to make the "lifetime employment system" far more flexible than it might at first appear, they do not fully account for the incentives on the part of the firm to maintain it. Returning to the issue of firm specific training, if we accept that this pattern of training has been the norm among large firms in the postwar period, then we must also recognize that each employee in such firms represents a large human capital investment. From the firm's perspective, terminating such an employee, even in financially difficult circumstances, is a difficult decision. While termination may help to alleviate temporary cost pressures, the firm will ultimately have to hire and train anew. Such implied costs of termination to the firm rise in direct proportion to the amount of firm-specific training embodied in the worker, and, as such, separation is a decision the firm will not take lightly. The result will be relatively long tenure and low turnover.

Although the preceding discussion has helped clarify why there is an inseparable relationship between the first two pillars of Japanese labor relations and the economic purposes they serve, we must still explore more fully why it is that firm-trained workers find it in their interests to remain with that firm for the long term. Specifically, we must consider the incentives workers face with respect to their participation in the "lifetime employment system." Part of this effort, albeit the smaller part, rests with the fact that firm-specific training in Japan makes an employee more of an asset to the firm that trains him or her than to a competing firm where the employee will be less of a known quantity. More important than this, however, is the role played by the third pillar of labor relations in postwar Japan, namely seniority wages.

As stated above, compensation patterns in Japan follow a rather sharp seniority profile as opposed to a lifetime productivity profile. Because of this, not only is it the case that the firm is willing to pay the costs of specific training, but it is also the case that workers have an incentive to stay with the firm. If a worker leaves a firm, he or she will have to begin anew at the starting point in the earnings profile. With seniority wages, this will imply a significant cost to a worker with any amount of tenure with a firm. Add to this the fact that the worker will have signaled to future employers that he or she cannot be trusted to repay the costs of retraining to the firm, and it is likely that the best that worker will be able to do on leaving his or her primary firm is to join the "secondary labor market." In Japan, this has meant moving from a well-paid job with a large firm to a low-paying job with relatively poorer working conditions in a smaller one, making the price a very high one indeed (Beason, 2000).

The situation we have described can be exemplified graphically (Figure 4.1). The curved line represents the hypothesized productivity profile of a typical worker in a firm characterized by "lifetime employment." Initial marginal product is low during the training phase and lies below the (seniority) wage profile. During this phase, the firm is paying the cost of the worker's training. Eventually, marginal product surpasses the wage, and the firm is

Wage, marginal product

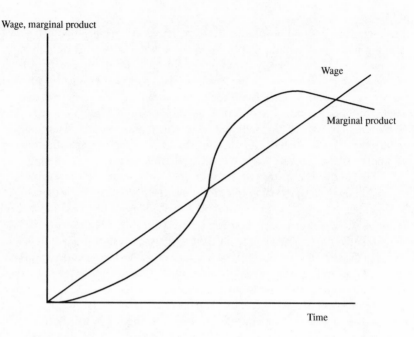

Time

Figure 4.1 Lifetime Employment Earnings-Productivity Profile

paid back for the costs it incurred in training the employee. Ultimately, the worker's productivity begins to wane and is once again surpassed by his or her wage. At this later point in the worker's career, the firm has an incentive to retire the worker, and indeed Japanese firms have been well-known for their mandatory retirement systems, typically around age fifty-five for most of the postwar period. The obvious reason for such early retirement is that if the worker continues with the firm for too long, it is possible that the present value of the stream of marginal product may become less than the present value of the stream of wages paid, something the firm wishes to avoid. We should note here that many firms move these "retired" workers to subsidiaries at a lower rate of pay, essentially removing elderly workers from the seniority wage system.

What we have shown here is that a labor market like Japan's, which is characterized by a high degree of firm-specific training for human capital, is one most likely also to be characterized by lifetime employment, labor peace, and seniority wages. This is not because such an arrangement of labor market institutions is part of a cooperative government-business design intended to give Japanese firms a comparative advantage over those of other nations. Rather, such an arrangement represents the only economically sensible response Japanese firms could pursue in the context of their human capital needs and the supply conditions that defined the Japanese labor market early in the postwar period. As such, lifetime employment, labor peace, and seniority wages are not really three separate pillars but rather the three faces of the single column that has supported labor relations in Japan throughout most of the postwar period.

JAPANESE-STYLE MANAGEMENT: PREROGATIVE OR INCENTIVES?

Like the three pillars of labor relations in postwar Japan, descriptions of the specific corporate practices that combine to form Japanese-style management are roughly correct. Japanese firms have appeared to behave in ways that distinguish them from the standard model of firm behavior in microeconomic theory. Moreover, Japanese firms appear to engage in levels of inter- and intrafirm cooperation that are generally not witnessed in the United States. Authors who point to such features of Japanese management are not incorrect in concluding that these kinds of features are specific to Japan. Where problems arise, however, rests with the way that the origin and importance of Japanese-style management are explained. Specifically, most treatments of Japanese-style management explain whatever differences characterize the behavior of Japanese firms as the result of managerial decision-making (management prerogative), and, moreover, they contend that Japanese management practices are different enough to form a competing model of firm behavior compared to what one finds in neoclassical treatments of the business firm.

Like discussions of Japan's labor market institutions, however, what is missing in treatments of Japanese-style management is attention to how the origins of Japan's different management practices are inextricably tied to the performance of certain economic functions. This has led Japan scholars focusing on this important topic to underappreciate the extent to which Japanese-style management is the expected response of Japanese firms to the economic incentives they faced in the postwar period and not the result of purposive managerial decision making. This has also led such scholars to overstate the extent to which management practices in Japan, as manifested in the actual behavior of Japanese firms, are unique and something quite apart from the way firm behavior is characterized in microeconomic theory.

The idea that Japanese firms are distinctive in their day-to-day behavior is based on the argument that, because Japanese managers have long-term bonds with their respective firms, they are more likely to focus on long-term economic goals. In this context, long-term goals refer to such maxima as sales, market share, or value added rather than profits whose maximization is said to be the singular concern of American firms.[25] Part of the reason for such ostensibly contrastive firm behavior in Japan is that management in U.S. firms is focused on short-term issues because its ranks have no particular long-term bond to the firm.

This particular characterization of American and Japanese firms is appealing in a superficial sense, and it is nurtured by the individual and company anecdotes that one often finds in the popular business press. Unfortunately, it is inaccurate both as a description of the behavior of Western firms in microeconomic theory and as an evaluation of how firm behavior in Japan is ostensibly different. Concerning the former, the behavior of U.S. or Western firms and, more specifically, the way the behavior of these firms is described in economic theory, is not the same as certain analysts of the Japanese economic challenge have asserted.[26] Short-term profit maximization is a far less accurate way to describe the behavior of American firms than the maximization of the firm's net present value. This is important to understand not just in the interest of empirical accuracy but more importantly because net present value is by no means a short-term concept.

By describing the behavior of Japanese firms as distinctive, analysts of Japanese-style management have missed two important points. First, much of what has been taken as modal behavior among Japanese firms is nothing more than an artifact of high levels of economic growth over a long postwar interval. It is true that Japanese firms often operate on lower rates of profit, especially when compared to their American counterparts. This empirical distinction, however, has been misconstrued to suggest that Japanese firms somehow ignored profits in pursuit of sales growth and market share expansion. What this argument has missed is that, throughout the high-growth period and up to the post–economic-bubble period, Japanese firms' profits were more than sufficient to cover their associated costs of producing the goods and services they exchanged in the market. Consequently, while Japanese firms were freed from making profits their principal goal, they in no way relegated firm profits to a level of insignificance. Again, this view of the behavior of Japanese firms mistook artifact for archetype.

Second, despite the many insights that have been provided, treatments of firm behavior in Japan are based on explanations for Japanese management practices that are not fully developed. What is missing from these treatments is a discussion of corporate governance issues. More specifically, what needs to be addressed in this area of corporate governance in Japan is how the takeover mechanism in Japanese firms has historically been weak. With a weakened takeover mechanism, managers of firms may be able to deviate from the primary shareholder objective of maximizing the net present value of the firm. Arguably, if shareholders are weak, then managers may operate the firm in a risk averse fashion, maximizing management tenure rather than profit. Simply put, if the takeover mechanism is in fact weak in Japan, then it might indeed be the case that managers may run the firm in a risk averse fashion and deviate from present value maximization.

A full treatment of the nature of postwar Japan's system of corporate governance system is beyond the scope of this chapter. Nonetheless, relying on the work of economists like Aoki (1984, 1987, and 1990) and Sheard (1996), certain points can be made, the most important of which concerns the fact that Japan's financial system can be characterized as bank-centered. This is significant because, in Japan's bank centered financial system, the equity market has been comparatively underdeveloped and, thus, has not historically served in the same capacity as a market for corporate control and management discipline that equity markets have served in other countries. This has meant that, while there are takeovers in Japan, the takeover mechanism and ability of shareholders to discipline managers is diluted. In such a context, some mechanism must emerge to discipline management, otherwise we would expect the moral hazard problem present in such situations to put firms on a collision course with failure. Since many Japanese firms became highly successful over the postwar period, it is certain that some substitute for the equity market discipline of managers had emerged. Historically, the monitor of Japanese firms became the banking sector and specifically the so-called main banks.[27]

As we stated earlier, the Japanese main bank system is highly complex and involves several bank-centered groups held together by cross–share-holding arrangements with the main bank at the center of these cross share holding nexuses. The main bank serves as monitor of the firms within its group or *keiretsu*, and it can be observed to exercise its monitoring capacity during periods of financial distress of member firms.[28] The cross–share-holding relationship, contrary to many popular representations, does not imply greater concentration and anticompetitive behavior among Japanese firms. Indeed, the result is quite the opposite. Since member firms in these corporate groupings come from a variety of industries, there is actually very little scope for concentration or collusive behavior. On the other hand, the close relationship between firms across various industries actually presents an opportunity for Japanese firms to achieve an alternative to vertical integration.

During the first five decades of this century, American firms generally became more vertically integrated, acquiring their suppliers in an attempt to end supply disruption and ensure quality control. For Japanese firms where large scale represents a cost disadvantage due to the high price of land and improvements, incentives existed for companies to rely more intensively upon outside suppliers for their inputs. Given that the subcontracting supply firm has some affiliation with the *keiretsu* grouping, or is at least subject to some control by the same main bank, many of the attendant disadvantages of utilizing subcontractors can be controlled. This means that, while reliance on outside subcontractors would reduce costs associated with large scale in Japan, it might increase costs associated with quality control of the inputs. If, however, the parent firm has some degree of control or leverage over the supplier, then these quality-related costs can be minimized. To the extent that the main bank can act together with the parent firm to monitor these subcontractors, and to the extent that group affiliation can effectively serve to blacklist the subcontractor in the event of failure to deliver quality inputs on time, the subcontracting system can emerge as an effective alternative to vertical integration in Japan.

By implication, in the United States, the corporate governance structure centers instead on the discipline of managers by the equity market. Potential subcontractors necessarily maintain a more arm's-length relationship to the parent by virtue of the fact that they typically do not belong to the same closely related group. In this context, vertical integration becomes the best alternative for monitoring input quality and cost. Combined with the fact that land costs are significantly less in America, there was generally speaking more incentive to achieve large scale. Returning to the issues of subcontracting and just-in-time management, it should now be clear how the interaction of the Japanese management training system, economic incentives, and the corporate governance structure combined to produce this one very famous Japanese management technique. The key conclusion, at least with respect to this technique, is that it was not the prerogatives of Japanese managers on the basis of knowledge gathered from the management literature that this technique came to be widely applied. Instead, it was the natural result of the relationships that existed among training systems, the corporate governance structure, and the economic incentives faced by Japanese firms.

Similar arguments can be made with respect to other Japanese management techniques, and the point is essentially the same, namely that in-firm training, economic incentives and the corporate governance structure essentially dictate their emergence and success and limit whether they can be transplanted as a management prerogative. What is often missed in discussions of management prerogative in Japan is that Japanese managers can be disciplined on two levels, one in the market for corporate control and again in the product market. This is important because, even if the market for corporate control does allow managers to act in a risk averse fashion, those same managers must produce products and compete in the market for those products. This second level of discipline, competition in the international product market, will necessitate the equivalent of profit maximizing behavior, rendering pressures toward risk aversion moot. The question raised here concerns whether or not the idea of Japan having a special system of corporate governance is actually devoid of content? It is fully possible that Japan's main bank system does not imply universally risk averse behavior on the part of firms but still implies that the ultimate monitor is the main bank. If so, any potential benefits to the Japanese corporate governance system must dissolve. This means that it is possible for the takeover mechanism's discipline to be absent without necessarily giving the risk averse operation to firms, something that might be beneficial to other stakeholders besides the firm's shareholders. The key issue therefore revolves around the issue of bank monitoring. The current economic crisis suggests that we should carefully consider how effective such monitoring might be.

While supporters of a Japanese-style corporate governance system tended to focus on the potential benefits of the main bank system to stakeholders other than shareholders, they failed to understand the moral hazard problem inherent in the system. While it may be true that banks can in principle serve well as monitors, especially during periods of financial distress, it is also possible that moral hazard is likely to result in what Japanese macroeconomists used to call "overloan" and "overborrowing." Specifically, the bank as monitor is also the bank as lender which, in the presence of deposit insurance, can create a potentially dangerous problem. Specifically, during periods of rapid economic growth under a regime of generous deposit insurance, the profit maximization problem for a typical bank becomes that of loan growth maximization. Simply put, with generous deposit insurance and rapid growth, banks focus on the revenue (loan) side of the equation with little consideration for the cost side, at least with respect to costs associated with default and risk. This general moral hazard problem is not unique to Japan, and is essentially at the heart of banking crises worldwide, such as the thrift crisis in the United States, the banking crises in Scandinavia, and past problems in Mexico. When we add this moral hazard problem to the corporate governance structure in Japan, we arrive at a situation where the combination is potentially deleterious.

Consider the monitoring and banking relationship during the bubble period in Japan. A corporate customer might see his or her main bank in order to arrange a syndicated loan for new capital expansion. The plan might be approved by the main bank, but, in accordance with its incentives to maximize loan growth, it might add the caveat that the capital expansion plans seem too conservative. In such a scenario, it is suggested that a more aggressive capital expansion plan be undertaken. Since the main bank serves as both monitor and lender to the firm, it has little choice but to accept the modification. So long as this situation is repeated by thousands of other firms, and economic growth remains robust with no exogenous events to disrupt the equilibrium, the situation becomes a self-fulfilling prophesy as employment income and therefore consumption spending grows rapidly enough to bring the new capital expansions up to capacity. This is the situation that Japanese macroeconomists referred to as "overloan" and "overborrowing."

What defenders of this kind of system failed to grasp was the great potential for disaster inherent in such a system, especially where monitor and lender coincide, the fox watching the chicken coup so to speak. While there were some fairly serious crises associated with the oil shock,[29] no major glitches disrupted the fragile equilibrium that characterizes this system because economic growth remained generally robust. In 1989 and 1990, however, fears about overheating of the economy combined with concerns about the government's fiscal position caused the bond market to sell off. Over a mere eighteen months, this bond sell off led to a dramatic rise in long-term interest rates. Simultaneously, Governor Sumita of the Bank of Japan handed the reigns over to the much more conservative Governor Mieno, who hiked short rates as well. The entire yield curve shifted upward in a very short time.

Not only had the interest rate environment suddenly become more pricey, but the sell off in bonds caused a crash in equity and other asset prices. Unlike similar crashes earlier in the postwar period, the Japanese household had become exposed to asset prices, at least through land holdings and often through equities, and the dramatic fall in the value of such assets gave rise to what economists call negative wealth effects. The average household saw the value of its wealth decline, and it responded by consuming less and raising precautionary savings. The economy slowed, and the major capital expansions urged by the main banks were no longer running at capacity. Many loans went bad, and the recent financial and banking crisis was the result.

It is because of this chain of events that we approach the suggestion that Japan's corporate governance system is to be emulated as a model of economic and management superiority with skepticism. We similarly find that other Japanese management practices, as useful as they might be given the functions they performed, result from the manner in which firms responded to the economic incentives and disincentives they faced early in the postwar period. Indeed, the Japanese system of human capital training and its system of corporate governance are the result of firms responding to the economic imperative they confronted in the postwar period. Failure to recognize the essential role played by incentives and markets led many mistakenly to suggest that they are the result of some overarching political-economic design and management prerogative and, thus, institutions that can be transplanted to help improve the comparative advantage of firms in the borrowing nation.

Chapter 5

THE POSTWAR JAPANESE ECONOMY

From High Growth to Structural Adjustment

The "no-miracle-occurred" school of analysis . . . came from the realm of professional economic analyses of Japanese growth and therefore in their own terms are generally impeccable, but they also regularly present extended conclusions that incorporate related matters that their authors have not studied but desperately want to exclude from their equations.

—Chalmers Johnson (1982)

I am of the school which interprets Japanese economic performance as due primarily to the actions and efforts of private individuals and enterprises responding to the opportunities provided in quite free markets for commodities and labor. While the government has been supportive and indeed has done much to create the environment for growth, its role has been exaggerated.

—Hugh Patrick (1976)

In an effort to discover why Japan's miracle soured, analysts are finding that they have to go beyond the "revisionist" and "traditionalist" debate that has polarized, and paralyzed, U.S. analysis for the past two decades . . . This bitter schism . . . did not always exist . . . Even in the worst moments of the 1980s, academic investigations were producing illuminating new understandings of Japan . . . Unfortunately, that work was consigned to the ivory towers while the two poles captured the op-ed pages.

—Richard Katz (1998)

A s we have argued thus far, the explanation for the economic course that Japan followed throughout the postwar period can be understood as a combination of two factors. The first is political and centers on the electoral imperatives that Japan's politicians have faced throughout the postwar period. Specifically, the changing electoral circumstances faced primarily by politicians in Japan's Liberal Democratic party throughout the postwar period led them to use the tools of economic policy in ways that would promote their electoral interests. The result, as we showed in chapter 3 and devleop further in the following section of this book, was specific and predictable patterns in the overall direction and content of economic policy making, especially those that defined Japanese industrial policy. While this area of economic policy making was said to be beyond parochial political influences, the data that were presented above showed that the patterns manifested in the distributions of well-known industrial policy tools could only be explained by the unmistakable influence of electoral politics.

The second factor concerns private actors making business decisions in response to the economic incentives they faced in their respective markets earlier in the postwar period. While there are many economic outcomes that fall into this category, we have examined two in particular, management practices and labor relations in large Japanese firms. We examined these fundamentals of large firm behavior in Japan for a number of reasons but mostly because Japan's management practices and labor market institutions have come to symbolize the manner in which Japan is different from the West in its essential business practices. This is also because Japan's differences in these areas have been treated as part of a larger institutional framework that was designed to give Japanese firms a comparative advantage and, thus, help them achieve national economic development goals that were set forth by the bureaucracy.

In the previous chapter, we identified and discussed the specific patterns that combined to form the manner in which management practices and labor relations have been conducted in postwar Japan. In this discussion, we explained that these patterns are best understood as expected outcomes that can be explained by Japanese firms responding to the economic incentives they faced, particularly in their efforts to acquire and train human capital and, more important, to retain those employees who have been the beneficiaries of the training provided by large Japanese firms. The importance of the discussion we provided is witnessed in our demonstration that the management and labor patterns that symbolize Japan's differences are in fact a common institutional response to a specific set of economic conditions. They are not separate practices, and, thus, they are not really transportable, in whole or part, to help firms in other nations compete against their Japanese counterparts.

These are undoubtedly important intellectual issues in postwar Japanese political economy, but we are still left with what is perhaps the most important issue in studies of postwar Japan, specifically, why its patterns of economic growth and development followed the course they did. This is a rather involved issue that necessitates attention to such specific questions as why Japan's postwar rates of economic growth were as high as they were for as long as they were and how we can understand Japan's remarkable economic performance in light of the last ten or more years of little or no growth. It also requires that we examine the dramatic structural changes that occurred in the Japanese economy from the time of that country's economic resurgence in the high-growth period to the adjustments made in the post–oil-shock years as well as those which have been occurring in the period that was ushered in by the collapse of the bubble economy.

Like the other political and economic issues that we have examined thus far in this book, scholarship on Japan's postwar economic trajectory is also characterized by the problem of "the Japan that never was." In the case of Japan's postwar economic performance, this intellectual problem can be summed up as the difficulties one encounters attempting to reconcile explanations for the period of high growth with the economic problems Japan has faced since the collapse of the bubble economy. This is undoubtedly true for explanations that have relied on revisionist ideas, the inadequacies of which were brought to light by the events of the 1990s, and it is also true for recent explanations like the "system that soured" explanation of Richard Katz (1998). Moreover, this is at least party true for treatments of the Japanese economy that appeared before the advent of Revisionism, albeit for reasons that are far less troublesome than for the previous two classes of scholarship.

On the one hand, treatments of Japan's economic resurgence that appeared earlier in the postwar period were correct in their attempts to explain the period of high growth principally as the result of economic factors.[1] On the other hand, these same explanations also focused on factors in their evaluations of Japan's economic growth that were said not simply to have contributed to high growth but, more important, to be by and large specific to Japan.[2] Most important among these factors are close cooperation between business and government and special behavior that was attributed to Japanese firms. This is problematic because such factors, to the extent that they are even specific to Japan, have not noticeably changed throughout the postwar period, which leads us to ask why they have had no enervating impact on the current crisis and, thus, whether they were important in the high-growth period in the first place. More recent "system that soured" explanations for Japan's postwar economic trajectory are quite thorough on the economics of Japan's current problems. Unfortunately, they replace the few weaknesses of earlier explanations with the most notable weaknesses of Revisionism. This is true because they have incorrectly specified the manner in which political influences impacted on postwar economic outcomes. Perhaps the most notable is how Katz (1998) and scholars with similar views, like Yamamura (1982), have asserted that Japanese industrial policy was partly responsible for the rates of growth and structural changes that took place during the period of high growth.

As we stated at the beginning of this chapter, both of these explanations are inadequate because of how they involve the intellectual problem of "the Japan that never was." Our purpose in this chapter is to eschew this problem by offering an explanation for Japan's postwar economic trajectory that both connects the economics of the high-growth years with those of the current period of structural adjustment and avoids the use of misunderstood political influences and special factors that are said to be unique to Japan. To accomplish this, however, it is useful for us to devote some time to a mapping of Japan's postwar economic trajectory so that we can be clear about what exactly we need to explain.

A PERSPECTIVE ON JAPAN'S POSTWAR ECONOMIC TRAJECTORY

The story of Japan's postwar economic development is no doubt a remarkable rags-to-riches drama. There are many chapters in this story, indeed, too many to recount here in detail. Nonetheless, there are certain notable parts to Japan's postwar economic trajectory that capture the essential details of its ascendance to becoming the world's second largest economy. We have identified three parts in particular, one pertaining to the growth rates that characterized its postwar development, a second concerned with the manner in which the structure of the Japanese economy changed throughout the postwar period, and a third focused on the relationship between Japan and the international economy.

The single most talked about feature of the postwar Japanese economy, one that has been repeatedly held up as that which distinguishes Japan from its developed counterparts in the West,[3] is its ability to have sustained rapid rates of economic growth over the greater part of the postwar period. This is perhaps best expressed in annual changes in real GDP which, from 1960 to the first oil shock in 1973 averaged over 10 percent.[4] While growth turned negative in the year after the first oil shock, it rebounded almost immediately and continued at a rate that was unmatched by any other developed nation with perhaps the exception of Norway. From the mid-1970s to 1992 when the problems of asset deflation began to show up in the real economy, Japan's annual growth in real GDP was nearly 5 percent. This rapid rate of growth in Japan's real GDP was highest among the world's developed nations. Japan is now the world's second largest economy, and in spite of its nearly decade-long period of economic stagnation, it produces 18 percent of the world's GNP, second only to the United States, which accounts for one-quarter of the goods and services produced in the world today.

The second part of Japan's remarkable postwar economic development concerns the manner and speed with which its economic structure changed throughout the postwar period. This is the well-known story of how Japan's manufacturing sector in particular evolved from reliance on the production of light industrial products like textiles to heavy industrial products, such as steel and chemicals, to increasingly more sophisticated high-technology products like consumer electronics, automobiles, semiconductors, and composite materials. Perhaps the best illustration of this in witnessed in the dramatic reversal that took place between the roles played by textiles and machinery in the totality of Japan's manufactured products. In 1950, textiles and machinery accounted for almost the same proportion of products manufactured in Japan. At that time, textiles were 25 percent of what Japan manufactured while machinery was just over 30 percent. Twenty-five years later, the situation was dramatically different. In 1975 textiles were just over 5 percent of total Japanese output while machinery was close to 60 percent.

The third part of Japan's economic development refers to its reemergence as an important player in the international economy. This occurred for many reasons, but perhaps the most important indicator of Japan's international economic importance rests with the way its exports in certain manufactured products came to dominate international markets. Data on Japan's growing export prowess is provided in Table 5.1, which covers the nearly forty-year period beginning in 1946. The data show that export growth was fastest in the first twenty years of the postwar period, a time when Japan's comparative advantage was in textiles and other low-tech goods. Export growth continued to slow from this point to the present, the one exception being the years immediately following the first oil shock when Japanese automobiles

Table 5.1 Growth of Japanese Exports, 1946–1995

Year	Export Index	Period Change
1946	1	—
1956	398.3	+398%
1965	1,346.3	+238%
1970	3,007.2	+123%
1975	7,320.9	+143%
1980	13,001.1	+78%
1985	18,564.5	+42%
1990	18,343.8	−1%
1995	18,376.5	+0.2%

Source: *Japan Almanac* (1999).

and machine products, among other things, proved to be price and quality competitive on the international market.

Like the changes that occurred in the structure of the postwar Japanese economy, how the content of Japanese exports evolved throughout the postwar period is aptly illustrated comparing textiles and machinery. In 1950, textiles made up nearly 50 percent of total Japanese exports while, in that same year, manufactured goods occupied only a little more than a quarter of Japanese exports. Twenty-five years later, however, the story was dramatically different. In 1975, textiles accounted for a little more than 5 percent of what Japan exported while machinery had risen to nearly 60 percent.[5]

Japan's postwar economic accomplishments have been dramatic to be sure, and they are not to be relegated lightly. Very few nations experienced the rapid and sustained levels of economic growth that Japan achieved throughout the postwar period. Nonetheless, given that it is our purpose to provide an explanation for Japan's postwar economic trajectory in a way that appropriately connects the earlier period of high growth with the current period of structural adjustment, it is necessary that we discuss these three parts of Japan's postwar economic development in a broader comparative-temporal perspective. This will help us see that economic trends in the postwar period are not all that unique but rather patterns that both defined Japan's economic evolution in the nineteenth and early twentieth centuries and that characterized other developed nations, particularly as they emerged from the ashes of the Second World War.

On the one hand, that Japan's rates of economic growth in the postwar period were remarkable is not to be doubted. On the other hand, there are many reasons to conclude that, while comparatively high for a relatively long period of time, they are not the extraordinary economic events that many have portrayed them to be.[6] The most obvious reason for this is that, from the 1870s until the start of the Pacific War, Japan had established itself as one of the World's fastest-growing nations.[7] Moreover, like Japan's economic growth in the prewar period, postwar growth rates, albeit high, were characterized by cyclic ups and downs that have invariably characterized rates of economic growth in the world's other developed nations. The fact of the matter is that Japan's postwar economic growth rates were quite cyclic and its fluctuations were very often tied to discernable events, particularly well-known external shocks. In fact, from 1945 to 1997, Japan's Economic Planning Agency identified twelve business cycles that the Japanese economy experienced despite its overall high rates of growth.[8]

In the opening years of the Occupation period, Japan's economy was moribund and nearly 100 percent dependent on aid from the United States. The first significant upward jump in economic growth came after June 1950 when the Korean War set off a notable "boom" in economic growth. This boom lasted only a short time and was followed by a near six month decline that was, again, followed by a nearly two-year period of fairly strong, war-induced period of growth. This pattern of strong growth and decline also characterized other stretches of the high growth period. While the Economic Planning Agency identified eight business cycles between 1960 and 1990 inclusive, perhaps two stand out as being most notable. The first of these occurred in the wake of the Tokyo Olympics, which was preceded by two years of strong economic performance only to be followed by over a year of economic downturn. The other cycle, in fact two cycles, are tied to the rise in the price of crude oil that took place in the 1970s. These as well as other economic shocks affected Japan's economic cycle in rather predictable ways.

The same kind of perspective can be applied to the manner in which the structure of the Japanese economy became transformed throughout the post-war period and how Japan became a very important player in the area of international trade. One aspect of Japan's postwar economic transformation involved a decline in the economic importance of agriculture. Between 1960 and 1990, the percentage of the Japanese workforce in agriculture declined from 26.8 percent to 6.2 percent, and parallel with this decline was an almost as significant a drop in agriculture's share of nominal GDP. In 1960, 9 percent of Japan's GDP came from agriculture. While this was not all that significant, it had dropped to an even less significant 1.8 percent by 1990. What makes this less remarkable is that the decline of agriculture in Japan had begun in the later decades of the nineteenth century and has continued up to the present day. This is the case in spite of the manifold forms of protection that Japan's farmers have received from the government which makes Japan not unlike other developed nations in the West. Moreover, the contribution of agriculture to nominal GDP in Japan has remained at the less-than-2 percent level through-out the 1990s which also makes Japan like other developed nations.[9]

With respect to its relationship with the international economy, Japan has been characterized as a nation that imports raw materials and exports finished products. It has also been argued that this pattern of Japanese trade can be explained as the result a government (bureaucrat) planned and imple-mented "neomercantilist" design to promote Japan's manufactured exports abroad while keeping its domestic market free of potential competitors in the same products.[10] This characterization of Japan's trade patterns has come to take on a life of its own that is sustained mostly by anecdotes of the difficulties that certain foreign exporters have conveyed about their attempts to penetrate the Japanese market. While there are both formal and informal barriers to trade that make selling certain products in Japan difficult, this characteriza-tion of Japan's relationship with the international economy has in a sense

eclipsed important postwar developments which show clearly that, if Japan
has increased imports of any product area, it is in manufactured goods. In
1981, for instance, one-fourth of what Japan imported was in the form of
finished goods.[11] By 1997, however, nearly 60 percent of what Japan imported was in the form of finished goods. Japan's import bill in finished
goods at this time amounted to $194 billion, and the largest category of
imported items was machinery and equipment which exceeded Japan's imports of mineral fuels by $30 billion.[12]

EXPLAINING POSTWAR JAPANESE ECONOMIC GROWTH

Our purpose in discussing these notable features of Japan's postwar economic
development is to show that, while remarkable in many ways, they were not
as extraordinary as many have suggested, especially when viewed in a broader
comparative-temporal perspective. This perspective is important for helping
us define Japan's postwar growth patterns not only because the period of high
growth has been held up as an extraordinary phenomenon that renders the
Japanese experience distinctive but also because Japan's postwar economic
trajectory has been offered as evidence of the limits of neoclassical economic
explanations for the postwar miracle.

While most challenges to the standard growth accounting approach
have appeared as some vague assertion that the rates at which the Japanese
economy grew and the length of time that growth continued must involve
more than the work of the "invisible hand,"[13] a more serious challenge can be
found in the work of Johnson (1982). In the introduction to his provocative
study of Japan's Ministry of International Trade and Industry, Johnson re-
views the weaknesses of extant explanations and notes that the neoclassical
approach, which he correctly labels the "no miracle occurred" school, is
among this group. Johnson's criticism of the growth models employed by
neoclassical economists is that they explain only 60 percent of Japan's growth
rates during the period of high growth. Johnson then concludes that the large
unexplained portion of Japan's economic growth that the standard economic
model does not capture must be attributable to government policy, the positive influence of which economists have either ignored or understated.

In his declamation against the neoclassical approach to growth accounting, Johnson is referring specifically to the results of estimating a standard
growth model with Japanese data, as presented in Dennison and Chung (1976
and 1977), and their conclusion that the application of greater amounts of
labor and capital, the standard factors of production, account for 60 percent
of the variance in Japan's growth through the early 1970s. While at first

glance, this may seem to represent a major challenge to neoclassical economics, what Johnson fails to understand is that the percentage of growth in Japan that is explained by the standard growth model is about the same for all the advanced industrial democracies.

Johnson is referring specifically to the R-square statistic from a traditional growth model, which explains growth in terms of a country's application of the standard factors of production—labor and capital stock—as well as other corrective factors such as time trends. In their studies of Japan, Dennison and Chung (1977) found that the standard model explained about 44 percent of Japan's economic growth for the period up to the early 1970s. Such results, however, are not so different from what we witness in studies of growth in other developed countries since the same models explain 52 percent of the variance in the case of the United States and 61 percent in the case of Canada. For France, Germany, and the United Kingdom, the variances in growth that are explained by the model for the same period of time are 26 percent, 44 percent, and 46 percent respectively.

Such data indicate that the approach taken by neoclassical economists performs no worse with Japanese data than with data from other developed nations. This tells us that, even in terms of its high levels of economic growth in the earlier part of the postwar period, Japan is not the exceptional case that many have suggested. However, this conclusion does not mean that simple growth models, with their emphasis on increments in the utilization of factors of production, have captured all that is interesting in Japan's postwar economic development. Neoclassical growth theory would be very simplistic indeed and would not form an entire subfield of its own if it merely studied how more inputs of essential factors of production translate into more outputs of goods and services. Indeed, if anything, most of the interesting aspects of growth theory focus on the unobservable factors in a simple regression models of economic growth. This means that most of the development in growth theory over the past forty years has occurred through a study of those factors that are not captured in the simple R-squared from the regression model of growth and factor utilization.

Robert Solow (1956 and 1957) long ago noted that it was the residual from the growth regression model that was of interest. We all know that utilizing more inputs increases economic output, albeit at levels of decreasing return, but what is the more interesting issue is how economies manage to make economic inputs more productive over time. It is the increased productivity of factors of production, the so-called Solow residual, which is of much interest in growth theory. Measures of this residual have been refined over time, and economists have dedicated much time and effort to trying to explain what factors influence it because it is this measure and not the simple relationship that exists between raw inputs and output that is the essence of modern productivity analysis and neoclassical growth theory.

Understanding that it is the residual element, which is known as total factor productivity growth, that is the key component of explaining the difficult aspects of economic growth is what helps us debunk the view that Japan's postwar economic performance was quite extraordinary. If, for example, there is a natural tendency for economies to experience a "spurt" in the efficiency of their utilization of factors of production during part of their development process (i.e., a spurt in total factor productivity growth), then a corresponding period of rapid economic growth should not be so bewildering. Given that the simple utilization of more factors seems to explain roughly only half of economic growth in most developed countries, including Japan, we should not conclude that Japan's high-growth period was extraordinary. A better starting point for an investigation of the high-growth period in Japan would be a systematic analysis of the causes of high–factor-productivity growth during the period that economic growth rates were high.

The importance of the Solow residual and total factor productivity growth has been well understood in the growth literature for several decades. More recently, however, research in growth theory has focused on wholesale technological shifts and the impact of innovation on economic growth.[14] In the crudest possible terms, these technological shifts might be understood as a shift in the intercept term in a linear growth model. While this description does a disservice to the substantive and statistical thinking that has gone into such models of economic growth, it helps us to understand some of the key implications of technological change and innovation for a simple linear empirical growth model. Moreover, it also helps us understand why such models fail to explain a greater proportion of economic growth.

By way of illustration, suppose we estimate a model of economic growth for Japan using data from the 1955–1975 period. During this period, it is certainly true that increasing amounts of labor, capital, and other factors of production were utilized, and, as we saw earlier, the greater utilization of such factors explains roughly half of the economic growth that Japan experienced throughout this period of time. Consider, on the other hand, the more accurate notion that, during this twenty-year period, there was significant innovation and technological change that affected the nature of the productive process. In other words, the functional relationship between inputs and outputs would have changed, perhaps significantly, throughout this twenty-year period, but the empirical model that we use to estimate these impacts does not. Indeed, by definition, the simple type of growth model we described above is static, which means that, when a technological change occurs but the model remains in its original linear form, the result must be that the amount of variance that model explains, the R-squared of the estimated model, must fall. Again, this is because when a shift in the functional form of an empirical model occurs while, at the same time, it is estimated with a static functional form imposed on it, the amount of variance explained must decline. In such a case, rather than being surprised that the model explains so little of economic growth, we should be surprised that it explains so much!

Such technological change and innovation in the production process in concert with unobserved improvements in the quality of the factors themselves, all of which affect the functional relationship that exists between inputs and outputs, will naturally impact on the explanatory power of empirical growth models. Recent developments in growth theory, however, have provided a way to model the impact of such technological changes,[15] and proper implementation of such developments will no doubt increase the proportion of observed variance in economic growth that such models can explain. Again, the inability of a simple linear growth model to explain more than about half of observed growth in Japan during the high-growth period is consistent with the explanatory power of such models applied to most other countries. There is absolutely nothing about the results which suggests that Japan's economic development was extraordinary during the period of high growth. However, in spite of our position that economic growth in the high-growth period is easily understood in the context of standard neoclassical approaches, we must still ask why growth continued to decline throughout the postwar period and whether or not government policy played any role in bringing on the current period of structural adjustment.

Despite our emphasis on market forces in explaining Japan's period of high growth, we are not taking the position that government policy was neutral throughout the postwar period. In addition to our showing how the Liberal Democratic Party set the direction and content of economic in broadly discernible ways throughout the postwar period, we should add here that the great amount of government largesse that was distributed throughout the postwar period also served to boost economic growth rates. More specifically, when the Japanese government pumped public money into the economy, as it did in substantial amounts throughout the postwar period for political and economic reasons, the net effect on growth was to raise it, at least temporarily. Nonetheless, acknowledging this is not the same as saying that industrial policy had a strong, positive impact on productivity growth in targeted industries. While we have already shown this not to be the case, we are still left with the question of what impact government policy had on bringing about the current period of structural adjustment.

THE NOT-SO-SURPRISING CRISIS OF THE 1990S

Given that Japan's rapid and sustained levels of economic growth in the postwar period were considered to be the hallmark of its distinctiveness, it should come as no surprise that the collapse of its economy and postwar political system in the 1990s was unanticipated by most scholars who study that country. It is for this reason that responses by such scholars to the economic problems Japan experienced in the 1990s have taken on certain characteristics. The first of these is best described as delay. What this means is that, because so many Japan specialists saw that country as being better able to produce high levels of economic growth than the other developed nations of the West, most reacted to the onset of economic crisis in the 1990s as if were a nonevent or, at a minimum, not all that serious. This at least characterized the initial response of Japan specialists to the economic problems of the 1990s, and, to be fair, we should say that many did want to be sure that the economic problems of Japan's current structural adjustment were in fact real before venturing to address such questions as how long such problems would last and what brought them on.[17] On the other hand, when Japan scholars did respond, their assessments of that country's postbubble economic crisis tended to be characterized by two distinct views that can be differentiated in terms of how much their respective proponents viewed the postwar Japanese political-economic system as being substantively different from its counterparts in the remainder of the developed world.

On one end of the spectrum, we have the opinions of those who either are Revisionists or relied heavily on revisionist ideas. Quite predictably, assessments of the current economic crisis in Japan provided by such individuals were a mixture of silence and denial. For example, Chalmers Johnson is perhaps the most notable representative of the denial view. In the "Introduction" to his collection of essays, *Japan: Who Governs?*, Johnson asserted that the deepening economic crisis Japan has been experiencing in the 1990s is partially the result of a government plan to "punish speculators" and buy time before Japan would have to accede to more American demands.[18] While Johnson's assessments stands well outside the penumbra of believability, we must note that it is the only explanation that he could offer for Japan's current crisis if he were to remain consistent with the revisionist view he has long promoted.

While other promoters of revisionist-views of Japan were also silent or at least delayed in their failure to acknowledge the severity of Japan's current crisis, they were in fact less consistent than Johnson because they ultimately provided assessments of Japan's economic crisis that in many ways contradicted their earlier views. One illustration of such an individual following the path of silence is found in James Fallows's statement about how the political-economic system of Japan, as well as that found in certain parts of Asia, are utterly different from what is typically found in the West.[19] The point is that, while the crisis was well underway when he was writing his book, it received virtually no mention at all.

An example of the breaking the silence with an assessment that contrasts greatly with earlier opinions is perhaps best captured in an Op-Ed piece that Clyde Prestowitz wrote for the *Financial Times*. Commenting on the recent wave of foreign investment in Japan, Prestowitz stated that "what 30 years of jawboning and threats by trade negotiators could not accomplish in terms of opening the Japanese auto market is being delivered by the consequences of seven years of recession and failing financial institutions."[20] Prestowitz's assessment is essentially correct, but it contradicts the view of Japan that he advanced in the past and continues to advance even now. Mr. Prestowitz has long been a strong advocate of the "jawboning" approach because, as he has written, Western economic doctrine with its emphasis on markets is not a useful guide for the postwar Japanese experience.[21] The question Prestowitz unintentionally raises and then ignores is how it is that markets, which did so little in Japan in the past, are accomplishing so much now?

It is important to note that such problematic assessments of Japan's current crisis are not exclusive to Japan scholars advancing essentially revisionist points of view. On the other side of the intellectual spectrum are scholars who wrote about the Japanese economy prior to the rise of Revisionism and those who came later and espoused what we have referred to as "system that soured" views. Representative scholars in both groups have written assessments of Japan's postbubble economic problems that are accurate in their understanding of the problems that Japan currently faces. This is because they have generally understood the economic problems that Japan currently faces, and, at the same time, they have generally gotten the economics of high-growth period correct as well. As mentioned above, however, their treatments of the high-growth period involved emphasis on other factors that, if truly important, should have either militated against the current economic crisis occurring at all or, at a minimum, reduced its length and severity.

These are troublesome explanations to be sure, but they are not as serious as those that see Japan's political-economic system as having worked well in the past only to "sour" in the postbubble period. This is because of their underlying assumption that industrial policy and other distinctive features of the Japanese political-economic system worked well earlier in the postwar period, contributing to the postwar economic miracle. The problem as we have stated above is not that so much that such assertions are inaccurate, which they are, but rather that accepting that government policies were effective in the past requires that we also accept that policy making worked in a particular way, a way that should have been able to avert, or at least mitigate, the current crisis far more effectively than has been done thus far.

Much less intellectually problematic than these assessments are those of Japan's postwar economic resurgence that appeared before the advent of Revisionism. Nonetheless, they still raise the issue of whether or not certain noneconomic factors that authors in this tradition have said played an important role in Japan's postwar economic resurgence did in fact play the role they suggested. Among the more important of these noneconomic factors are government-business cooperation, long-term goals being the focus of corporate Japan, and a consensus that economic growth was the most important national goal. Again, the problem is not simply that using such factors to identify Japan as a nation that contrasts significantly with its counterparts in the West is not wholly defendable but rather that, if these factors were as important in the past as suggested, they should also have been important enough recently to prevent the current crisis or at least render it less severe than it has been thus far.

To make this point in a more defendable way, however, requires that we determine if there were sings of Japan's impending economic problems. In other words, were signs of Japan's postbubble troubles readily identifiable or were they no where to be found? Moreover, we can also ask if it was the case that the models of Japan that guided so many watchers for so long blinded them to events as they had been unfolding for some time.

Our view is that the signs of looming trouble in Japan's political-economic system were there, and we make this statement in such a straightforward fashion because no nation, no matter how remarkable in its economic performance, can defy the economic laws of gravity. With the appreciation of the yen in the 1980s, the growth spurt Japan experienced at the time did not rest on its fundamental economic strengths but rather on borrowed time. The background is simple and carries many lessons. In the autumn of 1985, finance ministers and central bankers of the major powers met to deal with what was seen as an undervalued dollar and, by implication, a weak yen. It was agreed that the authorities of world's advanced countries would work together to strengthen their respective currencies against the dollar. All involved generally believed that the agreed-on plan of intervention would act as a catalyst for what the markets already recognized.

The yen appreciated from nearly ¥300 to the dollar in the mid-1970s to ¥150 in 1985 to close to ¥100 to the dollar by the end of the decade. This was a rise that was faster and higher than anyone had expected would ever occur, including the Americans who were strong advocates of such a change.

While many in the United States viewed this as evidence that Japan's economy does not respond to macroeconomic fluctuations as other advanced economies do, officials at the Bank of Japan worried about the high yen's impact on the economy. As a result, the Bank of Japan officials cut the official discount rate (ODR) and committed themselves to keeping it low. Surprisingly, Japan's economy showed only short-term signs of weakness, and it quickly rebounded. By late 1986, it was clear that Japan had weathered the storm. At such a time, the appropriate response would have been to raise interest rates, but the Bank of Japan, contrary to expected wisdom, continued to hold them down. This was partly due to Bank Governor Sumita's desire to see the Japanese economy heat up, and partly because there appeared to be no inflationary pressures in the real economy. Indeed, the rapid appreciation of the yen had created deflationary pressures due to falling import prices.

It is interesting that many American policy makers viewed the situation in much the same way, albeit for reasons that were quite different. They felt that expansionary monetary policy was a useful way to raise demand for imports from the United States. Nonetheless, this state of affairs led to nearly euphoric optimism throughout all of Japan, and, at the time, officials on both sides of the Pacific were generally content. The economy grew at an average of just less than 5 percent during the 1985–1990 period, and the Nikkei average rose to nearly 40,000 in 1989. Unfortunately, signs that there was much less to celebrate about were difficult to ignore. It is true that wholesale prices were falling, and there was no inflation at the consumer price level, but the excess of economic activity created by low interest rates leaked into asset prices. Consequently, they rose rapidly in value, indeed, well beyond what the fundamentals would support in the long run. The problem is that, when asset values deviate significantly from their underlying productive capacity, their prices must ultimately fall. Despite all the rhetoric, the Japanese economy was not immune to this economic law of gravity. All that was needed was a catalyst to bring down what was a house of cards.

That catalyst came in the form of subsequent interest rate hikes. On the short end, the hike came in the form of a new Bank governor, Mieno, who did not share his predecessors' views that Japan could defy the economic laws of gravity. When he took office in 1989, he quickly moved to hike rates. Standard market valuation models tell us that the current price of an asset should reflect the present discounted value of its future stream of earnings. When expectations of future earnings fall, or when the discount (interest) rate rises, the price of those assets must fall. Looked at another way, an increase in interest rates raises the cost of productive investment, making claims on those assets less attractive. In the last months of 1989 and the winter of 1990, the entire Japanese yield curve shifted dramatically upward, and, as should have been expected, the equity market collapsed. Within no time, the market for land collapsed as well.

What followed these events is well known not simply because it is now recent history but also because economic logic predicts the exact course that Japan followed after the bursting of the economic bubble. The average Japanese who had bought property during the bubble suddenly saw the value of his or her investments disappear. In response, households dramatically raised their precautionary savings, leading to a slowdown in rates of consumption. This is similar to the British "negative equity" episode of the late 1980s, and it is what economists call a negative wealth effect. Ultimately, it led to a slowdown of economic activity, forcing firms to cut back on capital expenditure, and sending the economy into a tailspin, from which the country has yet to recover.

III. POLITICS AND POLICY MAKING IN A DEMOCRATIC NATION

Chapter 6

THE ELECTORAL ORIGINS OF JAPAN'S ECONOMIC POLICIES

Parties formulate policies in order to win elections rather than win elections to formulate policies

—Anthony Downs (1957)

The role of politicians in the making of economic policy becomes, then, largely one of ratifying rather than shaping the consensus which emerges from the—very open and public—debates between the main "organized interests."

—Ronald Dore (1986)

It is an unfortunate but indisputable fact that politics in any country is a dirty business that does more to raise the ire of the average citizen than it does to earn his or her respect. Indeed, in our daily discourse, the word *politics* itself functions much more as a term of opprobrium than as a benign concept designed to capture the affirmative process by which collective decisions are rendered in a society. Arthur Lupia, a political scientist at the University of Michigan, discussed six reasons why "politics is designed to break your heart while making you really angry at the process."[1] Among his reasons are such facts as politics involving disagreements about the means of solving social problems as well as disputes about which problems merit government attention in the first place. Lupia also noted that politics is troubling because the process by which collective decisions are rendered invariably results in some groups and individuals emerging as winners and others being losers.

These negative characteristics describe the practice of politics in any democratic country, which means that politics is a process without peer. In other words, there is no available alternative to politics for rendering collective decisions in a society and, thus, setting the direction and content of national policy. In light of this, the question before us is how this process has worked in Japan, leading to the outcomes we have witnessed in the postwar period. More specifically, how have the political concerns that have ever consumed the elected officials who controlled Japan's postwar governments disposed those same individuals to use the tools of economic policy to serve their essential interests. The answer to this question begins with the way political concerns shape the interests of ruling parties and their members, an answer that takes us first to the nature of democratic politics.

DEMOCRATIC POLITICS AND POSTWAR JAPAN

The intellectual questions that have characterized the study of democratic politics, particularly the theory of democracy, are numerous, indeed, too numerous to recount here. Nonetheless, we can say that scholars who have studied the theory and workings of democratic politics can be divided into those doing normative theory and those doing deductive and empirical theory. Although somewhat oversimplified, it is true that scholars involved with the normative side of the study of democratic politics are principally concerned with such things as the philosophy of democratic politics, specifically, why certain values advance the ideals and practice of democracy better than others. Deductive and empirical democratic theorists, on the other hand, are much more focused on how democratic politics is structured and actually practiced in the world and how the different patterns that one observes might be explained.[2]

Since our purpose is to understand how the electoral imperatives faced by a nation's politicians persuade them to use the available tools of economic policy to advance their essential interests, we are naturally more interested in the work of those in the tradition of deductive-empirical democratic theory. By observing how democracy is actually practiced throughout the world, we learn just what enormous variety there is in the way that nations have assembled their political institutions and, consequently, practice democratic politics.[3] More important for our purposes here is that, in spite of the many differences that do exist, we know well that leaders in all democracies have certain behavioral tendencies that render them similar across the many institutional forms of democracy that we witness in the world. This is because all democratic political systems have certain features that help mold the behavior of their principal political actors.

Perhaps the most important of these concerns the manner in which individuals are selected for a nation's highest political offices, specifically, the fact that in democratic nations, this is done in free and fair national elections.[4] That Japan has selected its top national office holders in free and fair national elections is neither controversial nor ambiguous because even such critics of Japanese democracy as Chalmers Johnson, who believes that Japan is "softly authoritarian" rather than democratic, does not argue that it is without free and fair elections. The problem that revisionist and other critics have with

Japanese politics concerns certain features that are ostensibly unique to Japan and render its electoral processes less democratically meaningful than they are elsewhere in the developed world. These features relate, first, to the supposedly unusual outcomes the electoral process has produced in postwar Japan and, second, to the attendant power Japanese politicians are said to lack.

Concerning the former, it is true that national elections are a necessary but not a sufficient condition for a nation's politics to be democratic. This makes sense when one recalls that elections for the highest national offices were held in the former Soviet Union and that they are currently held in China but that neither the former Soviet Union nor China is democratic. This is because elections in both countries are neither free nor fair since they are monopolized by a single party (each nation's Communist Party) which prevents the organization of any real opposition and, thus, limits the extent to which citizens are able to select the individuals who will occupy those nations' highest offices. Revisionists and other critics of Japanese democracy have not argued that Japan's electoral politics are like those witnessed in China or the former Soviet Union, but they have suggested that the outcomes produced by its national elections are a manifestation of citizen input being less meaningful than in other democracies.

Postwar Japanese electoral politics have been referred to as "dominant party" politics, that is, as a pattern of electoral politics where one political party wins all elections, the fact that the process is formally free and open notwithstanding.[5] In the Fall of 1955, Japan's Liberal and Democratic Parties united to form the Liberal Democratic Party or the LDP.[6] When the party was formed, it controlled over 60 percent of the seats in both houses of the National Diet, and it won the next twelve elections that were held between 1958 and 1990 inclusive. While the LDP's vote and seat shares did experience a secular decline throughout the 1960s and 1970s, the party was nonetheless able to maintain control of the Diet and continue as the nation's single ruling party.[7] Revisionists and other critics of Japanese democracy interpreted LDP predominance as a nearly permanent feature of the Japanese political system and presented it as evidence of Japan's citizens having a limited choice in elections and small, if any, impact on political outcomes.

This is not a new criticism because some comparative politics specialists, like Harvard University's Samuel Huntington, have asked whether or not it is necessary for the election process to produce an alternation of political parties in power for a nation to be truly democratic.[8] An affirmative answer to this question is a point of view with few supporters, and the Japanese case helps us understand why it has never become widely accepted. Criticizing Japan in this way requires us to forget that its thirty-eight years of single-party predominance were preceded by more than a decade of intense electoral competition where different parties in different combinations controlled the government. Equally important is that this criticism requires us to evaluate democracies in terms of the outcomes they produce instead of by the procedures they utilize, even if the outcomes do not correspond with the choices made by a nation's citizens. In the case of Japan, this criticism discounts the fact that the LDP's long period of electoral predominance was the result of the Japanese electorate making choices among competing candidates in free and fair elections.

The second problematic feature of Japan's electoral politics that has been mentioned is perhaps more troublesome because it touches directly on the meaningfulness of Japan's national elections. The idea is that, in addition to a nation's highest political offices being filled through elections that are free and open, it must also be the case that the positions filled through the electoral process have attendant political power so that the individuals who are elected can actually run the country. There is no dispute that a nation would hardly be democratic if those elected to its highest public offices were, for whatever reason, prevented from actually determining the direction and content of national policy. While this has been an ongoing criticism of Japanese politics because of the power attributed to the country's educated and skilled bureaucrats, our discussion of the research conducted on economic policy making in the recent past has pointed out how this is not the case.[9]

In addition to institutions which provide for a country's highest offices being filled through free and fair elections, there are other legal-institutional features that one witnesses in democratic nations that are also influential in helping mold the political behavior of those officials who seek election to their highest offices. The reference here is to those legal and institutional features of a country that help ensure that its politics remain democratic, that is, those features that help make certain that national elections are conducted in a free and fair manner. There are many legal-institutional features of a nation that work toward this end, but two appear to be most important. The first of these relates to the formation and transmission of relevant political information, and the second concerns the direct political behavior of individuals involved in the electoral process.

First, for national elections to be sufficiently free and fair contests to qualify as democratic, citizen and leader alike must have access to information. It is through the availability of politically relevant information that such things as candidate and party positions, the issues and problems that define the political agenda, and the preferences of citizens become known. Any restriction of the generation and dissemination of political information is tantamount to a reduction in the quality of democratic politics. Overall, this means that, for elections to be truly democratic, legal-institutional features that promote a free press and protect access to information by all citizens must be in place.

Second, for a nation's electoral politics to be truly democratic, national elections must be free and fair in a way that eliminates, or at least reduces substantially, barriers to participation in electoral processes at both elite and mass levels. This means that a nation's citizens are not formally prevented from acting individually in their own interests or from organizing groups to accomplish the same ends.[10] In other words, individuals and political parties must be extended guarantees that their efforts to participate in the electoral process, either as potential candidates or as voters, will not be thwarted in any extralegal or otherwise arbitrarily discriminatory manner.

Very few individuals, be they scholar, journalist, or policy maker, would argue that Japanese citizens, either as voters or as potential candidates, encounter such formal restrictions in pursuit of their respective political interests. Some might argue, on the one hand, that Japanese politics involves informal restrictions, or restrictions that are manifested in the self-restraint of individual behavior. Indeed, such scholars have contended that, as a result of such informal restrictions, Japanese citizens do not really participate in politics to the extent that citizens of other democratic nations participate in politics.[11] On the other hand, it is only a very few Japan specialists who take the position that Japanese politics, as a result of such informal restrictions, is rendered less democratic than the politics of other advanced nations.[12]

It is true that Japanese respondents register lower than their American and many of their European counterparts on indicators of a participant political culture.[13] We do not disparage this research tradition but nonetheless note that our observations lead us to say that political action in Japan is not only frequent but nearly ubiquitous. For instance, in the summer of 1998, we spent several weeks in a MITI office conducting interviews of bureaucrats and politicians for this book. At that time, we noted that every day some political group would show up on the streets of Nagatacho and Kosumigaseki (Japan's government districts) to make its preferences known. By way of another illustration, one should recall the nationwide political action that took place in response to repeated government attempts to reform Japan's tax system. The point is that if one looks beyond the way that Japanese culture has been mapped, one can see that Japanese citizens take their politics very seriously, engaging in extra-election behavior at a level that appears to rival that in any other democratic parliamentary system in the world in terms of its frequency and stridence.

Finally, while few would argue that Japan lacks a free press, there are those who would say that the norms under which the Japanese press operates render it a much less effective tool of democracy than elsewhere.[14] This criticism has less to do with Japanese television, be it commercial or public, which arguably airs more, or at least no less, news on politics and government than is aired elsewhere in the West, than it has to do with the country's principal newspapers.[15] The criticism is not that these newspapers are antidemocratic but that they function as government mouthpieces, eschewing the kind of criticism that one associates with newspapers in the West. Japanese dailies tend to be filled with information that, on issues of political and economic import, comes by and large from government agencies.

Nonetheless, this does not mean that Japanese newspapers are governed by self-imposed norms of conformity and, thus, do not serve the interest of democratic politics. Whatever conservative behavior these newspapers manifest is due to the fact that Japan's daily newspapers have very little market incentive to change their format because a deviation of any notable magnitude might risk the loss of the market share that they currently possess. Perhaps more important than this, however, is the fact that investigative reporting and criticism of the government does occur in Japan, but it is not generally done by Japan's daily newspapers. Rather, this function is performed by the country's many weakly and monthly magazines, many of which are interestingly enough owned by the country's major daily newspapers.

DEMOCRATIC POLITICS AND RATIONAL BEHAVIOR

Since Japan's political leaders are chosen in national elections and since its political system possesses the legal-institutional features that are necessary to render its elections as free and fair as they are in other democratic nations, we now turn to the question of how its democratic politics has persuaded Japanese politicians to use the policy process to serve their essential interests. This question begins with specifying how we expect the politicians and parties who controlled postwar governments to behave in that role. Our first expectation is that politicians are rational, that is, goal-oriented in their behavior and that the principal goal they seek is to achieve elective office. Our second expectation is that they will behave in this manner in a context-sensitive manner. This means that they will seek office in a way that is cognizant of how the cultural, historical, institutional, and other factors that define the environment within which they seek elective office will affect the specific opportunities and constraints they face.

We are well aware that specifying the expected behavior of Japanese politicians in the above manner has been partner to much controversy, especially in political science. As applied to Japan, criticisms of this approach have been launched on procedural grounds where assumptions of rational behavior have been deemed inappropriate because they describe the cognitive abilities of actors in unrealistic ways.[16] Criticisms of the rational decision model have also been advanced on substantive grounds, that is, on the assertion that the rational choice framework has provided no intellectual value-added in the explanations its proponents have offered.[17] These two criticisms of the rational decision model have included a number of interesting and provocative intellectual issues. Nonetheless, in the context of our analytic effort here, we note that the validity of our approach is best measured by the quality of the explanation it provides. On the other hand, our assumption that Japan's politicians pursue elective office as their principal goal is deserving of further explanation. This is because the specification of a single goal to be maximized that is at the heart of the rational choice approach more often than not appears to be at odds with the real world of politician behavior. The problem proceeds from the question of whether politician behavior can be accurately described as the pursuit of a single goal and, if so, whether that goal is the pursuit of elective office.

It is true that scholars employing the rational choice perspective have typically assumed that a single goal is maximized by actors, like profits for business firms, utility for individual economic actors, and elective office for politicians. This has been somewhat of a problem, particularly in Japanese studies, because a number of critics have argued that Japanese actors pursue different goals than scholars using this approach have generally assumed. For example, as we discussed above, it is often said that Japanese firms do not maximize profits like their Western counterparts,[18] but rather shares of the market in which their firms compete, or that Japanese consumers cannot be utility maximizers otherwise they would not tolerate the high prices they pay for products in Japan. We do not make light of this problem in the cases of office-seeking behavior but simply point out that it can be dealt with in a useful way by making three additional assumptions about actor goals.

The first is that economic and political actors can and often do choose to pursue more than one goal. For example, some business firms may choose to pursue sales growth, something that is close to expanding external market share, while politicians may choose to pursue policy goals. We have said here that actors may pursue multiple goals and not different goals, which is a point that we need to clarify by the addition of a second assumption. This assumption begins with the idea that certain behaviors are essential to the roles played by economic and political actors, which means that such behavior is necessary for institutional (parties, firms) and individual actors to be the economic and political actors they are. For an individual to be a politician, he or she must in fact be elected to office, and, for a political organization to be a political party, at least some of those individuals who wear its label during election campaigns must be elected to office. In the area of economics, what makes an organization that exchanges products or goods in the market a business firm is its capacity to survive. In other words, over a certain time horizon, the revenues generated by this organization's sales cover the costs of producing the goods or services it exchanges in the marketplace.

These two supplemental assumptions imply a relationship between the goals actors pursue and the essential behavior that makes individuals and institutions exactly what they are in their essential economic and political pursuits. However, to make this relationship explicit, we need the assistance of a third assumption, which begins with the idea that, if economic or political actors decide to pursue multiple goals, they must do so in obeisance to a particular hierarchy. More specifically, actors may pursue multiple goals as long as they give priority to that goal which makes them what they are in their essential economic and political behavior. Stated another way, subordinate goals may be pursued as long as they do not threaten the attainment of an economic or political actor's principal or defining goal. For Japanese firms, this means that they may pursue sales growth (market share maximization) as long as such a pursuit results in revenues covering costs in the long run. For politicians, it means that they can pursue certain policies, but they can do so only as long as their behavior keeps them in office and, thus, politicians.

This idea of a hierarchy of actor goals implies that there will be times when an essential behavior is more important than at others and, as a result, subordinate goals must be abandoned. For example, profits become a much more pressing issue when a firm is experiencing cash flow problems and, thus, difficulty covering the costs of producing the goods and services it exchanges in the marketplace. In the political sphere, vote maximization becomes an imperative when a politician is in danger of losing his or her seat or when a governing party's majority has declined to a point that it is in danger of losing its ruling status. We will demonstrate in the next chapter how it was the erosion of the LDP's majority in the National Diet that led it to intervene in the policy-making process in certain expected ways to stem the outflow of its support. Our task for the remainder of this chapter is to spell out how the goal-oriented behavior of political actors leads them to use the tools of economic policy in certain expected ways.

ELECTORAL INTERESTS AND POLICY MAKING

The Case of Japan's Ruling Party

Having discussed the assumptions that will guide our analysis of electoral politics and policy making in postwar Japan, we turn next to the specific ways that the electoral concerns encourage politicians and parties to use the available tools of economic policy. In this analysis, when we say parties and politicians, we are referring specifically to politicians in parties that have controlled postwar governments. In postwar Japan, we are referring more specifically to the Liberal Democratic Party, and our focus on the LDP begins with our noting that this party's role in the policy-making process has received a fair amount of scholarly attention in the last decade and a half.

For example, Samuel Kernell, a political scientist at the University of California, San Diego, edited a volume that compared economic policy-making processes in the United States to those occurring in Japan.[19] The essays in his edited volume cover many different economic policy areas, including such important substantive concerns as tax reform and structural adjustment. Opinions expressed in this volume about how Japan's policy processes compare to those of the United States are hardly uniform, but there is an underlying theme that the policy-making process in Japan, like the United States, is characterized by the "primacy of politics."[20] Indeed, the consensus expressed in this volume is that economic policy making in Japan takes place within a system where parochially oriented politicians, acting through such institutions as *zoku*,[21] exercise a great deal of influence.

More broadly gauged than Kernell's collection of essays is Kent Calder's treatment of policy making in postwar Japan which revealed an LDP imprint on a very broad range of policy areas.[22] Calder explains that, throughout the postwar period, the LDP faced a number of "crises" that in one way or another threatened its electoral interests. To reduce the negative electoral impacts attendant to such crises and help preserve its ruling status, the LDP responded with a variety of government initiatives to "compensate" those groups that were negatively affected by such "crises."

These and other works on policy making in postwar Japan are important because they showed how the Liberal Democratic Party has been at the center of that process in postwar Japan.[23] On the other hand, being at the center of the policy-making process does not mean that the influence of Japan' elected officials has been ubiquitous and detectable in every part of that process. Throughout the postwar period, the Liberal Democratic Party simply did not direct every single detail of every policy that it enacted because not all specific policy cases merited direct intervention on the part of the ruling party. Certain aspects of policy making and certain policy areas themselves are more directly connected to the electoral interests of the LDP politicians who controlled the majority of the governments that were formed throughout the postwar period. Those aspects of the policy-making process as well as those specific policy areas that directly impacted on the ruling party's electoral interests required aggressive intervention while those that did not could be delegated to the nation's bureaucrats.

This leaves us with the task of identifying those specific policy areas and electoral circumstances that rendered the aggressive intervention of politicians in the policy-making process necessary from those that did not. There are many ways to complete such a task, one of which involves itemizing the universe of postwar economic policies and the processes through which they were created and implemented. This would be a very thorough approach, but it is obviously one that is well beyond the scope of this chapter. For this reason, we employ an alternative approach that involves the construction of a theoretical framework, which will allow us to identify the policy areas and electoral circumstances that behooved LDP politicians in particular to intervene directly in the process of making economic policy.

To identify the policy areas and electoral circumstances that require politicians in a governing party to intervene directly in the policy-making process, we must first understand the electoral implications associated with being a governing party.[24] A political party gains control of a government by being at the head of a majority coalition, that is, a combination of group and individual supporters that allows it to control a majority of seats in, or at a minimum survive a vote of no confidence, in its respective country's legislature.[25] When a political party achieves governing status, either singularly or as part of a coalition, it brings to that position tendencies to be active in certain policy areas, and what these are depends on the characteristics of the groups that support it. Consequently, by identifying the characteristics of a governing party's group support, we can predict the policy areas in which it will be most active.

Identifying a governing party's group support is not always straightforward because the core support of governing parties often involves much variation. To be sure, a governing party's core supporters can range from a single group like farmers in the case of some early postwar agrarian parties in Scandinavia to those which are supported by a well-blended collection of diffuse socioeconomic groups like the Democratic and Republican Parties in the United States. Nonetheless, we can still say, first, that party support groups possess certain political interests that in large part derive out of their socioeconomic characteristics and, second, that the policy tendencies of governing parties will reflect the interests of their support groups.

On the one hand, for example, because of the working-class nature of their core supporters, social democratic parties tend to emphasize policies that lower unemployment, sometimes at the expense of higher inflation, and expand the welfare state. On the other hand, more conservative-bourgeois parties, especially those whose core supporters are owners of private businesses, tend to be more interested in policies that lower inflation—even at the cost of raising unemployment—keep taxes down, and promote good business conditions.[26] Consequently, if party politics in Japan is like that of other democratic countries in this essential electoral sense, we would expect the policy tendencies of the Liberal Democratic Party to reflect the interests of those groups that gave it the support it needed to rule the country for so long.

While the LDP's support base has changed throughout the postwar period, three groups with easily identifiable socioeconomic characteristics have been identified as that party's core supporters, and perhaps the most important of these support groups is farmers. Individual farm families in Japan became an important political force early in the postwar period when the Allied Occupation, through an extensive land redistribution effort, dramatically increased the number of farm households, creating a rather large class of small landholders. On the one hand, since their creation by the Occupation, Japan's farmers have undergone numerous changes, especially in terms of the proportion of households that are engaged in farming as a full-time occupation. In the 1950s, over 70 percent of Japan's farmers were either full- or part-time farmers who nonetheless derived most of their income from farming, while, in the 1980s, this proportion declined to less than 30 percent of all farmers.[27] What has not changed, on the other hand, is the importance of this group as an essential support constituency of the Liberal Democratic Party.

In Table 6.1, we present the national support rates for the Liberal Democratic Party as well as the rates at which farmers supported that party at different time points throughout the postwar period. The data are from the monthly party and cabinet support polls taken by Japan's Jiji News Organi-

Table 6.1 Farmer Support for the Liberal Democratic Party

Year	LDP Support: National Rate	LDP Support: Farmers	Difference in Farmer Versus National Support Rates*
1960–1961	38.2	48.9	+10.7
1965–1966	37.7	50.6	+12.9
1970–1971	32.6	51.7	+19.1
1975–1976	26.5	49.5	+23.0
1980–1981	33.9	60.0	+26.1
1985–1986	34.3	62.9	+28.6
1990–1991	34.7	62.3	+27.6

*These percentages are obtained by subtracting column 2 from column 3.
Source: Compiled by the authors from Jijitsushinsha (1981 and 1992).

zation (Jijitsushinsha), and are presented in the table at five-year intervals. These Jiji polls are taken monthly and, as a result, can involve substantial sample to sample fluctuations. To average out such fluctuations and present support rates that capture the LDP's electoral strength at the intervals presented in the table, we report the average of twenty-four polls in the fifth and sixth years of each interval.[28]

The support rates presented in the table indicate that farmers have always been strongly supportive of the LDP, remaining loyal to Japan's ruling party throughout the three-decade period for which we have data. Indeed, even as the Liberal Democratic Party became less attractive to other sectors of the Japanese electorate, its appeal to farmers remained strong. The evidence for this is that LDP support rates among farmers began to exceed the party's average support rates by increasingly large amounts in the 1970s and 1980s. As the data in the table indicate, in the 1960s, farmer support rates for the LDP were just over ten points higher than the party's national support rate, but they continued to be more than twenty points higher in the 1970s and more than twenty-five points higher in the 1980s and 1990s.

The second characteristic of the Liberal Democratic Party's support base is its reflection of a distinct urban-rural cleavage. Citizens who live in Japan's rural areas have been an important support group of the LDP since it was formed in 1955. While less dramatic than the case of farmers, the higher rates of support for the party in rural areas is illustrative of the party's electoral strength in those parts of the country. Table 6.2 compares the LDP's national support rates to those it received from residents of the nation's rural areas. The data show that LDP support rates in rural areas were very close to the party's national support rates in the 1960s, which means that it was not until Japan became increasingly urbanized that the rural bias in LDP support

Table 6.2 LDP Support from Japanese Living in Rural Areas

Year	LDP Support: National Average	LDP Support: Rural Dwellers	Rural Difference from the National Rate*
1960–1961	38.2	39.9	+1.7
1965–1966	37.7	38.5	+0.8
1970–1971	32.6	39.3	+6.7
1975–1976	26.5	34.4	+7.9
1980–1981	33.9	38.9	+6.0
1985–1986	34.3	40.0	+5.7
1990–1991	34.7	39.7	+5.0

*These percentages are obtained by subtracting column 2 from column 3.
Source: Compiled by the authors from Jijitsushinsha (1981 and 1992).

Table 6.3 LDP Support from Small- and Medium-Size Business Owners

Year	LDP Support: National Average	LDP Support: Business Owners	Difference from the National Rate*
1960–1961	38.2	50.4	+12.2
1965–1966	37.7	48.7	+11.0
1970–1971	32.6	43.4	+10.8
1975–1976	26.5	38.2	+11.7
1980–1981	33.9	47.9	+14.0
1985–1986	34.3	46.5	+12.2
1990–1991	34.7	45.1	+10.3

*These percentages are obtained by subtracting column 2 from column 3.
Source: Compiled by the authors from Jijitsushinsha (1981 and 1992).

rates began to show up in the data. Indeed, in the 1970s, LDP support rates among rural residents increased to nearly five points above the party's national support rates, and these higher-than-average support rates among residents of Japan's rural areas is something that has continued to the present day.

The third characteristic of the Liberal Democratic Party's support base concerns its dependence on the owners of small- and medium-size enterprises. In Japan, this is a very diverse sector with many competing business interests, but its substantial presence in the Japanese economy is difficult to overestimate. While the prevailing image of Japan's economy is one where large firms such as the Sony, Toyota, and other internationally competitive, leading-edge businesses predominate, the reality is rather different.[29] From the 1950s to the 1980s, over 99 percent of Japan's businesses qualified as small- and medium-size firms as defined above and an average of 80 percent of all Japan's workers worked in such small- or medium-size firms. As Table 6.3 shows, Japanese who owned small- and medium-size businesses were somewhat less loyal to the LDP than farmers, but they were nonetheless one of the ruling party's essential support constituencies. With the exception of a short period in the early 1980s, which we discuss in more detail in the following chapter, LDP support rates among small business owners were on average ten to twelve percentage points higher than the party's national support rates for the same period of time.

These three socioeconomic groups do not in and of themselves complete the LDP's electoral support profile. Throughout the postwar period, other individuals have contributed to the party's predominant party status, but given that these groups constituted the party's core supporters, we would expect them to receive special policy attention from the Liberal Democratic Party. More specifically, if our understanding of the electoral origins of economic policy is correct, we would expect the LDP's policy tendencies to reflect a decidedly pro-farmer, a pro-small business, and a pro-rural area bias. We explore each of these in order below.

That the Liberal Democratic Party has favored Japan's farmers in its policy priorities is well known. Because of Japan's mountainous geography and Occupation land redistribution policies, land under cultivation tends to be in small, family-owned plots which, because of their lack of scale, are noticeably uncompetitive by international standards. For these reasons, Japan's farmers are in need of much protection from the government, and, as perhaps the most important support group of the LDP, Japan's farmers have received protection from international competition through trade restrictions and government subsidies. The extent to which LDP governments would go to protect the country's inefficient but politically vital agricultural sector is perhaps best illustrated by the policies it enacted to protect Japan's rice farmers.[30] Japanese rice farmers have been shielded from any international competition through the banning of rice imports by successive LDP governments. The ban on the import of rice was lifted in 1994 but then only by a non-LDP government.[31] In the summer of 1993, the LDP was displaced by a multiparty coalition for the first since it was formed in 1955, and, under the prime ministership of Hosokawa Morihiro, the import ban on rice was ended.

In some ways, the protection from international competition that rice farmers received from the Japanese government was exceeded by the preferential treatment they received in Japan's domestic market. While domestic preferential treatment involved many policies and practices, the idea was to accord Japan's rice farmers a price for their product that was above what they would receive in the world market. This pricing system was accomplished through a legislative act that was passed during the Pacific War.[32] This piece of legislation allowed the government to buy rice at prices well above those set in the world market and then sell that same rice for prices that were a little lower than the purchase price but still above the world price for rice.

In much the same way that farmers have been the beneficiaries of preferential treatment by the Liberal Democratic Party, so have Japan's rural residents. While there are many manifestations of this special treatment, perhaps none is more impressive than the fact that the LDP maintained the overrepresentation of rural districts in the National Diet through a malapportioned election district system. All elections in Japan from 1947 to 1993 inclusive were held under a system of multimember districts—with an average of three to five seats per district—where voters cast a single nontransferable ballot. The system was created at a time when most of the Japanese population lived in small cities or rural areas.[33] As might be expected, the district boundaries in Japan's election system were initially drawn in a way that reflected the predominance of the country's rural areas early in the postwar period. This means that malapportionment in Japan became an emergent problem that increased as Japan's demographic profile changed, especially in the 1960s and 1970s. In these two decades, Japan's metropolitan areas virtually exploded with population growth while the country's rural areas remained unchanged or even declined. The LDP's response, as expected, was lethargic at best, and the country's rural districts became overrepresented. Between 1958 and 1967 alone, malapportionment increased by more than 100 percent.

On the one hand, given the support rural dwellers have extended to the Liberal Democratic Party, we would expect the LDP to be disposed to maintaining the election system's rural bias as much as possible. On the other hand, given the extensive population growth that Japan's metropolitan areas experienced at the expense of the country's rural districts, we would also expect that this would become increasingly difficult as the postwar period progressed. In fact, in a section of Chiba Prefecture that was essentially a growing bedroom community of Tokyo, a group of voters filed a law suit to force the government to end the problem of malapportionment. In a 1976 decision, Japan's highest court ruled that the system was unconstitutional and needed to be changed, and it was under these kinds of circumstances that the LDP introduced modest reforms.

As we would expect, the Liberal Democratic Party's strategy was to reduce the worst abuses of malapportionment but not to eliminate the asymmetric benefits that the system helped extend to its core supporters in Japan's rural areas. At several different times in the postwar period, the LDP added seats to metropolitan districts, expanding Diet representation in those areas and at only one of these times did it remove seats from rural districts. Such election system corrections did reduce malapportionment, but it never eliminated it, and the system remained biased in favor of rural districts until it was replaced by an entirely new system in January, 1994.[34]

Overrepresentation in and of itself is not really useful unless it becomes an instrument through which the overrepresented areas receive benefits that they might not otherwise receive. This is the case in Japan because it can be readily seen that rural districts in Japan received a host of government attention that is far out of proportion with what one would expect given their smaller populations. Specifically, as members of the country's ruling party, LDP politicians worked very hard at bringing benefits to their rural constituencies. Ramseyer and Rosenbluth (1993) have shown that members of the Liberal Democratic Party, who competed against each other in district elections, specialized in different policy areas to distinguish themselves from other LDP candidates in the same districts. They accomplished this by being specialists in different policy areas and, thus, being associated with different types of government transfers that could be brought to the district. By government transfers, we mean pork barrel projects and other government monies, regulations, and services that enhance the interests of residents in Japan's rural districts. As Ramseyer and Rosenbluth have stated, the use of pork "is the strategy on which the LDP capitalizes" because "[t]he party allows its candidates access to government resources with which to compete for votes."[35]

The third way that government policy under the LDP reflected the composition of the ruling party's electoral support base concerns economic policies directed to the nation's small and medium-size firms. To understand this connection, we must recall that, while it is such world-class corporations as Sony, Toyota, and Matsushita that come to mind when the average person thinks about the Japanese economy, it is such businesses as the local dry cleaners, bakeries, or the closet-size shops from which typically elderly individuals sell magazines, box lunches, and tobacco products that prevail in the economic life of the average Japanese. As stated above, most firms in Japan are of the small and medium variety, and they employ approximately 80 percent of the Japanese labor force. What we must also recall is that owners of Japan's small- and medium-size firms constitute one of the LDP's core constituencies, and, as a result, we would expect economic policies to reflect a distinct small-business bias. A quick scan of such policies reveals that there are many ways that small- and medium-size firms are protected in Japan, but three areas in particular have been singled out by the LDP for policy action.[36]

The first area where government policy has helped smaller businesses is in the area of access to finance. Throughout the postwar period, Japan operated a largely bank-centered finance system that was biased against smaller businesses.[37] This system forced small- and medium-size businesses to rely on government financial institutions to receive the credit they needed.[38] The second area where LDP policies benefited the owners of small- and medium-size firms is in the area of taxation. As we suggested in chapter 3 and as Kent Calder showed, throughout the postwar period, "[b]oth small firms and cooperative business associations, composed almost exclusively of small firms cooperating for some specific policy-related purpose, pay sharply lower rates of taxation than do large corporations."[39] The third policy area where owners of small- and medium-size firms experience government benefits is in the area of trade. Protection of Japanese agriculture is well known, but aside from farming, "the sectors of most vigorous Japanese protection . . . are those involving processing by small Japanese businesses of imported raw materials such as plywood, other processed lumber products, and silk textiles."[40]

Chapter 7

POLITICAL CHANGE AND ECONOMIC POLICY MAKING

The history of Japanese politics under LDP rule is as importantly a story of political change as it is of continuity and stability.

—Gerald Curtis (1988)

In an effort to win back its lost ground, the LDP began shifting a growing percentage of budgetary resources in the 1970s to the redistributive and public goods successfully championed by opposition local governments.

—Mark Ramseyer and Frances Rosenbluth (1993)

U nderstanding the characteristics of a governing party's support groups tells us about the policy mix most likely to dominate that party's agenda and which groups are most likely to be recipients of government largesse. Knowing a governing party's policy orientation, however, does not tell us how that governing party's policy profile is likely to change as its support base evolves over time. This is an important issue because it is an unfortunate fact of political life that the support base on which a party's ability to govern rests is in a state of nearly constant change. From the ongoing shifts that occur in the demographic profile of a nation and the sometimes dramatic political implications that accompany economic fluctuations such as oil and other supply shocks, to the inevitable replacement of older voters with young, new entrants, party support groups are in a constant state of flux. Consequently, when such changes touch directly on a governing party's ability to remain in power as they invariably do, parties in control of a government will endeavor to counter those forces and preserve their levels of electoral support.

Saying this, however, does not tell us exactly how governing parties use the policy process to preserve their support levels and, thus, ruling status in the most effective manner. This is the issue we must address in this chapter, and our effort begins by noting that an understanding of this aspect of ruling-party behavior must recognize certain substantive and procedural issues. Substantive issues, on the one hand, revolve around exactly what policies a governing party should use to keep socioeconomic change and exogenous

113

shocks from reducing its support levels to an extent that threatens its ability to rule. As we show below, the specific policies a ruling party responds with will depend on the manner in which political change reduces its level of electoral support. Procedural issues, on the other hand, concern how a governing party should time its use of economic policy to be sure that the government benefits it transfers have the best chance of achieving the desired electoral results. As we show below, while this will vary somewhat with the type of policy being used, the timing of economic policies is often tied directly to the procedures that define democratic politics.

DEMOCRATIC POLITICS: PROCEDURAL AND SUBSTANTIVE ISSUES

To answer the question, how a governing party should time its use of economic policies to preserve its level of support, we must recognize that in democratic politics some points in time are more important than others. For governing parties, no time is more important than that of a national election because it is at election time that a governing party's electoral majority is up for renewal. Indeed, it is a national election that provides a governing party with an unretouched snapshot of the level of support it possesses, determining whether or not that level of support is sufficient for it to continue governing. For this reason, if there were ever a time when we would expect governing parties to use the tools of economic policy to serve their electoral interests, it would be when an election is called.

Exactly how governing parties in parliamentary systems like Japan's link the policy process to their political interests at election time involves two specific methods. The first method is political surfing and refers to the sometimes limited but nonetheless important flexibility officials in governing parties have in scheduling national elections. The idea is to schedule a national election at a time when electoral conditions favor the governing party and, thus, raise its chances of performing well in the election. While there is no singularly optimal way to accomplish this, certain patterns make sense and tend to define the most often used governing party approaches to political surfing. The first method is connected to the country's domestic conditions and involves the idea that a governing party, if the laws and political conditions affecting the holding of elections permit, schedules the election before it is constitutionally required to do so when the economy is performing well so that its candidates can surf the wave of economic prosperity to electoral victory. The other variant of this is to schedule the election after some major policy coup or other domestic or international event that renders the governing party popular among members of the electorate. Again, the popularity associated with the event or policy coup leads the governing party's candidates to surf themselves to electoral victory.

When we consider the LDP's use of political surfing, we must keep in mind that the party did not have to worry that much about macroeconomic conditions being an electoral liability. For most of the postwar period, Japan's strong economic performance served the LDP's electoral interests, and, as a result, the ruling party tended to engage in political surfing in the second way defined above. At times, this second type of political surfing was unintentional, such as in the death of Prime Minister Ohira during the election campaign of 1980. At that time, the LDP was bitterly divided over issues of corruption, taxes, and its eroding electoral support. Ohira headed one of the LDP's factions and had called the 1980 election less than a year after the 1979 contest failed to produce a leader with sufficient support to run the party. The Prime Minister, however, died during the campaign, allowing LDP candidates to ride a strong sympathy vote to victory in 1980. At other times, however, political surfing has been intentional, and perhaps the best illustration of this occurred when former Prime Minister Tanaka Kakuei called the 1972 election more than a year before constitutionally required to coincide with his success in reestablishing diplomatic relations with China.

Political surfing is an effective electoral tool, but it is not without its problems in that governing parties cannot always hold a national contest when domestic or international conditions are electorally favorable. At times when extant political and constitutional constraints do not permit a governing party to dissolve its lower house and hold an election, parties can use a second method to link the policy process to their electoral interests. This second method involves a governing party engaging in a "targeted manipulation of a specific economic program,"[1] which means that a governing party pursues the option of timing transfers of government benefits to coincide with elections.

Two Japanese political scientists, Kohno Masaru and Nishizawa Yoshitaka, have studied the manner in which the Liberal Democratic Party manipulated certain economic policies to enhance its chances for victory at election time. They examined government spending on construction projects targeted to Japan's numerous election districts for the thirty-year period from 1955 to 1985 and found that, throughout this period of time, spending on construction projects increased dramatically in the month that an election took place. What we must understand here is that, when governing parties send direct transfers of public resources to members of their support constituencies in the same month that an election is held, they are doing so in response to certain electoral imperatives. If it is the case that a governing party holds a majority of seats in the lower house of its respective parliament that is not in imminent danger of being taken away in an upcoming election, then the principal challenge it faces at election time is getting its core supporters to turn out and vote. This means that its electoral strategy can be focused less on expanding its support base than on ensuring that its core supporters, who are sufficient in number to provide a parliamentary majority, go to the polls on election day and extend it their support. This is what we refer to as a governing party facing a *turnout imperative* on election day.

For at least the first decade and a half of its postwar rule, Japan's Liberal Democratic Party faced a turnout imperative in lower house elections. During this period, the ruling party's share of lower house seats was sufficiently large so as nearly to guarantee that it would emerge from the next elections with its majority preserved. As a result, when lower house elections were held at this time, the Liberal Democratic Party needed only to remind its supporters that it is their benefactor party, which has protected and advanced their interests by different mixes of public resources and is now in need of their electoral support. A strategy that involves government transfers, such as spending on district construction projects timed as closely to the election as possible is one that appears most able to accomplish this, and it is for this reason that Kohno and Nishizawa (1990) found that LDP direct spending on district construction projects increased dramatically in the month that an election was held.[2]

How a governing party times the benefits it provides to its supporters represents only the beginning of how its electoral interests motivate it to use the policy process. As stated above, the problem of political change also involves the substantive issue of what type of economic policy is best suited to counter a particular type of political change.[3] While the individual-level changes that occur in a governing party's support base over time are numerous, we can say that they impact on its ability to remain in that position in a combination of two ways. First, electoral change comes in the form of what we call *sectoral change*. This form of electoral change involves sector-specific shifts of partisan loyalties where a substantial number of members of a governing party's support groups simply stop being loyal to the party. Second, electoral change comes in the form of *ecological change,* a process where electoral change occurs without any movement in the partisan loyalties of a governing party's support groups' members. Instead, ecological change involves alterations in the size of a governing party's support groups relative to the sizes of other socioeconomic groups.

Ecological and sectoral changes occur in a nation's electorate for different reasons. The former is typically the result of alterations that naturally occur in the socioeconomic profile of a nation. For example, as a nation undergoes industrialization and urbanization, the size of its rural and farming populations decline. If a nation's governing party is dependent on farmers and other rural dwellers as core supporters, its support base will naturally shrink as a result of that demographic shift. Sectoral change, however, is not directly related to demographic change but occurs when a group of governing party supporters simply turns away from that party. Because there may be multiple factors that lead an individual to support one party or another, there may also be multiple causes behind an individual altering his or her partisan preferences. Nonetheless, we can usually tie partisan changes to one of two specific causes, especially when they involve members of an easily definable socioeconomic group. On the one hand, it is sometimes the case that the appearance of a new issue, one that cuts across a group's political preferences, leads to a weakening of partisan loyalties.[4] On the other hand, individuals in a group may also shift their partisan loyalties because their benefactor party, as a nation's governing party, fails to provide appropriately timed and sufficiently supplied government benefits.[5]

A governing party will naturally respond to any condition that undermines its ability to remain in power, but these two types of electoral change persuade it to use the instruments of economic policy in different ways.[6] Ecological change reduces a governing party's ability to stay in power by rendering the support level provided by its core supporters insufficient to keep it in power. As a result, to maintain itself as a governing party, it must expand its electoral support beyond its original core supporters. To do this, a governing party will have to identify members of the nation's electorate that have the potential to become new supporters, and, while it is possible that a certain socioeconomic group can be targeted with a specific set of policies, in most cases this process involves attempting to gain support from the amorphous mass of that nation's nonpartisans.[7] In such cases, the method of attraction will typically involve the use of broadly targeted public goods because these will include the kinds of benefits a large, undifferentiated mass public would desire.[8]

In the case of sectoral change, a governing party will be forced to use the policy process in different ways depending on why certain members of a core support group alter their partisan loyalties. If on the one hand, the problem is that core supporters are not getting the kinds of government benefits that adequately advance their interests, then the response of the governing party will be to provide more of the same kind of benefits that it has provided in the past. If, on the other hand, core supporters fall away because of the rise of some crosscutting issue that captures their preferences as much as or more than their existing preferences, then a governing party will be persuaded to respond with policies that remove that crosscutting issue from the political agenda.

SMALL BUSINESS AND ENVIRONMENTAL POLICY:
THE LDP'S RESPONSE TO SECTORAL CHANGE

Throughout the postwar period, the LDP was forced to deal with challenges to its majority as the result of both types of electoral change, and, more than this, the sectoral changes it faced involved the loss of supporters' loyalties both because of the rise of crosscutting issues and because of dissatisfaction with the level of benefits its members were receiving. Concerning sectoral change that occurs through the rise of a crosscutting issue, a useful illustration of the LDP's expected response concerns the problem of environmental pollution that Japan experienced in the postwar period.

By the middle-1960s, Japan's reputation as a polluted country had achieved international notoriety. While none of the country's major political parties really championed the environment as a national issue, local officials did make pollution an issue in their respective campaigns. The result was a rise in non-LDP executives and assembly members at the municipal and prefectural levels, especially in those local areas where pollution was a serious problem and the issue was pushed by opposition candidates. While other factors were simultaneously at work, at least part of the secular decline the LDP experienced in the 1960s and early 1970s was due to the environment issue forcing Japan's voters to look outside the party for relief. For example, in a national sample taken during the 1976 general election, 60 percent of respondents who did not think the environment was an important issue reported supporting the LDP. For those respondents who stated that the environment was an important issue, only 22 percent reported that they supported the LDP.[9] The LDP's losses at both the national and local levels eventually became serious enough that the party could no longer ignore the issue, and part of its effort to deal with its hemorrhaging electoral support involved policy action on Japan's severe environmental problems.

What is important here is not simply that the LDP eventually took action on the environmental problems Japan was facing but rather how it went about making an effort to eliminate pollution completely. Policy action to alleviate pollution problems invariably involves polluting businesses that are supporters of a major political party having to incur higher costs that environmental regulations necessarily involve. This has been the case for U.S. businesses that are supporters of Democrats and Republicans in the U.S. Congress, and it has also been true for businesses that supported Japan's Liberal Democratic Party. In the United States, this relationship between polluters and politicians has led to a kind of incrementalist approach as elected officials tried to grapple with environmental problems but, at the same time, protect their affected business constituents.[10] In Japan, on the other hand, government action to reduce pollution levels involved an entirely different pattern of response.

If the LDP's efforts to eliminate pollution in Japan were in fact an attempt to halt the political losses it incurred at the local level because of this issue, then we would expect it to have followed a strategy other than the incrementalist approach that we have long witnessed in the United States. Rather, if our view is correct, the party should address the problem with an eye toward eliminating it as a crosscutting issue that was impacting negatively on its electoral fortunes. This means that the issue must be dealt with in a comprehensive manner because an incrementalist approach would not remove it from the nation's political agenda, eliminating it as a source of undesirable sectoral change and, thus, allowing ersatz supporters compromised by this problem to return to the party's fold.

In postwar Japan, the LDP's response to the nation's pollution problems was no doubt belated, but, when the party's policy response did come, it occurred in exactly in the predicted manner. Beginning in 1971, the LDP-controlled government created an Environmental Agency, enacted more than a dozen separate laws to control pollution, and allocated a mass of public money to be sure that its newly enacted environmental standards were implemented without undue economic hardships. Because of the party's efforts and Japan's fortunate geography in this respect, the pollution issue was off of the national political agenda by the end of the decade.[11]

Concerning sectoral change that derives from the declining loyalty of core supporters, we must recall that, when the Liberal Democratic Party was formed in the fall of 1955, it controlled over 60 percent of the seats in the lower house of the Diet. While, in the next three elections, the party obtained vote shares sufficient to maintain this level of lower house control, its electoral fortunes began to change rapidly. A number of factors contributed to the LDP's electoral decline during this period, but one notable factor involved the loss of support from owners of Japan's small- and medium-size businesses. As we showed in the previous chapter, small business owners have been one of the LDP's essential support groups, but their loyalty to the ruling party has not always been unwavering. The monthly party and cabinet support polls conducted by the Jiji News Organization showed that the LDP began losing support from this constituency soon after the party was formed, slowly at first, but then rapidly.[12] This sectoral change occurred at a time when the LDP was experiencing an overall secular decline, which meant that the party could not afford to lose the loyalty of this core support group. Given this, if the understanding of electoral politics and economic policy we sketched out above is correct, then we should expect the Liberal Democratic Party to use the policy process to get small business owners to return to the party's fold.

To show that this is exactly what happened, we need to track the developments that characterize this sectoral change. The first of these concerns identifying why members of this essential LDP core support group turned away from their benefactor party, and at least part of the answer to this question rests with the economic problems small businesses encountered in the 1960s and 1970s.[13] Small firms in Japan have been disadvantaged in procuring capital, attracting high-quality labor, and acquiring technology and information relative to their larger counterparts. Moreover, small- and medium-size enterprises have always been particularly vulnerable to changes in economic conditions.[14] For instance, in 1964 and 1965, the time of the Tokyo Olympics and shortly thereafter, Japan experienced a severe recession when "bankruptcies soared, with small businesses taking the brunt of the downturn."[15] This is confirmed by the data presented in Table 7.1, which shows that between 1960 and 1981, the average number of business failures among all Japanese firms grew substantially but that small- and medium-size firms were hardest hit.

In the early part of the 1960s, the increase in the number of bankruptcies was on the order of 72 percent per year. Rates of increase slowed in the early 1970s but jumped again after the first oil shock in 1973. By the end of the decade, rates dropped again to an average of 2.5 percent per year. Because small- and medium-size firms are generally less efficient than their larger counterparts, we would expect small firms to be significantly affected by changes in the business climate. As the data in Table 7.1 indicate, what happened in the 1960s and 1970s is that small- and medium-size firms endured an increasing proportion of the business failures that occurred. The last column of the table shows that this was particularly true for the early to mid-

Table 7.1 Bankruptcy Data for Small- and Medium-Size Firms, 1960–1981

Years	Average Number of Bankruptcies Per Year for All Firms	Small- and Medium-Size Firms' Share of Bankruptcies (Percentage Change)
1960–1963	1,448	+52%
1964–1966	4,570	+200%
1967–1972	6,663	−8%
1973–1975	9,967	+71%
1976–1978	15,648	+33%
1979–1981	16,849	−13%

Source: Calculated by the authors from MITI, *White Papers on Small and Medium-Sized Firms* (1960–1983).

1960s and the years immediately after the first oil shock where the small- and medium-size enterprise share of all bankruptcies grew by 67 percent per year and 24 percent per year respectively.

The economic hardships faced by Japan's small businesses would appear to be sufficient motivation for their respective owners to reconsider their relationship with the LDP. Evidence that this is exactly what happened can be found in the political activities taken by members of this important grouping of businesses. While there were a number of umbrella organizations advocating for the interests of small- and medium-size firms,[16] perhaps the most important politically was the People's Association of Commerce and Industry or *Minsho*. Nominally affiliated with the Japan Communist Party, *Minsho* watched its membership grow 250 percent between 1965 and 1972, a period when business failures ravaged the small-business sector.[17] Originally, *Minsho* pressed the LDP and the central government for financial assistance, particularly access to no-collateral loans. When members of this "pressure group" deemed the LDP's response insufficient, they began supporting opposition candidates who agreed to help small businesses in their efforts to obtain more financial assistance.

The period of small business troubles and *Minsho*'s political activities certainly correspond both to the period of LDP sectoral decline and to the time when opposition parties performed much better electorally at both the national and local levels. It is most likely that these events are connected, but, to be sure, we need to track the partisan changes that characterize owners of small- and medium-size enterprises. Data collected by the Jiji News Organization show that small business support for the Japan Communist Party (JCP) increased by over 300 percent in the first half of the 1970s. In fact, by 1977, over one-quarter of all small business owners reported supporting the JCP. Given *Minsho*'s affiliation with the Japan Communist Party, these numbers suggest strongly that its efforts on the part of small business were successful.

Our understanding contends that the LDP should respond to this sectoral change and use the policy process to regain the loyalty of small business owners that it had been losing in the 1960s and 1970s. Since small businesses were clamoring for financial assistance in the face of the economic difficulties they faced, our expectation is that the LDP should have responded with exactly what members of this important support constituency demanded. To determine if the LDP's behavior accords to this pattern, we must provide a clear description of the party's expected response by explaining the manner in which small- and medium-size enterprises obtained needed financing throughout this period of time. This, in turn, requires a brief review of specific aspects of the Japanese financial system.

Small- and medium-size firms have relied on both private and public sources for their financing needs. On the private side, a number of institutions were created specifically to attend to the financial needs of small- and medium-size businesses. Principally, these have included regional banks, *sogo* banks, *shinkin* banks, and credit cooperatives.[18] Funds from these institutions, however, have been inadequate to satisfy the financial needs of Japan's small business sector mainly because of the manner in which the country's financial system discriminates against small- and medium-size businesses. Interest rates in Japan have been strictly regulated, and private banks often require that borrowing firms maintain a "compensating balance" in their institution which has had the effect of pushing effective rates on borrowed funds well above the nominal rates.[19] Compensating balances are higher for smaller firms because loaning money to them involves higher risks, and, as a result, small- and medium-size firms encountered great difficulty meeting the requirements for private borrowing. For example, in the early to mid-1960s, effective rates on borrowed funds for small firms were anywhere from 35 percent to 65 percent higher than those paid by large firms.[20]

To compensate for this bias in the financial system and help small- and medium-size firms obtain the financing they needed, a number of government financial institutions were created. Among these, three stand out as being most important. The first is the People's Finance Corporation, which was created in 1949 specifically to provide financing to small businesses, especially those that were considered to be uncompetitive internationally. The second financial institution is the Small Business Finance Corporation, which was founded in 1953 to provide long-term loans to small businesses to help them comply with government policies in such areas as pollution control and energy conservation and weather economic hardships when economic conditions were unfavorable. The third government financial institution is the Central Cooperative Bank for Commerce and Industry which was created in 1936 to provide funding for what are known as geographically concentrated industries. These include traditional industries such as pottery and silk weaving as well as other business areas occupied primarily by small firms.

In addition to these institutions, small- and medium-size firms in Japan have received central government financing from a number of specialized institutions. These include two regional development banks, the Hokkaido-Tohoku Development Corporation and the Okinawa Development Corporation, which play important financial roles for small businesses in northern Japan and the islands comprising Okinawa. In specially designated areas such as pollution control, the Environmental Sanitation Business Finance Corporation has funded small businesses and, in the area of loan guarantees, Japan's small business sector has been assisted by the Small Business Credit Insurance Corporation.

These public financial institutions are capitalized with funds the Japanese government gathers through its postal savings system and then places in the Ministry of Finance's Trust Fund Bureau. Postal savings funds are provided to these institutions, as well as many others, through what is known as the Fiscal Investment Loan Plan (FILP). Discussing the FILP as a public funding mechanism at the discretion of elected politicians goes against nearly everything specialists have written about Japan's financial system. It has become an accepted fact that not only is the FILP the most important tool of Japan's industrial policy, it is also outside the realm of electoral politics. Chalmers Johnson wrote that the FILP is a "very considerable financial institution to be totally in the hands of the bureaucracy for public investment and which is generally beyond the influence of pork-barrel politics."[21]

If this is an accurate assessment of political influence, it is true only for part of the postwar period because, in 1973, a law was passed that required Diet approval for the investment of Trust Fund Bureau monies and Postal Annuity Assets of five years or longer. While this effectively made each element of the FILP part of the budget plan subject to Diet approval,[22] there is reason to believe that political influence on the distribution of FILP monies existed before the passage of this law. First, FILP budgets have always been prepared by the Ministry of Finance, but the government financial institutions that have been the recipients of FILP funds have had to have their individual budgets and "annual plans" approved by the Diet.[23] Also, if one examines the types and distribution of expenditures made under the FILP, especially in light of sectoral changes that were occurring at this time, the influence of electoral politics appears to be undeniable.

Table 7.2 shows that the largest recipients of FILP funds have been public financial institutions, a category composed of public sector banks that were created to serve the needs principally of small- and medium-size businesses. Their share of FILP funds grew to nearly one-half of all the program's disbursements by 1980. Moreover, examining FILP disbursements by expenditure category reveals that the largest share by far did not go to the key industries that are associated with Japan's industrial policy but rather to what is known as "livelihood infrastructure and welfare."[24] This category includes such things as housing; health, welfare, and education facilities; and public financial institutions for small- and medium-size firms.

If the LDP wished to use the policy process to regain the loyalty of its ersatz small business supporters, we would expect it to commit increasingly larger amounts of government funds to the public financial institutions that

Table 7.2 FILP Recipients and Expenditure Categories*

	1965	1970	1975	1980	1985
RECIPIENTS					
Special Accounts	1.5	1.2	1.7	2.0	2.1
Public Corporations	11.6	10.1	10.7	7.8	6.6
Public Finance Corporations	26.6	32.3	32.9	45.2	42.9
Banks	16.2	20.3	11.2	8.0	7.0
Public Bodies	19.8	19.2	23.1	18.8	21.4
Local Government Bodies	21.2	15.2	19.4	17.1	18.2
Special Corporations	3.1	1.2	1.0	1.1	0.8
Other	—	0.2	—	—	—
EXPENDITURE GROUPS					
Livelihood Infrastructure and Welfare	52.8	56.3	64.1	71.8	69.8
Industrial Infrastructure and Land Management	31.9	27.4	25.5	19.6	21.9
Key Industries	15.3	16.3	10.7	8.6	8.3

Source: Patterson (1994).
*All entries in the table's cells are percentages.

traditionally served small businesses until that policy action achieved the desired electoral results. Moreover, if owners of Japan's smaller firms fell away from the party because they were dissatisfied with its performance as their benefactor party, we would expect them to return to the party's fold when their financial demands were addressed. It is interesting to note that Ministry of Finance data show clearly that the budgets of the above mentioned institutions increased dramatically during the period of sectoral change and that party support data provided by the Jiji News Organization indicate that, by the end of the 1970s, small business owners began to recommit themselves to the Liberal Democratic Party. The connection between the LDP's behavior and the partisan orientation of the small business sector then appears solid, but to be sure that this apparent connection is reliable a more thorough analysis is necessary.

Demonstrating the connection between the policy behavior of the LDP and the partisanship of small firm owners is a little more complicated than simply showing that the behavior of these two actors occurred in the way we expected it to occur. To be certain that the relationship is as strong as we have asserted, it is necessary for us to control for all other potential influences in an appropriately constructed statistical analysis. This process begins with us defining the variable to be explained as the sum of all loans extended to small- and medium-size firms through government financial institutions. The institutions whose funds we summed up for this variable are all capitalized with finds from the FILP and include the following public financial corporations that we discussed above: the People's Finance Corporation, the Small Business Finance Corporation, the Hokkaido/Tohoku and Okinawa Development Corporations, the Small Business Credit Insurance Corporation, and the Environmental Sanitation Business Finance Corporation.[25]

Our view is that the level of funding the government provided to these institutions and extended to the small business sector will be a function of the LDP's response to support losses from small business owners and the party's attempt to woo them back. This means that the amount of Fiscal Investment Loan Plan money given to owners of small- and medium-size firms should have increased as this group's support rate for the LDP declined, and this is a relationship that should hold up in the presence of other potentially important factors. Such factors include, first, bureaucratic influences that will manifest themselves in the form of that well-known public sector budget signature, namely incremental growth over time.[26] What this means for our analysis is that the budget of a government-funded financial institution in any given year will be related to that institution's budget in the previous year. To capture this, we include in our statistical model a term for the budgeted amount in the previous year or a lagged dependent variable.

The amount of government financing extended to Japan's small- and medium-size firms will no doubt also be related to economic conditions, particularly, the manner in which they affect both the supply of funds available for the FILP and the demand for public financing from firms in the small business sector. We capture the supply factor in our statistical analysis by adding to our model the amount of money available to the FILP. The relationship is straightforward in that we expect more money to be provided when the supply of available funds in the Postal Savings System is more generous. We measure this supply factor by totaling up the combined assets of the Ministry of Finance Trust Fund Bureau, which is the sum of assets in the Postal Savings system, the Post Office Life Insurance and Postal Annuity, and the Welfare Insurance Special Account. We should note here that funds from these sources averaged 65 percent to 85 percent of FILP funds with the remainder made up through government borrowing.[27]

Small- and medium-sized firms' demand for public financing is captured in two ways in our analysis. The first involves the business conditions that small- and medium-size firms faced throughout the period under consideration. We capture these conditions by adding real GNP growth rate to our analysis. For the period from 1960 to 1973, real GNP averaged 9.5 percent but dropped to a small negative value in 1974—the year after the first oil shock—only to rebound to an average of 4.2 percent per year through the end of the 1980s. By including this in our model, we intend to capture small- and medium-size firms' demand for financial assistance that is derived from macroeconomic conditions. In our analysis, however, it is also necessary that we attempt to capture the impact of economic conditions at the level of individual enterprises, and, for this reason, we need to include a second demand factor. The manner in which we accomplish this is by including the annual change in capitalization (*shihon kin*) for all manufacturing, commercial, and service enterprises in our analysis. Unfortunately, our data on changes in firm capitalization rates are not disaggregated by firm size, but given the enormous presence of small firms in Japan and their financial weakness relative to the country's large firms, these data serve as a more than adequate proxy for our analysis.

Aside from the bureaucratic and economic factors that we just described above, there is an additional control variable that we include in our statistical model. Because it is necessary to assume in our analysis that the amount of financing extended to small- and medium-size firms will be characterized by natural growth that is outside political, economic, and bureaucratic factors that our model is designed to weight, it is necessary that we add a variable that captures this. The standard way to capture such an influence is through the addition of what is called a time trend.

Finally, as we have stated above, the amount of money made available to Japan's small- and medium-size firms from the FILP through the country's various public financial institutions will be based on the political calculations made by the ruling Liberal Democratic Party. By political calculations, we are referring to the LDP's concern with the loss of its small business supporters, and, to determine the level of support that owners of small- and medium-size firms extended to the Liberal Democratic Party, we used the Jiji News Organization's party support polls, which are broken down by the occupation of respondents. As in the other instances where we used Jiji party support data, the annual data we use in our analysis are the average of twelve monthly polls taken in a year. When including this in our analysis, we had to keep in mind that the fiscal year in Japan begins in April and that the government budget is drafted at the end of the previous calendar year. This means that any LDP effort to bolster its support levels with increased amounts of financial aid to small firms will most likely show up in the time period (year) following a registered loss of support. For this reason, the political support variable in our analytic model is entered at a one-year lag.

What we have here is a standard time series model that allows us to estimate the impact of all the factors we discussed above on the amount of public finance that the small business sector received from LDP governments from the 1960s to the 1980s.[28] This is ordinarily done through an ordinary least squares (OLS) estimation with strict attention to the statistical issues that are necessarily involved in such time series models.[29] The results of our estimation are presented in Table 7.3 and confirm our understanding of how electoral politics drove the content and direction of economic policy in postwar Japan, and, in this instance of sectoral change, the results in the table tell us that the Liberal Democratic Party responded in exactly the way we expected it to respond.

As explained above, our understanding is that, as the support for the LDP from small business owners drops, the amount of public financing extended to the businesses in that sector would increase. This means that the coefficient on this variable should be large and negative, something that is confirmed by the estimate in the table. In fact, the data in the table tell us that the LDP's interests had more of an impact on the amount of money given to small- and medium-size firms than any other factor. This does not mean that other factors were irrelevant because the results in the table indicate that, with the exception of the capitalization variable, which was statistically insignificant,

Table 7.3 Political, Economic, Bureaucratic, and Time Influences on the Amount of Government Finance Provided to Small Business

Variable	Coefficient (Standard Error)	T Ratio
Constant	18912.08[a] (7445.93)	2.54
Previous Year's Budget	0.4544[a] (0.2078)	2.19
LDP Support from Small Business Owners	−319.86[a] (131.467)	−2.43
GNP Growth	−277.99[b] (117.963)	−1.93
Available Trust Fund Bureau Funds	0.055000[c] (0.0169)	2.99
Change in Capitalization	0.0684 (0.1261)	0.54
Time Trend	97.753 (194.104)	0.50

$R^2 = .99$; $F = 2496.97$
[a]$p < .05$; [b]$p < .10$; [c]$p < .01$.

signs on remaining coefficients were in the correct direction and statistically significant. For example, as expected, high GNP growth in the period under consideration was negatively related to the amount of public finance provided to small- and medium-size firms, while the availability of money in the Ministry of Finance's Trust Fund Bureau was related in a positive way to the amount loaned. In both cases, the relationships are statistically significant but substantively small. In light of these and other results in the table, we are able to conclude that the LDP used the tools of economic policy in the predicted manner, increasing the amount of public money extended to small- and medium-size firms to get back a committed, core supporters of Japan's ruling party.

FISCAL STIMULUS POLICIES: THE LDP'S RESPONSE TO ECOLOGICAL CHANGE

Our next case of the LDP using the tools of economic policy to serve its electoral interests concerns the party's response to ecological change. As discussed above, ecological change involves continuity in the loyalty of a party's support groups but a change in their size relative to other socioeconomic groups. This is a very troubling electoral change because it results in a governing party's core support declining in size to the extent that it becomes insufficient to sustain that party in power. In the face of such an electoral change, a governing party is forced to seek additional support from other members of the electorate, usually voters who are uncommitted nonpartisans rather than voters who are part of another party's core support constituency. It also means that, in order to attract new supporters, policy strategies designed to maintain the loyalty of old support groups are inappropriate. Ecological change then requires an entirely different use of public policy, and, to show what this strategy is and how Japan's LDP employed it, we must first show how ecological change affected the LDP's support levels.

Our discussion of the LDP's support groups focused on three in particular, owners of small- and medium-size firms, farmers, and residents of Japan's rural districts. The developments of the postwar period brought on a marked change in Japan's demographic profile, and, while the small business sector remained a steady proportion of the Japanese electorate, farmers and rural dwellers declined dramatically. In 1960, there were nearly 12 million farmers in Japan. Ten years later, this number dropped to 8.1 million and, in 1980, to just over 5 million. By the mid-1990s, Japan's farming population had dropped to 3.2 million, a three-and-one-half decade drop of nearly 400 percent. Paralleling this drop in the farm population was an equally dramatic change in the urban-rural nature of the Japanese population. Since the end of the Pacific War, Japan's population has become increasingly urbanized. Early in the postwar period, two-thirds of the Japanese population lived in one of the country's rural areas,[30] but four decades later this proportion had dropped to one-third with over 40 percent of the country's population living in one of Japan's three largest metropolitan areas, Tokyo/ Yokohama, Nagoya, or Osaka/Kobe.

In the first three decades of the postwar period, these two essential LDP support constituencies were reduced dramatically, contributing significantly to the party's secular decline. LDP leaders were well aware of how the demographic changes taking place in Japan were undermining the party's ability to control a majority of seats in the lower house of the Diet. In a 1963 *Chuo Koron* article, LDP member, Ishida Hirohide, stated that socioeconomic changes brought about by Liberal Democratic Party policies would lead to conservative-progressive electoral parity unless the LDP began to attract new supporters.[31]

As Japan's governing party, the LDP had at its disposal all of the tools of economic policy to attract new supporters, but the problem it faced was which policies would be most useful for attracting new supporters in the face of the demographic transformation Japan had been experiencing at the time. As mentioned above, governing parties with a waning majority due to ecological change face a *support expansion imperative* because, to maintain their governing status, they must attract new supporters into the party's fold in addition to maintaining the loyalty of their core supporters. Certainly, the policies used to bring owners of small- and medium-size firms back into the party's fold would not be adequate because, as we discussed above, they are designed to address the electoral implications of sectoral change. The voters who would be available for mobilization outside of the LDP's and other parties' core supporters would by and large be the politically unaffiliated members of a diffuse mass public, and the most effective strategy to attract such voters would involve broadly gauged, public goods–type policies.[32]

What distinguishes policies of the public goods variety from others is exactly what makes them useful as a support expansion tool in the hands of governing parties. The quality we are referring to here is that of nonexclusivity, which means that, once provided, it is not possible for individuals to be excluded from consuming that good.[33] This is important for governing parties seeking to expand their support bases because such policies will reach those nonpartisan citizens that the governing party wants to bring into its fold. There are numerous opportunities for ruling parties to use a public goods strategy to augment their support base, but the tricky problem they face concerns the substantive issue of which public goods policies to use and the procedural issue

of how to time their announcement and implementation so that they produce
the desired electoral results.

The problem of which public goods policies a governing party should
select can be resolved in a fairly straightforward fashion. If a party builds a
bridge where no river exists, such an action serves no discernible transporta-
tion end and, as a result, no political purpose as well. What this means is that
the electoral interests of a governing party are served only when it chooses
public goods that address some manifest policy problem. In other words,
although public goods policies are designed to serve the governing party's
electoral interests, they cannot do this if they do not address a real (perceived)
problem. For example, implementing policies to improve macroeconomic
conditions when an economy is booming or to expand on an already fully
developed welfare state will bring few if any electoral returns because there
is no public perception that such policy actions will bring much in the way
of needed benefits.

The problem of the appropriate timing of a public goods strategy is also
straightforward, but it does involve somewhat more guesswork than does the
problem of selecting the correct policy in the first place. One the one hand,
as we discussed above, to make the policy process serve a governing party's
turnout imperative, that is to remind party supporters to turn out and vote for
it in an election, it is necessary that the policy be timed as close to the
election as possible. On the other hand, using the policy process to convince
unaffiliated nonpartisans to vote for it at election time, a governing party
must, more than anything else, convince those nonpartisans that it is committed to implementing policies that address real (perceived) problems. This
means that a governing party faces the challenge of announcing the policy
close enough to election day so that its efforts are remembered and rewarded
at the ballot box but not so close that the public goods policy action appears
overtly political.

Throughout the postwar period, we have witnessed the LDP using public-
goods types of policies in a number of instances. One notable instance occurred
in the early 1970s and involved the ruling party's efforts to expand the Japanese
welfare state. Compared to the democracies of Northern Europe, welfare in
Japan was relatively underdeveloped, especially in the early postwar years, and,
by engaging in an expansion of welfare programs, the LDP was addressing an
existing social problem. The government's efforts included improving such
things as pensions and health care and involved a general effort to address the
quality of life concerns of Japan's burgeoning "middle mass" population. At the
same time, however, the LDP implemented these welfare state expansion policies in the hope of getting politically unaffiliated beneficiaries to become the
party's new supporters.[34]

Another notable illustration of how the Liberal Democratic Party—and the two coalition governments that replaced it in 1993 and 1994 for that matter—used a public goods strategy both to solve an existing public policy problem and to counter the deleterious effects of ecological change concerns its attempts improve macroeconomic conditions. It is true that Japan's economy performed quite well throughout most of the postwar period which means that related policy action at such times would not be effective politically. Nonetheless, from time to time, Japan did experience downturns in the business cycle which were sometimes severe enough to require concerted policy action. Moreover, following the bursting of the economic bubble, Japan's macroeconomic performance has been comparatively poor. Indeed, from the early 1990s to the present date, Japan has been experiencing a structural adjustment where the lackluster performance of the economy has become arguably the most important issue the government faces. In response to these periods of economic lethargy, the Japanese government employed fiscal stimulus packages, and, if our conception of how electoral concerns influence the direction and content of economic policy, then they should have been employed by the ruling party not only to address a real economic problem but also to halt the deleterious effects that ecological change was having on its support levels. This task begins with an explanation of how Japan's fiscal stimulus policies are put together, announced as policies, and then funded.[35]

Fiscal stimulus policies have been made known to the Japanese public through government announcements that a package of spending is being put together that will help stimulate demand and ultimately restore lagging economic activity to acceptable levels. Typically, such fiscal stimulus policies are funded outside of the general budgeting process in what is known as supplementary budgets (*hosei yosan*), which have been a regular feature of the Japanese budgeting system throughout the postwar period. The phrase itself refers to budgets that are typically adopted once per annum, late in the calendar year, by a parliamentary act outside of the nation's annual budget cycle.[36] Supplementary budgets are nonetheless related to the regular budget in that they have been enacted to address some aspect of the original budget. Often, they were prepared and adopted to make up for unanticipated shortfalls in tax revenue and, thus, ensure sufficient funding for items specified in the original budget. Supplementary budgets have also been enacted to provide monies for disaster relief efforts in the wake of Japan's sometimes destructive typhoon season, to fund gaps that have arisen in Japan's national debt, and to underwrite certain initiatives deemed important by the Diet.

Despite the manifest regularity of supplementary budgets, departures have occurred in both substantive and procedural ways. By substantive we mean that, from time to time in the past but with increasing frequency in the

1990s, supplementary budgets have been enacted to fund government economic stimulus efforts in addition to those other functions we listed above. Such instances initially involved no special announcement, which means that when a supplementary budget was enacted, reports in the media simply stated that, in addition to disaster relief or some other normally funded item, the purpose of the supplementary budget involved government attempts to stimulate domestic economic activity.[37] More recently, however, the procedures involved in funding economic stimulus policies also changed. After 1987, when supplementary budgets most often included spending for economic stimulus as well as other policies, the budgets themselves were assembled and adopted only after the government had already announced its intention to put together an economic stimulus package. In other words, the procedures changed in that the Japanese government reported its intention to promote domestic economic activity with an economic stimulus package of a certain yen value but then left the actual amount to be spent to a later time when a supplementary budget was adopted by the National Diet.

Since May of 1987, when Prime Minister Nakasone announced that he would propose a special spending package to increase domestic demand, the Japanese government has announced more than a dozen of these economic stimulus packages that, in order to be implemented, had to be included in subsequent supplementary budgets.[38] The dates and amounts of the first twelve of these packages are presented in Table 7.4 with the yen values of each presented in two columns. As the column designations indicate, the data in

---

Table 7.4 Japan's Fiscal Stimulus Packages, 1987–1998

DATE ANNOUNCED	ANNOUNCED AMOUNT (trillion yen)	ACTUAL STIMULUS EXPENDITURE (trillion yen)
May 1987	—	¥2.0
August 1992	¥10.7	¥8.6
April 1993	¥13.2	¥10.6
September 1993	¥6.3	¥5.1
February 1994	¥15.2	¥7.2
February 1995	¥1.6	¥1.6
April–May 1995	¥2.7	¥2.7
September 1995	¥14.0	¥7.9–9.0
December 1996	¥2.7	¥2.7
December 1997	¥15.9	¥2.9
April 1998	¥16.6	NA
November 1998	¥24.0	NA

Source: *Asahi Nenkan* (various issues) and *Asahi Shimbun* (November 17, 1998).

the middle column refer to the announced value of the fiscal stimulus packages while the column on the right represents our attempt to determine how much of the announced figures was actually spent. Similar attempts were made by the popular business press and by financial market analysts at the time, but the methodology of such analyses has remained unclear. Since the general goal seemed to be to remove previously announced spending and nonexpenditure items from the headline figures, in Table 7.4, we have simply excluded allocations from the FILP and any previously budgeted items from the estimate of hard spending.[39]

This is important because we notice immediately from the data in the table that the amounts actually spent were almost always lower than the amounts that were originally announced. We must consider the possibility that actual budgets were lower because upper-level bureaucrats, especially those in the Ministry of Finance, were decidedly opposed to these economic stimulus packages. Since the 1970s, MOF bureaucrats were primarily concerned with the solvency of the government's fiscal position.[40] For example, in April of 1993, when the Miyazawa government announced its second economic stimulus package, MOF Vice Minister, Ozaki Mamoru stated publicly that "[t]he Ministry of Finance 'will resist to the end' going into heavy debt again."[41] Moreover, many in the bureaucracy believed that such policies would be ineffective and, possibly, counterproductive.[42]

What we need to demonstrate here is that the announcement of the fiscal stimulus packages listed above was part of the LDP's electoral strategy, bureaucratic opposition notwithstanding. This requires that we perform a statistical analysis that weights all potentially significant factors, and, like the analysis we provided for LDP policies designed to bring back owners of small- and medium-size enterprises, the first step of which involves defining the dependent variable. For our purposes here, the variable to be explained is the timing of the government's announcement of the fiscal stimulus packages we defined above. We define this variable as a monthly series that begins in January 1975, and ends in December 1998. During this time period, a particular month is coded 1, if the Japanese government announced an economic stimulus package either as part of a supplementary budget, as it did several times as the end of the 1970s, or separately without any reference to a supplementary budget, as has been the case throughout much of the 1990s. All other months in the series are coded 0.

To demonstrate that these fiscal stimulus packages were motivated not simply by the desire to improve macroeconomic conditions but also by the hope of attracting additional electoral support, we note that the timing of the packages should correspond to the constitutional and political processes that define democratic politics in Japan's parliamentary system. What this means is that, first, the announcement of these fiscal stimulus packages should correspond to Japan's election cycle because, as stated above, no other time is as important for a governing party. This is an uncontroversial statement, but the unanswered question is just how these stimulus packages should be related to the holding of an election, and, to answer this, we must recall the electoral objectives of a party facing a *support-expansion imperative*.

Japanese governments announced economic stimulus policies to show the nation's voters, especially those who were politically uncommitted, that they were capable of taking appropriate action on the problem of improving macroeconomic conditions. On the one hand, by announcing a stimulus package in the same month that an election was held, the governing party would make itself vulnerable to charges that its motives were purely electoral and that it was not sincere in its attempt to address the country's economic problems. On the other hand, announcing an economic stimulus policy too soon before an election could keep the governing party from enjoying the electoral benefits such announcements were also designed to provide. For these reasons, we assumed that a package would be announced two months before an election, and, thus, include it in our statistical model as a dummy variable with a two-month lag.[43]

Politics in parliamentary systems also involves processes that behoove governing parties to be interested in the levels of support they possess even when no election is pending. This is because support levels are directly related to the ability of governing parties to put together cabinets that can govern effectively and implement their respective policy agendas. In addition to this, governing party support levels are directly related to the ability of the cabinets they head to avoid motions of no-confidence which, if successful, can force them either prematurely to go to the polls or to go into opposition. Such electoral conditions touch directly on the ability of governing parties to reform cabinets, particularly when an extant administration is unable to continue running the government for one or more reasons. In postwar Japan, this occurred in two ways. The first is the cabinet reshuffle, which involves the replacement of some or all ministers with others from the same party, and the second involves a cabinet change that results in the formation of an entirely different government, that is, one headed by a different prime minister.

Cabinet reshuffles have occurred in postwar Japan both frequently and routinely. For the period covered by our data series, cabinet reshuffles occurred slightly more than once per annum.[44] On the one hand, in light of this, we have little reason to expect them to be related to the announcement of the economic stimulus packages that were part of government attempts to increase support. On the other hand, for those cabinet changes that involved the formation of a new government, our expectations are different. New governments have tended to be formed when support for an existing cabinet had dropped to very low levels. Indeed, using the party and cabinet support polls conducted monthly by the Jiji News Organization,[45] we note that one and two months prior to a cabinet reshuffle, cabinet supporters were outnumbered by nonsupporters by an average of 7.05 percent and 5.59 percent respectively. This suggests to us that new governments were formed in response to low approval ratings and, as a result, would seek to begin their duties with as much support as they could acquire. For those times when the macroeconomy was a salient issue, this would mean that newly formed governments would want to demonstrate that they could take decisive action on this problem. Consequently, we would expect the announcement of an economic stimulus package to follow the formation of a new government.

While reasonable enough, this expectation does not tell us just how long after a new government is formed would we expect an economic stimulus package to be announced. Since the announcement of such a package is intended to increase governing party support in the new cabinet, it is most likely that a new government would want to assemble and announce the policy as soon as it was formed. The question, however, is how realistic this timing would be. Since new governments were formed when support for the cabinets they replaced was low, the formation of the new government itself was the product of much bargaining among either LDP faction leaders (LDP only governments) or the leaders of those political parties that were potential coalition partners (more recent governments). Negotiations would involve not simply the issue of who would be the new prime minister but also the issue of portfolio distribution. For these reasons, we concluded that the announcement of an economic stimulus package would be unlikely to occur in the month that a new prime minister took control of the government and, thus, we made the new government variable part of our amended model by including it at a one-month lag.

Finally, to be sure these two electoral politics variables independently raise the probability that an economic stimulus package will be announced, we add one other electoral politics variable to our statistical model. As suggested above, a governing party has an incentive to use the policy process to raise cabinet support levels when its support drops to levels that are potentially threatening. This is perhaps always true, but it is even more true when the other methods of raising support levels that we discussed above are for whatever reason unavailable. To capture such situations, we included a measure of support that incumbent governments possessed in any given month in our series. Using the *Jijitsushinsha* cabinet support data mentioned above, we subtracted the percentage of cabinet nonsupporters from the percentage of supporters. This produced an index of cabinet support with a mean value of

–0.811 percent over the months contained in our series and minimum and maximum values of –79.4 percent and 55.7 percent respectively. Decimals with negative values indicate a plurality of nonsupporters while those with positive values indicate the opposite.

For the purposes of entering this variable in our model, we first note that the results of the *Jijitsushinsha* polls are reported one month after they are taken. Moreover, it is highly unlikely that a governing party would use the policy process in response to a low support rating in a single month. Indeed, our expectation is that governing parties would use the tools of economic policy only after consistent months of low approval ratings. For these reasons, we enter the cabinet support control variable at four-, five-, and six-month lags.

To determine if the political factors we discussed above were responsible for the announcement of Japan's fiscal stimulus packages, we need to add more control variables to our analysis, one rather standard and another somewhat unusual. Taking the latter first, what we mean by an unusual control variable is that it is unique to the Japanese context and, thus, not typically used in such statistical analyses. We are referring here to foreign pressure or *gaiatsu*, especially that from the United States. Pressure has defined U.S.-Japanese relations from the beginning, but, in the 1980s, the U.S. government began pressuring Japanese governments to use fiscal policy to stimulate domestic demand, initially to draw more U.S. goods into the Japanese market but, more recently, to revive its own lagging economy. To include this control variable in our analysis in an appropriate manner, we must be able to say when Japanese leaders would be under the most pressure from the United States to use the policy process to stimulate domestic demand. Our answer is those months when a bilateral meeting between the U.S. president and the Japanese prime minister took place. In the period covered by our data, there were twelve instances of such meetings, and, consequently, those months when a meeting occurred were given a value of 1, while all other months received a value of 0.

The standard control variable we referred to above is added to our analysis to be sure that the specification of our statistical model is complete. The control variable we add is designed to capture to independent impact of macroeconomic conditions on the probability that a stimulus package would be announced. Including this control variable in our statistical analysis will tell us whether or not the political factors we have discussed above are operative over and above what we would expect any incumbent government to do given certain macroeconomic conditions. Our measure of macroeconomic conditions is derived from Japan's index of production measured as year-on-year changes, that is, how a current month's index compares to the same month's index in the previous year.[46] We note that production index figures are collected monthly but announced at a two-month lag. Given this delay, combined with our desire to capture any seasonal (quarterly) adjustments that may occur and any lead time a government would need to respond to worsened economic conditions, we enter this control variable in our statistical model at two-, three-, and four-month lags.

Since the dependent variable in the model is dichotomous, a maximum likelihood estimation procedure (logit) is necessary, and the results of our first estimation are presented in Table 7.5.[47] From the results of our analysis, we can say that the model has been appropriately specified as is indicated by the significance of the estimates provided at the bottom of the table. More important, however, is the fact that the results we present here confirm our understanding of electoral influence and economic policy as it pertains to a governing party facing a *support expansion imperative* due to ecological change. The evidence for this is found in the relatively large and statistically significant coefficient on the election variable. The coefficients on the *"Gaiatsu"* and

Table 7.5 Politics, Pressure, and the Use of Fiscal Stimulus Policies

VARIABLES	WITH A TEMPORAL DUMMY			WITHOUT A TEMPORAL DUMMY		
	ESTIMATE	SE	Z	ESTIMATE	SE	Z
Constant	-3.63^a	0.47	-7.70	-3.59^a	0.45	-7.91
Elections (t-2)	1.85^b	0.86	2.14	1.92^b	0.84	2.29
U.S. pressure	2.51^a	0.84	2.98	2.45^a	0.82	2.96
New Gov't. (t-1)	1.71^b	0.79	2.17	1.66^b	0.78	2.13
Cabinet Support						
(t-4)	-0.03	0.03	-1.09	-0.03	0.03	-1.05
(t-5)	0.04	0.03	1.14	0.04	0.03	1.37
(t-6)	-0.02	0.01	-1.31	-0.02	0.16	1.29
Economy						
(t-2)	0.23	0.15	1.54	0.24	0.15	1.16
(t-3)	-0.29	0.17	-1.74	-0.29	0.17	-1.70
(t-5)	0.01	1.43	0.08	-0.001	0.14	-0.01
Temporal Dummy	0.52	1.24	0.43			

Total Cases: 274   Total Cases: 274
Log Likelihood: -47.728 Log Likelihood: -47.811
Chi Square: 20.86   Chi Square: 20.69
DF = 264; Sig. = 0.00012   DF = 264; Sig. = 0.0057

$^a p < .01$; $^b p < .05$.

"New Government (t-1)" variables are also large and statistically significant which tells us that, when we consider the Japanese government's use of economic stimulus policies, domestic politics and foreign pressure have mattered. Concerning national elections, we notice from the coefficients in Table 7.5 that, two months before a national election is held, the odds that an economic stimulus package will be announced increases by nearly seven times. More than this, our results indicated that domestic politics raised the odds of a package being announced in one other way. Specifically, one month after the formation of a new government, the odds that an economic stimulus package would be announced increased over five times. The results in the table also show that pressure form the United States was quite important. Indeed, the holding of a meeting between a U.S. president and a Japanese prime minister raised the odds that a package would be announced 11.6 times.

THE POLITICAL IMPACT OF ECONOMIC POLICY

In the analyses provided above, we have shown how the political imperatives faced by politicians in Japan's governing parties impelled them to use available tools of economic policy in certain expected ways. While this has helped us understand how Japan's politicians have set the direction and content of economic policy throughout the postwar period, it has not told us why political trends took the turn they did in the 1990s. In other words, if the LDP used economic policy to preserve its electoral support at levels sufficient to maintain its ruling status, then why did its efforts ultimately fail?

The short answer to this question is that LDP efforts simply did not succeed in halting the loss of support that contributed to its secular decline throughout the postwar period. Part of the problem rested with how the LDP's attempts to maintain the loyalty of its core supporters, while at the same time attracting new sources of potential support, became increasingly contradictory over time. What this means is that the efforts the party made simultaneously to maintain and expand support had the unintended consequence of forcing the ruling party to use policies that, in an electoral sense, worked at cross purposes. Specifically, the party essentially employed policies that were designed to attract new supporters but, at the same time, hurt the interests of its core supporters. More than anything else, this involved two sets of policies, one that affected Japan's farmers and another that affected owners of small- and medium-size firms.

As shown in the previous chapter, Japan's farmers have always received a significant amount of government protection and largesse. This assistance helped keep this essential support group generally satisfied, but, as the postwar period progressed, the LDP was forced to confront growing pressure to reduce the support it extended to the nation's farmers. One source of pressure came from outside of Japan in the form of international pressure while the other sources were entirely domestic. International pressure came mostly from countries that were large producers of agricultural products like the United States which argued that, because Japan's manufactured exports benefited from relatively free international markets, it should take specific steps to open up its agricultural markets. While somewhat muted compared to international pressure, domestic pressure to reduce government support to the nation's farmers came from many sectors, including segments of the Japanese electorate on which the Liberal Democratic Party had become increasingly dependent as the size of its legislative majority shrank. Certain government agencies like MITI and the Ministry of Finance had advocated "rationalizing" Japanese agriculture, but more important than this for political reasons was the fact that large businesses and their respective organizational groupings—such as Keidanren and the Federation of Employers Organizations—and a cross section of diverse individuals and businesses that stood to benefit from lower agricultural prices also recommended that Japanese agriculture become more open to international trade and less dependent on government support.

While delayed and incremental when they did occur, changes in agricultural policy did come, and these took the form of trade liberalization (initially, citrus products and beef), reduced subsidies, and government efforts to rationalize agriculture by encouraging larger farm holdings and the diversion of lands under cultivation of rice to other crops. These changes, however, did not come without substantial amounts of side payments to the country's farmers in the form of loans for rationalization programs, subsidies to agricultural producers threatened by trade liberalization, and increased spending on local construction projects to employ the excess labor created by the changes that the government pursued. Mollification efforts were generally successful as farmers remained loyal, albeit grudgingly, to the LDP.

Unfortunately, the ruling party was ultimately forced to consider policies that represented a threshold over which Japan's farmers were not going to allow the LDP to cross. The issue was the liberalization of the rice market, and, when the LDP considered succumbing to international pressure to open this market, farm cooperatives throughout Japan made it known that they would place their political support elsewhere, specifically with those who pledged to continue protecting this market.[48] While the LDP did not end rice quotas, its consideration of this issue hurt it in the upper-house election of 1989 and the lower-house election of 1993, and it is for this reason that, when the LDP returned to power in 1994, it raised subsidies to rice farmers.[49]

The second policy area concerned tax policy and, as stated above, predominantly affected owners of small- and medium-size businesses. The genesis of the problem rests with Japan's tax system itself and the fact that it levied the heaviest tax burden on salaried employees.[50] In the early postwar years, the tax burden was relatively light, in spite of its biases, because fiscal policy was conservative and high levels of economic growth provided a generous amount of revenue for government use. This situation began changing in the 1970s as government outlays on such things as public works, environmental programs, welfare system expansion, and assistance to politically important sectors began to expand.

The increased fiscal commitments that such programs required produced large budget deficits, and the government initially dealt with the growing debt its policies produced by issuing bonds. Unfortunately, continued government deficits forced the ruling LDP to consider the difficult issue of how it raised its revenues, and the proposed solution ultimately involved the imposition of an indirect tax. On the one hand, changing the way that taxes are levied in such a way would undoubtedly make the system fairer for salaried workers. On the other hand, for small business owners and farmers who did much better financially under the current system, the proposal was something to be opposed. With extensive consultations and a number of fits and starts, legislation reforming Japan's tax system was eventually passed and put into effect.[51] The reform legislation took nearly a decade to enact and left many segments of the Japanese electorate unsatisfied, especially small business owners who once again began to turn away from their benefactor party.[52]

Another part of the problem associated with LDP attempts both to hold together its support coalition while at the same time increasing its size concerns the problem of costs. The point is that, as the LDP had to spend more to sustain itself as the nation's ruling party, the role that money played in the political process naturally increased. This was true both in terms of the government benefits that the ruling party extended to politically important sectors as well as the money that was needed by LDP candidates in their district campaigns, especially as margins of victory for LDP candidates in national elections began to erode.[53] The former aspect of the cost problem has been extremely important for how recent LDP governments have responded to the current structural adjustment while the latter part of the cost problem is directly related to the growth of corruption as an issue in recent elections. While the former aspect of the cost problem was discussed above, the latter has not been examined and is something we turn to in the next chapter in the context of how issues and other short-term factors contributed to the Liberal Democratic Party losing its status as Japan's predominant party.

Chapter 8

POSTWAR JAPANESE POLITICS

From LDP Predominance to Coalition Politics

One party was in permanent control, and factions within that party struggled for control of turf and appropriations. Elections had more to do with patronage and loyalty than with "issues" in the normal sense.

—James Fallows (1994)

There is little the political opposition can do to win political power. The question is whether the LDP will do something to lose it . . . For the foreseeable future, the end of LPD rule, if it is to occur at all, is most likely to result from a split within the LDP itself.

—Gerald Curtis (1988)

In Japan, from the founding of the LDP in 1955 until its dominant Takeshita faction split in late 1992, the LDP was created to prevent the Japanese Communists and Socialists from ever coming to power. This came to be known as the 1955 system.

—Chalmers Johnson (1995)

Scholarly assessments of postwar Japanese politics are based on descriptions of its best and worst features that are generally accurate, but they have nonetheless understated certain dynamic features that politics in postwar Japan has possessed. Specifically, assessments of Japan's postwar political trajectory have left us with an incomplete picture of what has driven election outcomes throughout the postwar period because they have largely ignored the role played by issues and other short-term forces in the LDP's struggle to maintian its electoral predominance.[1] There have been many consequences to this underemphasis, but the most important has been how discussions of Japanese politics missed the underlying trends that led to the Liberal Democratic Party being pushed out of power for the first time in thirty-eight years in the lower-house election of 1993. The principal reason for this rests with how studies of postwar Japanese politics have understood the election patterns that defined Japan's postwar party system, that is, the fact that Japan has been a predominant party system for most of the postwar period.

Since it was formed in the Fall of 1955, the Liberal Democratic Party won the next thirteen lower-house elections and headed every government in Japan for the next thirty-eight years. To be sure, the LDP's many years of strong electoral performances became the premier issue to be explained, but, in the face of the Liberal Democratic Party's manifest electoral prowess, scholars either explicitly or implicitly treated the LDP's electoral predominance as a nearly permanent feature of Japan's postwar political system. While the lower house election of 1993 revealed that the LDP's predominance was hardly immutable, it also revealed that this underlying assumption was problematic because of how it kept many Japan scholars from seeing the important changes that were occurring in postwar Japanese politics, changes that anticipated the end of LDP predominance long before it actually occurred.

To explain why the LDP's performance was poor enough to keep it from forming a government in the wake of the 1993 lower-house election, we must explain that party's entire postwar trajectory, that is, its rise, predominance, decline, resurgence, and, to a certain extent, dissolution.[2] Developing such an explanation requires that we interpret the LDP's electoral predominance as something that occurred over a specific period of time for a particular set of reasons, which are characteristic of elections in all parliamentary systems. This does not mean that electoral politics in postwar Japan can be approached in exactly the same way that we would approach the same subject in the United States or any other electoral democracy for that matter. Indeed, there are contextual differences that must be taken into consideration when dealing with postwar Japanese elections, and, for reasons like the unavailability of survey data for every lower-house election, explaining election outcomes in postwar Japan presents a distinct analytic challenge. Rather, what we are saying is that, despite the analytic challenges that Japan's postwar elections present, the pattern of predominant party outcomes they have manifested throughout the postwar period offers us an unparalleled opportunity to study the impacts that such long- and short-term forces as partisanship and issues have on election outcomes.

The LDP's relegation to the opposition in the summer of 1993, after thirty-eight years of uninterrupted rule, signaled that the tectonic plates of Japan's political system had shifted. This is because the LDP's return to power a short time later did not indicate that in any way that the old days when the party's electoral predominance was virtually unchallenged had returned.[3] In the next two general elections of October 1996 and June 2000, the LDP's share of the national vote was about what it was in the 1993 contest, suggesting strongly that it had not really recovered in an electoral sense.[4] The old ruling party was nonetheless able to form a coalition government in both instances but only because, first, the opposition was so fragmented, and second, because Japan's new electoral rules in those contests provided it with a very large seat bonus in the new mixed system's single member districts.[5]

That the LDP lost its status as the nation's predominant party in 1993 and has not yet been able to recover and rule again as a predominant party is curious. This is because, after a long period of secular decline from the time it was formed in the fall of 1955, the LDP entered a period of resurgence in the 1980s and was ostensibly as electorally strong as it had ever been. There were numerous articles and books, written in Japanese and English, which talked about the 1980s in Japan as a period of conservative resurgence or *hoshu kaiki*. In spite of this, the LDP lost its upper-house majority in the election of 1989, but the party seemed to recover well in the lower-house election of the following February.[6] This led analysts to observe that the 1990s would be just like the 1980s, a time of a reborn Liberal Democratic Party. Indeed, the LDP's return to favorable electoral circumstances in the 1980s, particularly its humiliation of the Socialist opposition in the double election of 1986, was touted by many as the denouement of a conservative realignment in the Japanese electorate.[7]

The problem here is that if the Liberal Democratic Party had recovered completely and returned to favorable electoral circumstances, it should not have performed so poorly in the 1993 and subsequent election contests. What must be explained is why the LDP experienced a resurgence in its support levels and appeared unbeatable in national elections in the 1980s and then why, in the 1990s, the LDP performed so poorly that it was either out of power or required the cooperation of other parties to govern. To accomplish this, we must separate the portion of the LDP vote that was due to long-term partisan support from that which was due to short-term, election-specific factors. By determining the share that each of these two factors contributed to LDP support in national elections, we can better trace the amount of underlying support the party had in the various electoral periods of the postwar years. Our task in this chapter then is to provide such an explanation, and it begins with a review of how Japan scholars have treated the LDP's changing electoral fortunes throughout the postwar period.

ELECTORAL PERIODS AND THE LDP'S CHANGING ELECTORAL FORTUNES

Although postwar Japanese politics has been stable throughout the postwar period, it was anything but static, and this is captured in the fact that the electoral position of the LDP looked very different at different time points in the postwar period. In fact, from the beginning of the Occupation to the very present, one can identify five distinct electoral periods that are defined by the different electoral circumstances the Liberal Democratic Party and its antecedent organizations faced in each. The first of these periods is known as the formative or presystem period and covers the years from the beginning of the American Occupation of Japan in 1945 to the formation of the postwar party system in Japan in 1955.[8] To the extent that this period is covered at all in writing on postwar Japanese politics, it is dealt with in a generally perfunctory fashion.[9] This is because Japan watchers have tended to cover the politics of this first electoral period much more as a time that anticipated the formation of the postwar party system than as a string of years that involved electoral patterns worthy of scholarly attention in their own right.[10]

The second electoral period in postwar Japan is known as the period of predominance and refers to the short span of years when lower-house elections resulted in the LDP being Japan's dominant political force. This period includes the election of February 1955, even though the Liberal Democratic Party was not formed until the following fall, and it ends with the lower house contest of 1963. This is because, in each of the elections that fall within this period of time, the LDP received over 50 percent of the national vote and an even higher share of lower-house seats. In the elections of 1958, 1960, and 1963, the Liberal Democratic Party captured 57 percent, 57 percent, and 54 percent of the lower-house vote respectively; in 1955, the combined vote of the Liberal and Democratic Parties was over 60 percent.

The period of predominance was followed by a third electoral period, one defined by the secular decline of the LDP. This LDP decline is captured by two low benchmarks, the first occurring in the lower house election of 1967, when the LDP's vote share dropped below the 50 percent level, and the second occurring in 1976, when its share of lower-house seats dropped below 50 percent, forcing the party to seek a partnership with the New Liberal Club and several unaffiliated conservatives. At the end of this third electoral period, the LDP was still the nation's ruling party, but the fact that it was a predominant party in decline is clear, something manifested by its performance in this period's elections. In the contest of 1967, the LDP captured 48.8 percent of the votes cast, an amount that still netted it over 55 percent of the seats in the House of Representatives. Four elections later in the lower-house contest of 1976, however, the party's vote share had dropped seven percentage points to 41.8 percent, a drop significant enough to prevent it from singularly controlling a majority of seats in the Lower House.

The next electoral period covers the five elections that occurred between 1979 and 1990 inclusive and is referred to as the period of conservative resurgence or, as mentioned above, *hoshu kaiki*. It is called the period of conservative resurgence because it represents a time when the LDP's electoral performance was better overall. It is not that the Liberal Democratic Party's average of lower-house vote shares was markedly higher compared to the period of decline but rather that the party's performance in the five contests of this eleven-year period followed an oscillating but nonetheless upward trend. Specifically, in the two double elections of 1980 and 1986, the LDP performed quite well, but the vote shares it captured in the 1979 and 1983 contests were mediocre at best.[11] This suggests strongly that the party's return to better electoral circumstances was tentative and perhaps something other than a true conservative resurgence, the fact that many scholars referred to this period in such a way notwithstanding.

Finally, the most recent electoral period, which begins after the LDP's marginal victory in the 1990 lower-house election and continues to the present day, is referred to as the period of dissolution. This most recent period is given this label because, beginning in 1992, the Liberal Democratic Party experienced its most serious bout of fragmentation when numerous LDP politicians bolted the party and formed several new conservative parties.[12] Most of the political parties that were created at that time or over the next several years have either disbanded or reemerged as new organizations in a Japanese party system that remains in a state of flux.[13] This recent electoral period is also given this label because, in the three lower-house elections that have occurred thus far, the LDP's vote shares are on average well below those it obtained at any other time in the past. As noted above, in the election of 1993, the LDP obtained 36.6 percent of the vote while, in the following contest of 1996, its performance was slightly worse. In the nation's single member districts, the party obtained only 32.8 percent while, in the PR districts, its vote share was 38.5 percent. In the most recent lower-house election of June 2000, the LDP's performance improved in the single member districts with the party obtaining 41 percent of the vote there, but its electoral fortunes soured in the PR part of the system as it obtained 29 percent of the votes cast there.

What is interesting is that attempts to explain the path followed by the Liberal Democratic Party's electoral fortunes throughout the postwar period are nearly equal to the number of electoral periods that must be subsumed. While this has left us with a collection of scholarly assessments that are as time-specific as the electoral periods we have identified above, this does not mean that there is nothing useful in the body of scholarship that has addressed the course followed by postwar Japanese politics. Rather, it means that what we know about the LDP's performance in postwar elections is incomplete, particularly when evaluated against the broad expanse that defines Japan's postwar electoral history. In fact, most attempts to explain the LDP's electoral fortunes have begun with neither the formative period nor the period of predominance but rather with the period of decline. This is because, as Masaru Kohno (1997) points out, most scholarly work on the subject has simply taken LDP predominance as a given.[14]

Consequently, initial scholarly attempts to deal with this topic are focused on why the LDP, shortly after it established itself as Japan's predominant party, began to decline electorally. Two competing explanations exist, the first of which is the ecological change explanation which, as was discussed above, emphasizes the role played by Japan's changing demographic profile. The idea is that the socioeconomic groups which formed the LDP's core support constituencies were a fairly substantial portion of Japan's population in the early postwar years, leading to the party's electoral predominance at that time. Throughout the postwar period, however, the country experienced a long wave of urbanization that caused the expansion of Japan's large cities and metropolitan areas. This resulted in the diminution of some of the LDP's core supporters, rural dwellers and farmers in particular, leading to their occupying a much smaller proportion of Japan's population. With the relative size of these two LDP support groups in decline, we would expect Japan's ruling party to experience a parallel decline in its level of electoral support, and, for a certain number of years, this is exactly what happened.

Unfortunately, while accurate in many ways, the ecological change explanation is incomplete. As mentioned in our above discussion of the party's changing electoral fortunes, the 1980s was a time that witnessed the LDP beginning an oscillating but nonetheless noticeable resurgence in the aggregate vote shares it captured in lower-house elections. The problem here is that, after 1980, the demographic changes that affected the ecology of the Japanese electorate slowed but in no way stopped. How is it then that the LDP's electoral fortunes improved while the size of some of its core support groups continued to shrink? The answer to this question rests with the idea that, while election outcomes are a product of long-term, secular trends, such as the partisan shifts attendant to ecological change, they are also molded by other factors that must be considered if one is to have a complete picture of the LDP's changing electoral fortunes.

The second explanation for the electoral decline of the LDP is an individual-level explanation that focuses on the relationship between election outcomes and changes in the value orientations of Japanese voters.[15] Scholars in this camp argue that Japanese voters, like their European counterparts, have become increasingly characterized by modern values. Modern values stress such norms as individualism, tolerance, and equality, unlike their traditional counterparts, which stress such norms as piety, conformity, and austerity. The changes that occurred in the value orientations of the Japanese throughout the postwar period have been deemed politically relevant because modern values have been linked with issue positions and voting preferences that favor parties of the Left. Moreover, the segments of the population most characterized by modern values in Japan—young, educated, urban dwellers— have grown throughout the postwar period relative to other groups which proponents of this view interpreted to mean that the center and left in Japan would continue to gain in electoral strength at the expense of the LDP.

The value change view appeared to be a powerful explanation, especially in light of the electoral changes that occurred in the 1960s and 1970s when the Opposition's performance in local and national elections improved substantially. Unfortunately, like its ecological change counterpart, it is quite incomplete as presented in the literature on voting behavior and election outcomes in postwar Japan. This incompleteness becomes evident when the value-change model is evaluated in a broader temporal perspective. The problem is simply that, if it was a change in values that created a more auspicious political environment for the parties of the left and center in Japan, then the Liberal Democratic Party should not have experienced the electoral resurgence it did in the 1980s.

Throughout the 1980s, changes in the distribution of Japanese value orientations followed the same path they did in the 1960s and 1970s, which means that, if values were responsible for election outcomes as Flanagan and others have asserted, the reversal that we witnessed in the LDP's electoral fortunes should never have occurred. What we have here is an inconsistency that becomes even more problematic when one considers that the segments of the Japanese public possessing modern values have also been identified as the groups that have been most responsible for the conservative party's resurgence in the 1980s.[16] It is most likely that proponents of this view have overstated the relationship that exists between the value orientations of voters and their political behavior. Specifically, the value orientations of individual voters are electorally significant only in the way they relate to salient election issues. If an election is not defined by issues that can be informed by a voter's value orientations, be they modern or traditional, such values will not be a significant force in that voter's electoral choice.

Attempts to explain the path of postwar Japanese politics did not stop at the decline of the LDP. In fact, when the party returned to more favorable electoral circumstances in the 1980s, analysts of Japanese politics offered a different story for the party's electoral fortunes. The most notable of these is what we refer to at the conservative resurgence explanation. As suggested above, this is a view of Japanese politics that focuses on the post-1980s period of Japan's electoral history and holds that, for a variety of reasons, a growing number of Japanese electors became more conservative in their political orientations and, thus, more electorally sympathetic to the Liberal Democratic Party.[17] These new conservative voters were not the active political participants that the party's small business and farming supporters have been. They were, instead, passive supporters of the LDP and, thus, have been referred to as latent conservatives. Their political behavior, specifically their support for the LDP, was tied to their turning out in general elections, which means that turnout became the critical variable for determining the probability of LDP success in an election.

It is true, as has been shown in a number of NHK (1992) survey studies, that a growing segment of unaffiliated voters selected the LDP as their party of choice when asked which party they support a second time, that is, in a manner that forced respondents to choose a party. Nonetheless, the problem with this idea is that it essentially assumes the outcomes it is supposed to explain. In other words, rather than attempting to determine what portion of the rise in the LDP's electoral support was due to long-term, partisan shifts, it simply begs the question that the period of conservative resurgence was brought on by favorable partisan shifts in the Japanese electorate. We must consider the possibility that such passive LDP voters are not latent conservatives at all because, as politically unaffiliated electors, they are much like the "peripheral" voters described in "surge and decline theory." This means that the presence of such voters at the polls will "swing the partisan division of the vote toward the party that happens to be advantaged by circumstances of the moment."[18] If this is the case, those voting for the LDP in 1986 did so because the short-term forces that were salient in that election favored the Liberal Democratic Party and not in obeisance to some recently acquired latent conservatism.[19]

We notice a similar trend when we consider what has been written on the most recent electoral period. Because election results in the last several years violated the views that were propounded to explain the patterns that characterized the period of conservative resurgence, there was a rush to develop a new understanding of Japanese politics and the manner in which the electoral process worked there. Two distinct views have made their way into the scholarly discourse in an effort to account for the ostensibly anomalous results of the posteconomic bubble period. The first emphasizes change and argues that issues such as corruption became so prevalent that the Japanese public finally decided to relegate the LDP to the opposition. This view also contends that the negative impact of the corruption issue was exacerbated by the fact that it was salient at a time when Japan's economy was performing poorly. Consequently, it is in combination that these two factors were sufficient to produce electoral results that spelled the end to Japan's predominant party system. The second explanation emphasizes the status quo and contends that the LDP's losses had more to do with the fact that so many former party members bolted the organization and sought support from their respective districts' voters either as unaffiliated candidates or as members of an alternative political party.[20]

By and large, both arguments are factually accurate. Candidates who bolted the LDP and stood for office in their old districts performed quite well in the 1993 election. Also, corruption and the state of the Japanese economy were important issues in the minds of most Japanese and did influence their electoral choices.[21] Being factually accurate, however, does not mean complete as an explanation, and this is something that characterizes both arguments, albeit for different reasons. The status quo argument is incomplete because it assumes that district-level candidate effects are all that matter in Japanese elections.[22] Moreover, this argument assumes that those candidates who bolted the LDP would have won whether they were affiliated with the LDP or some other party or whether they simply would have presented themselves as unaffiliated candidates. The problem is that candidates performed well in the past with the LDP, among other reasons, because of the constituency benefits they were able to deliver. As members of other parties, these candidates' ability to perform with the same level of effectiveness was hardly a sure thing.

The issues and economic performance argument is problematic because it is also incomplete. One reason for this is that it emphasizes only certain issues, such as corruption and Japan's recent economic problems, and not other issues that, as we show below, have long influenced election outcomes in postwar Japan. Another reason this argument is incomplete refers to the inconsistent treatment issues and other short-term forces have received in assessments of Japan's postwar political trajectory. The problem is that issues have been weighted heavily in recent elections but not in past contests when they were also salient. For example, corruption has been a leitmotif in postwar Japanese politics, but it has not been treated as being as electorally significant in past elections as it has in recent contests.

As stated above, our solution to these problems involves providing an explanation that can account for the LDP's changing electoral fortunes throughout the entire postwar period. This means that an explanation that accounts for the party's electoral predominance in the early part of the postwar period should be part of an explanation that can account for the party's decline, resurgence, and dissolution. To be sure, Japan scholars such as Richardson (1997) have mapped the behavioral tendencies of Japanese voters in a consistent way across the electoral periods defined above. His and similar efforts have been insightful and are generally consistent with the explanation we provide. On the other hand, such efforts are different from the approach we employ because they have focused on mapping the Japanese electorate at the individual level. The explanation we provide below proceeds from the notion that election outcomes are an aggregate phenomenon that requires a different theoretical perspective than has been used hitherto in studies of election outcomes in postwar Japan.

SHORT- AND LONG-TERM COMPONENTS OF ELECTION OUTCOMES

To understand why the Liberal Democratic Party became Japan's predominant party only to suffer a long period of secular decline that resulted in the eventual unraveling of the postwar party system, we must begin with the factors that influence election outcomes in the aggregate. While somewhat oversimplified, election outcomes are a function of two essential components, one systematic and long-term and the other election-specific and short-term. The long-term and systematic component refers to the distribution of partisan preferences that define a nation's electorate while the short-term, election-specific component refers to salient issues and party/candidate effects that distinguish one election contest from another.

Concerning the former, the electorate of any democratic country can be described in terms of the partisan attachments of its voters. While hardly immutable over long time horizons and variant in strength across individual electors, partisanship can be measured in a fairly accurate manner. Specifically, we can distinguish between those electors who have a partisan attachment, that is, those who are disposed to support a particular political party (party supporters or *shijisha*) from those who do not, that is, those who are independent in partisan terms (unaffiliated electors or *mushozoku*), and we can also distinguish among strengths of partisan attachments. The former distinction is significant because partisans are predisposed to vote for those political parties to which they have acknowledged an attachment while nonpartisans or unaffiliated electors have no such propensity. The second distinction, that between strong or committed partisans and weak or passive partisans, is significant in terms of probabilities. Specifically, it is important because the probability of being loyal to the party of one's choice on election day where such a probability of voting in accordance with one's partisanship is directly proportional to the strength of one's partisanship.

The short-term, election-specific component begins with the idea that elections are like a window on a society through which one may peer and witness the conflicts and problems that define that nation's politics at that particular time. To see this idea in action we need only to recall how different the Bush-Dukakis election in 1988, with its emphasis on who was tougher on communism and crime, was an entirely different affair than the following Clinton-Bush election where the defining problem is perhaps best expressed in the famous line, "It's the economy, stupid." Japan is no different from the United States or any other democratic country in terms of how the tenor of its national elections change from contest to contest. For example, the double election of 1980, when Prime Minister Ohira Masayoshi passed away while campaigning had an entirely different character than the following contest of 1983 when the issue of corruption of the former Prime Minister Tanaka, reappeared with a vengeance. These different short-term, election-specific factors not only give elections their individual tenor, they also carry partisan consequences that affect the outcomes of elections in profound ways.

Since all election outcomes can be thought of as being a combination of these long-term and short-term factors, the analytic task we must complete involves sorting out the contribution of each component to the distribution of aggregate support a political party receives in an election. To accomplish this, we must first recall that the impact that short-term forces will have on election outcomes will be inversely proportional to the number of a nation's electors that are characterized by strong partisan attachments. We must also note that the standard way of isolating the impact of partisan factors from short-term forces has involved identifying the partisan component of an electorate with national surveys, determining what share of election outcomes that component explains, and then assuming the residual is due to election-specific, short-term factors.[23] This has been done in the United States because we have a National Election Study for every presidential and midterm election held since 1950, but in Japan such a consistent array of national samples does not exist for each election. As a result, to sort out the impact of issues and other short-term factors from the long-term component of postwar Japanese elections, we must proceed in a different manner.

The approach we use here to estimate the impact of issues and other short-term forces on election outcomes is informed by a body of work known as "saliency theory."[24] As we discussed above, political parties in a governing position use the policy process to reward the groups that support them. This is consistent with the tenets of saliency theory, which adds that the implication of such political party behavior is the acquisition of certain policy images over time vis-à-vis the electorate. In other words, because of their efforts to promote the interests of their core supporters, political parties become affiliated with certain policies and, in a sense, become the owners of certain issues. On these owned issues, members of nations' electorates associate them with a certain level of proficiency and credibility, and it is for this reason that social democratic parties are considered more proficient at promoting welfare policies while conservative bourgeois parties are better at policies that are favored by businesses.

The idea that voters view political parties differently with respect to their ability to handle certain problems is important for how the salience of certain issues in elections influences voting behavior. Saliency theorists have argued that political parties in the parliamentary systems of the developed world can be divided into two general types, bourgeois or conservative parties and socialist or social democratic parties. Moreover, proponents of saliency theory have also classified the universe of potentially salient election issues as belonging to one of fourteen categories, with each category being further defined as a socialist or bourgeois issue area.[25] In other words, issues in each category are owned either by bourgeois parties or social democratic parties, which means that when specific issues in these categories become salient during a national election, they benefit the party that owns that issue.

Understood this way, analyzing the impact of issues becomes a process of identifying salient issues, determining which party will benefit from their salience, and then calibrating the electoral impacts associated with each identified issue. For example, when welfare issues are salient in an election, they should benefit social democratic parties, since welfare forms the crux of the social democratic program. On the other hand, when defense issues are salient, they should benefit bourgeois parties since it is these parties who have established themselves as the ones with a record of proficiency in this issue area.

This framework represents a great advance in the study of aggregate issue effects because it permits a study of such electoral influences across electoral democracies as well as over time. Unfortunately, it has certain problematic features that must be reworked if it is to serve our purpose here of explaining the changing electoral fortunes of Japan's Liberal Democratic Party. The most important concerns the fact that issue effects are assumed to be consistent across countries, even those whose experience is different from what we have witnessed in West European electoral history. The best illustration of this concerns constitutional issues that Budge and Farlie (1983) argued benefit conservative parties when salient in an election. This assumption is defendable for the European context because conservative parties there have traditionally defended the constitutional status quo while socialist parties have traditionally pushed to change them to effect various socialist goals. In Japan, however, the postwar experience has been just the opposite.

First, Japan's constitution was written by the Occupation authorities and then imposed on a National Diet that had little choice but to ratify the document. Moreover, the postwar constitution contained certain prohibitions that many conservatives found to be anathema and, thus, sought to change at different times throughout the postwar period. Article IX, prohibiting Japan from possessing offensive forces is perhaps the most notable, and, from time to time, it came under attack from certain conservative politicians. These attempts were always resisted by Japan's parties of the Left, particularly the Communists and Socialists, which in turn earned those parties a reputation as protectors of the Japanese constitution. For this reason, constitutional issues are not a conservative issue and do not benefit the LDP when salient in an election.

We deal with this problem in the discussion that follows by treating issue effects in postwar Japanese elections as an empirical problem that can be solved by completing two tasks. The first task involves determining which issues were salient in which elections so that we can provide a consistent and accurate mapping of the electoral history of the postwar period. Our approach involved an examination of certain Japanese language reports for all lower-house elections in the postwar period. Specifically, annual editions of *Asahi Nenkan* [Asahi Yearbook], *Yomuri Nenkan* [Yomiuri Yearbook], and *Jiji Nenkan* [Jiji Yearbook] were used because they describe in detail the issues that defined Japan's postwar elections and the positions taken by Japan's various political parties on these issues. These yearbooks were content-analyzed to determine which issues were salient in each of the elections and identify the issue positions the various parties emphasized in their respective campaigns. We examined the three above-named yearbooks to be certain that our selection of salient issues was consistent across elections. Specifically, if an issue was not mentioned by all three yearbooks as being one that was important, then it was not reported as being salient.[27]

The second task in our empirical analysis involved developing a method to calibrate the direction and impact of issues that were found to be salient in Japan's postwar elections. To determine whether or not a salient issue should work to the LDP's electoral benefit or detriment in a postwar election contest, we must first know the party's position on the issue and then the distribution of public opinion on that salient issue as well. Again, the three yearbooks mentioned above tell us the positions of all parties, and they were consulted to provide an issue profile of the LDP in each postwar election. Next, to determine the distribution of public attitudes on salient issues we consulted all available public opinion polls. Some of these involved published sources like the three yearbooks mentioned above and *Yoron Gekkan* [Public Opinion Monthly] published by the Prime Minister's Office while others involved individual election studies available for secondary analysis.[28] From these public opinion data, we determined whether the Japanese public was favorably or unfavorably distributed on a salient issue or whether it was evenly divided. The result of these efforts allowed us to determine whether the LDP's positions on salient issues were on the majority side of public opinion, in which case it would benefit electorally, on the minority side of public opinion, in which case it would be hurt electorally, or in a neutral position, in which case there would be no electoral impact.

With this information in hand we then coded each salient issue in an election a +1 if it was beneficial to the LDP or a −1 if not, and a 0 if its impact was expected to be neutral. These issue-specific impacts were then summed up for each election, resulting in an integer that indicated how the balance of election-specific, short-term factors was expected to impact on the LDP electorally. Before showing this in a more systematic way, however, we want to emphasize that by identifying and calibrating issue impacts in this way, we avoid the shortcomings of the otherwise very useful saliency theory framework discussed above. Specifically, we know that public attitudes are not static and change over time with respect to different issues. One must only recall how certain political issues, anathema at one time, become more and more politically acceptable at later dates to know that change is an ever-present reality of electoral politics. Our method assumes that public attitudes on important issues may change over time, which allows us to trace how the Japanese public may have changed its issue attitudes over the course of the elections conducted throughout the postwar period.

In the same way that public attitudes on issues may change over time, it is also the case that the same salient issue may take on different substantive meanings in different elections. This is extremely important because, although remaining in the same issue category, issues that take on different substantive meanings in different elections may be attendant to entirely different electoral impacts. By way of illustration, consider the issue of defense that has been assumed to be an anti-LDP issue throughout the postwar period. This is the case when the defense issue manifested itself as the LDP's efforts to remilitarize the country, which it did from time to time. Given the legacy of the Pacific War, if LDP efforts were too enthusiastic and accompanied by rhetoric that made reference to the nation's imperial past, this would raise the specter of militarism. This is a sensitive and unpopular issue among Japanese, and, when defense was defined with such militarist overtones, it put the conservative party on the minority side of public opinion. On the other hand, the defense issue has also manifested itself as the government's legitimate self-defense efforts in the face of external threats. One example of this occurred in response to the former Soviet Union's military build-up in the Far Eastern part of the country in the waning years of the Cold War. When defined this way, the LDP's efforts were on the majority side of public opinion and, thus, worked to the party's electoral benefit.

EXPLAINING THE LDP'S RISE AND DECLINE

Using this framework, we identified two categories of issues and the impacts they had on the LDP's electoral fortunes in national elections held since 1958 (Table 8.1). The first category involves issues that are derived from the performance of the LDP as governing party during its term in office prior to an election, and for this reason issues in this category are called performance issues. In a sense, all elections serve as a referendum on the manner in which governing parties managed their own affairs and the affairs of the nation while in office. More than any other issue, this involves the state of a nation's economy such that, if the economy performed well in a period leading up to an election, a governing party should benefit while holding an election during a recession would be associated with a negative public reaction. It is for this reason that the electoral impacts associated with the economy as a performance issue are labeled erratic.

The next performance issue in the table is "party effects," which refers to the manner in which the behavior of Japan's political parties affected the issue climates of postwar elections. When salient, party effects impacted on the LDP's electoral fortunes in both positive and negative ways. The former most often occurred when the behavior of individual LDP politicians compromised the unity of the party, undermining public confidence in its ability to continue as the nation's governing party. Such times occurred when the LDP's leadership was manifestly split and competing faction leaders put up different sets of candidates in the same election and also when the party formally split as in the cases of the New Liberal Club in 1976 and the formation of other

Table 8.1 Salient Issues and Their Electoral Impacts

ISSUE TYPE	ELECTORAL IMPACT
Performance	
Economy	Erratic
Party Effects	Erratic
Corruption	Negative
Candidate Effects	Positive
Substantive	
Foreign Affairs	Positive
Defense	Erratic
Constitutional	Negative
Civil Order	Positive
Social Welfare	Negative
Environment	Negative
Taxes	Negative

conservative parties in the early 1990s. Party effects, on the other hand, also carried positive impacts on the LDP. Such times occurred when the New Liberal Club rejoined the LDP in 1986 and when certain opposition parties approached the LDP as potential coalition partners in the same 1986 election, leading to disarray in the Opposition camp.

The third and fourth performance issues carry opposite electoral impacts, despite the fact that both involve individual politicians. On the one hand, the third performance issue, "corruption," has been a virtual leitmotif in postwar Japanese politics, and, when salient, it has universally hurt the LDP. "Candidate effects," on the other hand, have carried positive impacts on election outcomes although they certainly have the potential to be negative. Moreover, we separate this class of performance issue from party effects because they revolve around the activities of one or more individual candidates and because they occur independently of political parties. Perhaps the best example of this occurred during the lower-house election of 1980 when Prime Minister Ohira died while campaigning, encouraging an outpouring of sympathy toward the former prime minister and, as a result, benefiting the LDP electorally.

The other category of issues is listed separately in the remainder of the table and is referred to as substantive issues. Issues in this category cover that set of political issues that one typically finds being salient in the elections of any democratic nation. From the table, we notice that the only substantive issues that were consistently pro-LDP were foreign affairs and civil order. The former, on the one hand, was salient from time to time throughout the postwar period and benefited the LDP because no party outside of the LDP was a credible leader of the nation's international interests. The latter, on the other hand, was salient only in the 1960 election when the autocratic manner in which a revised security treaty with the United States was ratified by the Diet led to violence that the Japanese public tended to blame on leftist groups. Except for defense, which was erratic for the reasons described above, the remaining substantive issues worked to the detriment of the LDP when salient in elections.

Having identified the performance and substantive issues that were salient in postwar Japanese elections, we must now illustrate more clearly how these issues are related to the Liberal Democratic Party's changing electoral fortunes. To accomplish this, we calculated the issue scores of each postwar election from 1958 to 1996 inclusive and then compared these scores to the LDP's vote shares in the same elections. These results are presented in Table 8.2 where the election-specific issue scores and LDP vote shares have been divided into the four electoral periods that correspond to the times for which we present data. Even a perfunctory glance at the table reveals a strong

Table 8.2 Issue Scores and LDP Vote Shares, 1958–1996

Electoral Period/ Election Years	Issue Score	Vote Shares
Predominance		
1958	+1	57.8
1960	+3	57.5
1963	+1	54.6
Decline		
1967	0	48.8
1969	−1	47.6
1972	−2	46.8
1976	−5	41.7
Resurgence		
1979	−1	44.5
1980	+2	47.9
1983	−1	45.7
1986	+3	49.4
1990	+1	46.1
Dissolution		
1993	−5	36.6
1996	−3	35.1*
		*weighted PR & SMD

relationship between the issue scores and the LDP's share of lower house votes in the same elections. Specifically, in the period of predominance, issue scores were low but positive which contrasts greatly with the periods of decline and dissolution when issue scores were decidedly negative. Finally, the period of resurgence is actually a time when a strong LDP showing tended to be followed by a weak showing, and the issue scores for the elections of this segment of electoral history follow the same oscillating pattern.

Although the issue scores of Japan's postwar elections appear to correspond strongly to the LDP's changing electoral fortunes, we must note that it is one thing to pair issue scores and election outcomes together and assert that the former accounts for the latter and quite another to calculate the average impact that a change in an election's issue climate had on the LDP's vote shares. Doing this is essential both to be sure that salient issues carried the electoral impacts that our theoretical discussion says they did and, more important, to be able to develop a method to isolate the short-term issue impacts from the long-term partisan factors that operated in Japan's postwar elections. This requires a statistical analysis where vote shares are regressed on issue scores for the elections that occurred from 1958 to 1996 inclusive, and it also requires that one other influence be included in the analysis. Given existing research on the topic, it is clear that the ruling party's underlying support changed throughout the postwar period. For statistical purposes, this means that each of the electoral periods we identified above will exert an independent influence on the average level of support the LDP received in that electoral period. To capture this in our analysis, we have to include these electoral periods in our statistical model as dummy variables, something we do for the second, third, and fourth electoral periods.[30]

The relationships discussed above are straight forward and represented by the following linear equation:

$$V_i = \alpha + \beta_1 X_i + \beta_2 P_2 + \beta_3 P_3 + \beta_4 P_4 + e$$

where, V_i is vote share for the LDP in the ith election,

X_i is the issue score for the ith election,

P_2, P_3, and P_4 are dummy variables for the second, third, and fourth electoral periods,

α is the intercept,

β_1 to β_4 are coefficients, and

e is an error term.

This equation was estimated using the issue scores and vote shares presented above, and the results are presented in Table 8.3.

From the results presented in the table, we can say that the model is sound in a statistical sense and that it has much explanatory power, accounting for 95 percent of the variance in the LDP's changing electoral fortunes for the period under consideration.[31] Moreover, all coefficients in the model are statistically significant, with signs in the expected direction, which tells us that our understanding of elections as the product of short-term and long-

Table 8.3 Issue Impacts on the LDP's Electoral Fortunes

Variable	Coefficients	T-Ratios
Constant	54.87*	62.84
Issues	1.06*	−4.82
Period of Decline	−6.52*	−4.82
Period of Resurgence	−8.99*	−8.96
Period of Dissolution	−14.77*	−8.07

*P < .01

Model F 78.01   Prob > F 0.0000   Adjusted R^2 = .9596

term components is intellectually sound. In addition to the general performance of the model, several specific aspects of the results presented in the
table are of interest and in need of further explanation.

The first term in the table is the intercept, which should be interpreted
as the LDP's expected share of lower-house votes for the entire postwar
period. More specifically, this is the share of lower-house votes we would
expect the LDP to obtain either when no issues are salient in an election or
when issues are salient but their attendant positive and negative impacts can-
cel each other out. The value of the constant is 54.87 percent, which tells us
that, given no issue effects and no corrections to the LDP's support base for
the electoral periods that have been identified, Japan's ruling party entered the
average postwar election with a very significant vote advantage, one that was
more than sufficient to give it a majority of lower-house seats. What we learn
for these data is just how electorally strong Japan's ruling party has been
throughout the postwar period, helping to explain why it has been able to
survive so long as Japan's ruling party.[32]

Our statistical analysis has also shown quite strongly just how important issues and other short-term effects have been in postwar Japanese elections. This is captured in the coefficient on the "issues" variable, which is
1.06 and statistically significant at the 99 percent level of confidence. The
size of the coefficient tells us that a unit change in the issue climate of an
election, that is the salience of one additional issue with a positive or negative
impact, is associated with a change of just over 1 percent in the LDP's
aggregate share of the lower-house votes. For example, staying away from
corruption, keeping factional squabbles in check, and being certain that the
economy runs well would add more than three points to the party's expected
vote shares in a lower-house election. With these results, we can conclude
that issues have always been important in postwar Japanese elections but that
what has been missing is a design that has been able to capture their impact
with the level of accuracy presented above.

In our discussion of the LDP's changing electoral fortunes, we divided
postwar elections into groups corresponding to specific electoral trends for the
ruling party, and, in our statistical analysis, we included a variable for the
periods of decline, resurgence, and dissolution. In the language of statistics,
these are known as intercept dummy variables which means that, in our analysis, they can be interpreted as how the progression of time from one electoral
period to the next affected the LDP's underlying support. With no ambiguity,
the coefficients for the period dummy variables tell a story of continual predominant party decline. By the end of the 1960s, the LDP's significant vote
advantage had been reduced by 6.5 percent and by another 2.5 percent over the
next ten years. The hemorrhaging of the LDP's underlying support did not halt

in the 1980s even though the party generally performed better in the elections of that decade. In fact, from the time of its resurgence until it was pushed out of power in the summer of 1993, the party's underlying base of support was nearly 15 percent lower than it was when it entered its first lower-house election in 1958.

Given what has been written on postwar Japanese politics, the results we have presented make two rather controversial points about the LDP's changing electoral fortunes. The first is that issues have always mattered in postwar Japanese elections, and the failure of many scholars either to acknowledge this or account for their electoral impacts in a systematic way for the entire postwar period has been a problem of design and not something specific to the Japanese electoral process. Second, having shown that the LDP's base of support continued to erode in a monotonic fashion, we must now provide a different explanation for the party's return to more favorable electoral circumstances in the 1980s. The explanation we provide here is simply that the LDP's stronger performances in the 1980s were not a true conservative resurgence but rather the result of short-term factors in those elections. The LDP's underlying support continued to wane in the 1980s, and this paved the way for its very poor performances, at least in terms of vote shares, in the lower house elections of the 1990s.

To show that this is exactly what happened, we need to take the LDP's lower-house vote shares and break them down into their long-term and short-term components. The analysis presented above provides a way for us to calibrate that portion of the LDP's vote shares that was due to issue and other short-term effects and those that were due to underlying partisan effects. Specifically, this can be done by determining the percentage of votes in each election that is attributable to issues and then subtracting this amount—or adding in the case of a negative value—from the party's actual vote share. The results of this analysis are presented in Table 8.4

The percentages in the table's second column are the actual vote shares the LPD received in the lower house elections indicated in column 1. The percentages in the third column are the shares of lower-house votes the LDP would have received had there been no issue or other short-term effects salient in those elections. They were obtained by removing election-specific, short-term effects from the party's actual vote totals, raising the party's vote shares when issue effects were negative and lowering them when they were positive.[33]

These values provide us with an accurate estimate of that portion of the LDP's aggregate vote totals that are due to its underlying support, and, from the data presented in column 3, we can see that the party's underlying support declined continually throughout the postwar period. To indicate just how much the party's underlying support declined, we calculated averages for

Table 8.4 LDP Lower-House Vote Shares:
Long-Term and Short-Term Components

Election Period/ Election Years	Vote Shares: Period Average/ Individual Elections	Underlying Support: Period Average/ Individual Elections
Predominance:	56.6	54.9
1958	57.8	56.7
1960	57.5	54.3
1963	54.6	53.4
Decline:	46.2	48.4
1967	48.8	48.8
1969	47.6	48.7
1972	46.8	48.9
1976	41.7	47.0
Resurgence:	46.7	45.9
1979	44.5	45.6
1980	47.9	45.8
1983	45.7	46.6
1986	49.4	46.2
1990	46.1	45.0
Dissolution:	35.8	40.1
1996	36.6	41.9
1996	35.1	38.2

each electoral period. As expected, the party's underlying support was above the majority point in the period of predominance but had dropped to 48 percent in the period of decline. Period averages presented in the table indicate that the LDP's electoral decline continued, slowly at first (45.87 percent in the period of resurgence) but with rapidity in the next two decades. By the 1990s, the LDP's expected vote from underlying support was reduced to 40 percent, and, while this is a substantially lower level of underlying support than the party received in the first ten years after it was formed, this is still a sizable level of underlying voter affirmation. In fact, it is substantial enough for the party to obtain a lower-house majority even with a moderately positive issue climate.

The electoral events of 1993 caught many Japan watchers by surprise. After nearly four decades in power, the LDP was pushed aside by a fragile eight-party coalition. The analysis presented above shows that surprise was unwarranted because such an event was more likely to occur in the late 1980s and early 1990s than at any time previously. The preceding has also provided a useful way to understand how electoral politics in postwar Japan evolved to its present state. Accomplishing this involved challenging the conventional wisdom about postwar Japanese elections in a couple of ways. First, the foregoing has shown that conservative resurgence in the 1980s was ephemeral if not mythical. Despite its resurgence in the 1980s, the LDP's core support continued to hemorrhage away. The foregoing has also suggested that the purpose of establishing a new election district system involved more than simply cleaning up electoral politics, as individual proponents and the media most often stated. The introduction of a new, two-vote, parallel election system in 1994 was also consumed with solving the LDP's problem of electoral decline. As we have shown above, the LDP's vote shares in the most recent election recovered but not quite enough to give it the majority of lower-house seats it had long possessed. With the large seat bonus it receives in the 300-seat, single-member district portion of the new system, Japan's Liberal Democratic Party has been able continually to form all governments since the election of 1996.

IV. JAPAN IN THE NEW MILLENNIUM

Chapter 9

THE PAST IN JAPAN'S
POLITICAL-ECONOMIC FUTURE

Out of the ferment of the postwar era we already can see new forces arising, which, if they mature, will modify the entire relationship of civilized nations. These elements of historic process cannot be studied adequately by the means, and through the instruments at our disposal at present. They cannot be referred to the casual or incidental interests of those who make this field an academic avocation.

—A 1927 SSRC Report

A very large mass of writers . . . have accepted the basic distinction between East and West as the starting point for elaborate theories, epics, novels, social descriptions, and political accounts concerning the Orient, its people, customs, "mind," destiny, and so on.

—Edward Said (1979)

I n the study of politics and economics, it is much easier to impose an explanation on some past record of events than it is to specify with any accuracy the course that political-economic events will follow in the future. There are many reasons for this, but perhaps most important is the notion that forecasting naturally involves controlling for so many more unknowns than does any attempt to account for what has already occurred. Indeed, few will disagree that planning for the unforeseen contingencies that must be considered and attempting to specify those factors that must be weighted renders projecting into the future an effort fraught with error. On the other hand, acknowledging such difficulties does not mean that speculating on the course certain events are likely to follow in the near future operates more in the realm of sorcery than of science and, thus, can result in nothing that is both reliable and fruitful. Moreover, acknowledging the difficulties associated with projecting the course political-economic events may follow does not mean that the comparative ease of explaining a set of past occurrences always results in assessments that are accurate or useful.

More than anything else, projecting the course that certain political-economic events are likely to follow requires that one understand something about how those events will be determined in the future, and, to be accurate and reliable, this must proceed by appreciating how closely related the forecasting process is to the process of explaining what has already happened. Indeed, while different in purpose and scope, these two intellectual activities are utterly dependent on each other because projecting political-economic events into the future derives from how well the past occurrence of those events has been explained. This means that the forecasting process is necessarily guided by historical antecedents. In this sense, history is not just the path one takes on a retrospective journey to try to understand the roots of the present, it is also a guide for what we can expect to occur in the near and, with less certainty, distant futures.

As we have endeavored to show in the preceding chapters, much of the scholarship on postwar Japan that appeared in the last two and one-half decades does not offer a basis on which we can project the course that political-economic events are likely to follow over the next several years. The most important reason for this is that the explanations that became prevalent in the last two and one-half decades simply did not anticipate the troubles that the 1990s would bring to Japan. As a result, they are simply not reliable as guides for how Japan's political-economic course will unfold in the future. This criticism is supported by the fact that proponents of the views discussed above have rushed to alter the perspectives they previously advanced to accommodate the problems that Japan has been experiencing in the last decade. In most cases, these explanations do not pass even the loosest of consistency tests, and, consequently, most have been amended beyond recognition or completely abandoned.

The task of suggesting, first, how the Japanese government is likely to respond to the political and economic reform imperatives it currently faces and, second, how actors in Japan's private sector are likely to respond to the economic challenges they face must proceed from a solid understanding of what will determine their behavior in the context of the country's ongoing political and economic crisis. Past explanations for Japan's postwar political-economic trajectory are unable to accomplish this not because their proponents have failed to recognize the challenges that Japan's political and economic leaders face in the postbubble period but rather because they have not offered an adequate explanation for how the 1990s occurred in the first place. Again, as we have been arguing throughout this book, much of the literature on the postwar Japanese political-economic system that appeared in the last two decades described a "Japan that never was."

To be sure, the future itself will be the final arbiter of any effort to project the course that political-economic events will follow. Nonetheless, we can say that a projection's potential for success in the problem at hand rests with how the underlying ideas that guide it perform across the entire expanse of Japan's postwar political-economic history. In other words, as we have said above, those ideas must explain how a once ably functioning political system collapsed under the weight of its own corruption and ineffectiveness and why an economy, once the envy of the developed and developing worlds, stagnated for such a long period of time. Ideas that are best able to accomplish this are those that do not have to be constantly qualified or amended in the face of events that they did not, and indeed could not, anticipate. It is only in this way that we can get beyond the problem of "the Japan that never was."

In his book, *The Armchair Economist: Economics and Everyday Life,* Steven Landsburg discusses how one should think about human behavior that appears to violate the rationality assumption that guides neoclassical economic analysis.[1] To accomplish this, Landsburg uses a thought experiment involving a theoretical physicist who is well versed in the theory of gravity but then encounters a helium-filled balloon for the first time. Because this objects floats in the air, ostensibly in violation of the theory of gravity, the theorist's understanding of the meaningfulness of gravity is challenged. In the face of this theory-defying object, the gravitational theorist has two choices. The first involves the theorist continuing to adhere to the theory of gravity in a general sense but recognizing that there are cases (conditions) that the theory cannot subsume. From the perspective of the theorist, this is certainly not a desirable alternative because a true exception undermines the reach of the theory, and enough true exceptions will lead to the development of competing theories that eventually replace the existing paradigm.

Fortunately, there is a second option that allows the theorist to investigate whether or not the anomalous case functions as a true exception to the theory. In the context of the above example, this involves the counterintuitive course of trying to account for the helium-filled balloon within the confines of the theory of gravity. As we know well, helium-filled balloons do not violate the theory of gravity. Although a seemingly solid object floating in the air would seem to present such a disconcerting challenge, we know that this is hardly troubling because helium, as a component element of the earth's atmosphere, is simply lighter than the atmosphere around the balloon that has captured it in a concentrated form.

While this thought experiment may seem a long way from the political-economic trajectory of postwar Japan, it is illustrative of the intellectual course we should follow if we are to avoid the problem of "the Japan that never was." Specifically, Japan encountered the political-economic problems it did in the 1990s not because it experienced a transformation that rendered its "developmental state" essence ineffective in the face of changing conditions. Japan happened on troubled times in the last several years simply because its essential political and economic actors have been behaving in the current period of crisis exactly as they have throughout the entire postwar period. Saying this means that we have captured two very disparate sets of outcomes without amending the ideas that guided our perspective. This does not mean that consistency is some abstractly sacrosanct concept that functions as the singular measure of the quality of all social scientific theory. Rather, it simply means that a perspective that has to be amended well beyond recognition or abandoned altogether in light of the events it does not subsume cannot be a sound basis for projecting the course that future events will most likely follow.

We believe that we have provided the best way to judge the manner in which the Japanese government and private sector will behave in response to the crisis. This is because, in the preceding chapters, we explained Japan's postwar political-economic trajectory as the result of its essential political and economic actors behaving in expected ways. Consequently, we believe what is most likely to happen in the future will also be the result of these same actors behaving in the current period of crisis essentially as they have been behaving throughout the postwar period. This is important because it is only by understanding how the political and economic behavior of Japan's essential actors resulted in very different outcomes over the entire postwar period that we can grapple with how they have responded to the crisis in the way they have thus far. Moreover, it is only by understanding how and why Japan's leaders have responded to the current political and economic problems in the last decade and a half that we can suggest with any accuracy how they are likely to behave in the near future.

THE POLITICS OF POLITICAL-ECONOMIC REFORM

On the one hand, we have been clear in our criticism that much existing work on Japan did not explain that country's postwar political-economic trajectory in a satisfactory way. On the other hand, we have also said that, in recent assessments of Japan's current troubles, Japan scholars have correctly identified the challenges that Japan's public and private leaders face today. Treatments of the postbubble period have reflected an understanding that Japan currently faces a structural adjustment that is quite different from problems associated with downturns in the business cycle. In this way, current assessments have also been correct in specifying the policies that the government could enact to implement meaningful economic reform and, thus, hasten the end of the current structural reform as well as address those problems that led to the postwar party system collapsing. Rather, our point is that scholarship that has talked about Japan's current problems has not fully appreciated how difficult it would be for Japan's elected officials to depart in any notable way from what they have been doing since the economic bubble burst.

While no longer the nation's predominant political party, the Liberal Democratic Party has been the largest party in a three-party coalition. In this context, we would expect it to prefer a course of action that would increase its support levels as much as possible. While this would most likely fall short of returning it to the earlier days of electoral predominance, it would certainly allow it more governing flexibility than it currently possesses. Obviously, being able to take credit for enacting policies that hasten the end of the long period of economic stagnation the country has been facing would serve this preference. Unfortunately, enacting the economic and political reforms that are necessary to accomplish such a goal would require a substantial departure from the manner in which the ruling party conducted its political and economic business in the past. Specifically, reforms that are to be politically and economically meaningful would require the party, at a minimum, to begin rolling back in a substantial way the supports and protections its governments have extended to so many of its supporters in the country's inefficient small- and medium-size firms.

In light of this, the way Japan's politicians have responded to the current crisis thus far is exactly what we would have expected. The political constraints LDP politicians have faced in the last several years have rendered any policy action that departs radically from what we have witnessed partner to very high political costs. Since the party is no longer a majority party, and its preference would be to gather enough support to regain its majority status, it cannot afford to enact any policy that would alienate any of its existing support. This is important because it tells us that the government's ability to enact a course of policy that addresses the problems Japan currently faces, is due neither to a lack of policy creativity nor to bureaucratic intransigence. Rather, it is due to the LDP, or any other party for that matter, not being able to alienate any of its existing support.[2]

The same kinds of constraints exist with respect to Japan's actors in the private sector. It is true that owners of Japan's large-, medium-, and small-size firms want to survive as business enterprises and that, in the context of the economic problems Japan has faced in the last decade, this has become an increasingly difficult task. Unfortunately, having a desire to endure as a profitable business firm and do what is necessary to make that happen does not mean engaging in behavior that will necessarily result in a stronger, reformed economy in the aggregate. In fact, given that Japan has notable excess capacity in certain areas and that this capacity is the result of the continued operation of many inefficient firms, economic reform overall will impact negatively on the goal of many firms to survive.

Moreover, it is well known that inefficient firms have survived in postwar Japan for political and organizational reasons. The former refers to the extensive rent-seeking that occurs in the Japanese political-economic system and the fact that many inefficient firms have survived because of the benefits they have received from the government. These benefits have taken many forms, and as we have shown above, their distribution has by and large benefited the nation's slow-growing and inefficient producers. The latter refers to the special upstream-downstream supplier-producer relationship that many of Japan's small- and medium-size firms enjoyed throughout the postwar period. These special *keiretsu* relationships advantaged these firms by giving them access to technology and markets that they may not have gotten in a market that was structured differently. While there are extensive costs associated with these relationships and larger firms have been moving out of them in the last several years, there are reasons to believe that this will not go as far as we would expect given the balance of market incentives at this time.

Large firms in Japan at this time are certainly facing strong incentives to cut costs given the losses they experienced in the wake of the bursting of the economic bubble. Naturally, we would expect the cost-cutting measures they seek to involve finding cheaper suppliers of the inputs they need in their daily production activities and, thus, the severing of relationships with some of the upstream suppliers. Unfortunately, upstream suppliers in Japan's subcontracting system involves small- and medium-size firms that constitute one of the Liberal Democratic Party's core support groups. This means that members of the ruling party are not going to sit by and simply watch them go bankrupt and disappear. Indeed, LDP Secretary General Nonaka Hiromu, argued this point of view in a short but strongly worded *Chuo Koron* article where he noted that "abandoning the weak is not the politics of strength."[3]

It is for this reason that we would expect the government to continue to provide protection and assistance to supporters in small- and medium-size firms to the greatest extent possible. Unfortunately, continued government support means that large firms will not be able simply to sever any and all relationships with such firms without any consideration of the political impact that such actions will bring. Moreover, this overall constraint is reinforced by the fact that many large firms are troubled with financial and restructuring problems of their own, and, thus, are still dependent on the government for support, particularly as that support relates to their access to capital. This means that the government still has some leverage over how large firms treat their constituent suppliers in its approach to the structural problems that the country faces.

There is one other aspect of Japan's current economic problems that lead us to believe that there is little chance that any radical economic reform will occur in the near future. The reference here is simply to the fact that Japan is a wealthy country, which is important because being wealthy has allowed Japan to endure during this period of crisis without suffering a complete economic collapse. This has obviously been helpful to the average Japanese, but it has come at the price of the current structural adjustment continuing as long as it has. Indeed, being a wealthy country has encouraged a kind of muddling through attitude that is sustained by the simple fact that Japan has endured and most likely will continue to endure throughout the current crisis. As long as the economy stays afloat and the social consequences of economic stagnation are not utterly disruptive to the current sociopolitical state of affairs, there is little incentive for either public or private actors to engage in some radical policy action.

These expectations are important, but they do not mean that no action can be taken on the part of the government or Japan's principal actors in the private sector. Indeed, we expect that at least some reforms will be devised and implemented not simply because of the length and severity of the current crisis but also because not all political and economic actors are facing exactly the same constraints against taking concerted policy action. There are certainly politicians who will find it in their political interests to champion meaningful political and economic reforms, and there are certainly businesses that are better positioned to emerge from the structural adjustment in a strong competitive position.

These statements may seem to violate our earlier statements explaining why deep and meaningful reforms are unlikely, especially in light of the fact that a number of seemingly important reforms have taken place already. This is true in both the economic and political spheres where some arguably substantial changes have been made. This leads us to ask whether or not our prediction that no substantial policy action would be taken is misplaced and, absent some dramatic occurrence like the complete collapse of the Japanese economy, there is little reason to expect any dramatic departure from the course that the country has been following since the bursting of the economic bubble. In light of this, our task in the remainder of this final chapter is to take the important actions that have occurred and evaluate how well they fit with the perspective that guided our analysis thus far and determine what they tell us about the future course public and private action is likely to follow.

PROSPECTS FOR POLITICAL REFORM

As explained above, the most serious political problem facing Japan today concerns the ineffectiveness of the governmental (policy) process in the face of the current crisis. This political problem has two aspects, the first of which concerns the unsatisfied demand of the Japanese public for the government to do something to enervate the problems that the country has been facing. This aspect is complemented, or more accurately aggravated, by a second aspect which is defined by the propensity for corruption that has character-ized Japanese politics throughout the postwar period. As the economic cer-tainty that characterized the life of most Japanese in the postwar period melted away in the wake of the postbubble crisis, so has the Japanese public's rather extensive tolerance of politician malfeasance. These two aspects of Japan's reigning political troubles led to calls for politicians to change their behavior, but the policy they actually helped engender led to the very insti-tutions of Japanese democracy becoming nearly universal targets of criticism.

The dual problem of corruption and political ineffectiveness is under-standable in terms of how electoral politics evolved throughout the postwar period. As explained above, the essential political problem facing the LDP and LDP-led governments from the mid-1970s to the present concerns the decline of support for the formerly predominant Liberal Democratic party. The loss of LDP predominance has carried two implications that are largely responsible for this political problem. First, as a political party with a thin majority prior to the bursting of the economic bubble and without a clear majority in the last ten years, the LDP can ill afford to alienate any of the electoral support it currently retains. Given that the desired political reforms will negatively impact on the party's ability to provide benefits to a dwindling supply of core supporters, it has been very reluctant to enact any policies that would radically depart from the course it has been following. This problem aggravates the second problem, which concerns eliminating, or at least reducing corruption. Since corruption was given greater encouragement as the party's support levels dwindled and the costs of maintaining itself at the nation's predominant party increased, the roots of the problem remain untouched.

This situation has presented the LDP with a dilemma in that, while it cannot afford to engage in a reform effort that departs radically from its current course, it cannot at the same time afford to ignore the strong public demand that exists in the country for concerted policy action. There are strong political reasons for the party to refrain from engaging in any radical alteration of the political system, but, at the same time, the party also faces strong incentives to do more than simply pay lip service to the political impasse within which Japan's democracy seems to be stuck. In light of this, we are left with the question of exactly what we would expect the LDP and other parties in power to do in the area of political reform, and our answer contains two parts. The first is that we would expect the LDP, and any other political party that served in the government, to push for political reforms that can be interpreted as addressing the woes that have immobilized the political process in Japan, but only at a time when the costs of taking such action are surpassed by the costs of taking no action. Second, we would expect the party to emphasize only those reforms that would advance their electoral interests or, at a minimum, hold them harmless.

While there have been a number of efforts in this area from various parties that have been in government since the bursting of the economic bubble, perhaps the most notable has been the replacement of Japan's old system of electoral rules with an entirely new election system. The discourse on political reform has long been centered on Japan's old election system where individual candidates stood for election in multimember districts and where electors cast a single nontransferable vote. Under this system, LDP candidates ran against not only members of the opposition, but also other LDP candidates. As a result, this system arguably encouraged elections that were candidate-centered rather than party-based and emphasized the distribution of pork rather than substantive discussions over how to solve the nation's pressing problems. Political reform proponents have argued that if the election system could be changed, many present-day political problems would disappear because new electoral rules would lead to the emergence of a two-party system where there would be a greater emphasis on substantive problems and the policies most likely to solve those problems.

Election system reform is nothing new in postwar Japan as both the LDP and the Opposition endeavored to change the old multimember district system in a way that gave them greater political advantage. It was not until the Japanese Supreme Court stepped in and declared the old system unconstitutional that certain minor reforms were enacted.[4] The momentum for political reform in the late 1980s, however, centered around replacing the entire system, and, because public demand became so strong for some kind of political reform, it became virtually impossible for a political party to oppose election system change, at least in principle.[5] This situation made some kind of institutional reform inevitable, but it left as a subject for political debate the exact kind of system that would be selected to replace Japan's old electoral rules. This was a debate that took the appointment of a nonpartisan election system commission five years of investigation and deliberation to propose a politically workable formula. Throughout this five-year period, multiple proposals were introduced and rejected, but it was the Hosokawa government, the first non-LDP administration in thirty-eight years, that approved the legislation that scrapped Japan's old multimember district system. The new system was a parallel system where Japanese voters cast two ballots, one for a single candidate in one of 300 single-member districts and the other for a party list in multimember, proportional representation districts where seats are distributed by the d'Hondt method.

Replacing a country's electoral rules is no small task, and as such as it may seem like a political reform effort that violates the expectations we set out above. It is true that nothing touches more directly on the electoral fortunes of elected officials than manipulations in electoral rules, rendering any election system change something to be taken seriously. Moreover, this change in the rules of the game was part of a group of political reforms that altered the way that elections in Japan were not only conducted but also financed. Nonetheless, there are three principal reasons to conclude that this change in Japan's electoral rules does not violate our expectations about the scope of expected reforms we would have expected politicians to introduce and enact. These reasons concern the timing of the reforms, the type of system that was adopted, and the manner in which the new district's boundaries were drawn.[6]

Our expectation is that political reform would occur only if such a process could enhance the electoral interests of the parties that would be involved in the process. Proposals to change Japan's election system had occurred at numerous times in the past, but they were realized only after a five-year debate that ended with a non-LDP administration enacting the necessary reform legislation. Events followed this course because demand for the type of institutional change that occurred did not exist until the late 1980s, creating an environment where there were strong electoral incentives to push for electoral reform. In other words, there were strong electoral incentives for political parties to push for reform of the nation's electoral rules.

Second, when we examine the different proposals that were propounded by Japan's various political parts throughout the five years of debate that occurred, we notice that there were a number of different proposals. Nonetheless, the different configurations that were offered can be explained only by how the new system would be expected to affect a party's electoral interests. On the one hand, as Japan's largest party, the LDP would benefit from a nationwide single-member district system or a mixed-member system where the preponderance of candidates would be elected in mixed-member systems. The parties of the opposition, on the other hand, were on average much smaller than the LDP and, thus, would benefit much more from a system where all seats are allocated by some type of PR formula or, in a mixed system format, where most seats are in PR districts. As is now well known, the final form of the new system would take involved a compromise, specifically, the one originally proposed by the non-partisan election system commission, where 300 seats were in single-member districts and 200 would be allocated by proportional representations.

The final reason that this grand institutional change does not violate our expectations concerns the manner in which the new system's district boundaries were drawn. The problem facing designers with respect to the new system's single-member district boundaries, was how to accommodate incumbents. All incumbents that would stand for office under the new rules had been elected in a district that was essentially their home base.[7] This involved over 500 seats that could certainly not be accommodated in the new system since there were only 300 seats available in single-member districts. Since the new 300 single-member districts would be carved out of the old 130 multimember districts, we would expect incumbents to stand in new districts where they would have the greatest chance for reelection. A review of the data, which shows where incumbents were electorally strongest, revealed that just over three-fourths of incumbents stood in districts where they were electorally strongest.[8]

For those who could not be accommodated in this way, we would expect some other institutional innovation to be available to protect these candidates' incumbent status. The institutional innovation that was used to accomplish this is known as overlapping candidacies. This means that many candidates were allowed to run on party lists in a PR district at the same time that they were candidates in one of the new single-member districts. A review of the data mentioned above revealed that, for incumbents who could not be allowed to stand in a single-member district where he or she was electorally strongest, 60 percent were allowed to run simultaneously in their corresponding PR district. This leaves only a few unaccommodated exceptions that can be explained away in a fairly simple manner. Of the incumbents who were not accommodated in the above manner, 87 percent were members of the New Frontier Party which made it a part of its platform not to allow overlapping candidacies. When these candidates are subtracted out of the total number of incumbents not accommodated under the new rules, this leaves only four incumbent candidates.

Among other things, it is because the new election system was designed to accommodate the desires of the parties that competed over its format and included boundaries that were drawn in a way to protect all incumbents that it has not fulfilled its promise to the Japanese public that institutional change would change the Japanese party system. Nonetheless, even if the process proceeded differently than it did, Japan's mixed system format would never have resulted in a two-party system or other political outcomes that many said it would help bring because of what are known as contamination effects. According to Herron and Nishiakwa (2000), parties that have no chance of winning a seat in a single-member district still put up candidates in those districts. This is because doing so gives them greater visibility in the PR districts where they present party lists and, thus, can and do win seats. This means that the large number of parties that plagued the last system will continue under the current system, but knowing this gives us insight into the manner in which political reform is likely to continue.

Our expectation is that there will continue to be public demand as long as the economic crisis continues and the government refrains from what is perceived to be concerted policy action. This will give those parties that can survive a motion of no confidence in the Lower House of the National Diet and run the government an incentive to continue to manipulate the country's new election institutions under the banner of continuing to promote political reform. In fact, this is exactly what happened as a coalition government led by the Liberal Democratic Party lowered the number of seats available in the PR districts from 200 to 180. In light of this, our expectation then is that genuine political reform will continue to be defined as the need to alter political institutions that will result in a continued manipulation of the rules of the game.

ECONOMIC REFORM AND STRUCTURAL ADJUSTMENT

Our expectation that political reform efforts occur when the costs of inaction exceed the costs of implementing policies that carry negative electoral impacts and that specific policy recommendations be designed to advance the political interests of the governing party (parties) that introduce them can also be applied to the economic reforms that we have witnessed thus far. To explore this idea more fully, we must first understand that the policy imperatives that face a government during a time of a structural adjustment are quire different from those that occur during a downturn in the business cycle. In the case of the former, which has characterized the economic problems Japan has been grappling with in the postbubble period, the best policy is to get out of the way of the adjustments that need to occur but to use the policy process to assuage the social dislocation that are often partner to these kinds of adjustments.

Given that this involves dismantling the kinds of supports that have protected the inefficient producers that are an important part of the LDP's core support, our expectation is that the LDP and the coalition governments it has been leading would not engage in any kind of policy action that would depart radically from what has been occurring throughout the last ten years. Saying this, however, does not mean that parties and politicians in LDP-led governments would have no incentive to depart from the course they have been following in the last several years nor does it mean that all governments should behave in exactly the same way with respect to economic reform. In fact, a look at what has been happening in the last ten years reveals that the governments of the postbubble period have behaved in different ways, and this tells us that every future government will not behave exactly as its predecessor.

Perhaps the most important differences we have witnessed thus far are those that distinguish the behavior of the LDP and non-LDP governments that have held power since the collapse of the economic bubble. Since the summer of 1993 when the LDP was pushed from power for the first time in thirty-eight years, two non-LDP coalitions controlled the Japanese government. The first was a seven-party coalition under the Prime Ministership of Hosokawa Morihiro, and the second was a minority government headed by Hata Tsutomu. At least initially, these two governments enjoyed a large amount of support from Japanese voters who held very different policy priorities than traditional supporters of the Liberal Democratic Party. For example, supporters of the Hosokawa government were most concerned about political reform while nonsupporters were most concerned about business conditions and the continued protection of agriculture.[9] Given this, our expectation is that these two non-LDP governments would move decidedly on the problem of economic reform.

While in power for a short eight months, the Hosokawa government did exactly this, enacting several important reform bills that, among other things, ended the ban on rice imports, reformed the tax system, and established a new tone in U.S.-Japanese economic relations by refusing simply to acquiesce in American pressure as its predecessors were wont to do.[10] The Hosokawa administration was as successful as it was in such a short time not simply because its supporters were in favor of the reforms his government put forward but also because the non-LDP coalition government he led possessed a comfortable majority in the Lower House of the Japanese Diet.[11] This is important because it helps explain why the non-LDP government that was put together in the wake of Hosokawa's resignation over allegations of receiving money from the Sagawa Kyubin company accomplished very little. Hata tsutomu succeeded Hosokawa as Prime Minister, and, while his government's supporters were as pro-reform as those who supported his predecessor, he was not able to advance the reform agenda in an effective manner simply because his minority government did not control a majority of lower house seats.

The remaining governments of the postbubble period have been LDP governments where the erstwhile predominant party ruled either alone or in coalition with other political parties. There have been five LDP administrations since the fall of the Hata government in June 1994, and, when we say that these governments did much less than the non-LDP governments that preceded them, we are not suggesting that they did nothing nor that each responded to the current crisis in exactly the same way. This is particularly true of the Hashimoto (January 1996 to July 1998) and Koizumi (April 2001 to the present) governments, which have not only been more verbally committed to the painful process of reform than the two lackluster LDP administrations that separated them, they have also been more visibly aggressive at trying to implement economic reforms.[12]

Hashimoto's dramatic policy pronouncements were motivated by his desire to lead the erstwhile ruling party back to its position of predominance by luring back former party members and attracting new support form an increasingly impatient Japanese electorate. His efforts in the former area gave the party a razor-thin majority in the Diet's Lower House, but the reforms he implemented, especially his consumption tax increase at a time when a weak recovery had begun, helped plunged the economy back into a state of stagnation. The result was a disastrous showing in the upper-house election of 1998 and Hashimoto's replacement with a much more cautious leader, Obuchi Keizo. The LDP more or less marked time over the next two years, surviving a challenge from the composite New Frontier Party in the lower-house Election of 2000.[13] Nonetheless, the party was not able to rule on its own, which made gaining additional support in the Upper House in the next election critical. It is for this reason that, three months before the next upper-house election, the LDP selected the outspoken Koizumi Junichiro as its next party president and Prime Minister.

Koizumi's commitment to ending the current crisis has been viewed in Japan and elsewhere as sincere because, among other things, his pronouncements have included talk about the pain that would necessarily be partner to meaningful economic reform. His manifest commitment and straight-talking style were initially rewarded with very high support rates for his administration and a decisive victory in the 2001 upper-house election. Unfortunately, Koizumi does not possess his own base of support within the LDP, and, as a result, he is dependent on the support of party leaders for his continuation as party president and Prime Minister. As long as he remains popular with the Japanese electorate, however, his position as Prime Minister is most likely safe because potential challengers will hurt the party's positive image if they act to remove him. This is why Koizumi has worked hard to maintain his popularity with Japanese voters, but this is also why his statements and style worry many other LDP leaders.

On the one hand, paying lip service to the need for meaningful economic reform that is convincing to the Japanese public will be supported by LDP leaders. On the other hand, concerted action to implement such economic reform will be resisted by most party leaders because of how it will negatively affect the LDP's core supporters. It is for this reason that, while viewed suspiciously by many of his own LDP colleagues, Koizumi will continue as LDP president as long as his leadership benefits the party. Unfortunately, over the last twelve months, Koizumi's popularity has undergone dramatic changes. From the time he assumed the Prime Ministership until the end of 2001, Koizumu supporters outnumbered nonsupporters by an average of 50 percentage points. By April of 2002, however, these two groups were nearly even with 42 percent supporting his cabinet and 40 percent in the no support column. Certainly, part of the problem is how Koizumi caved in to party pressure, especially with respect to his popular Foreign Minister, Tanaka Makiko. Unfortunately, his independence from party influences is what helps make him popular among Japanese which means that, his ability to act on Japan's current problems will depend on the levels of support the Japanese public extends to his cabinet.

While this captures the way that our perspective of postwar Japan would deal with the economic policy patterns that have occurred thus far in the postbubble period, we still need to discuss the economic patterns that are most likely to unfold over the next several years. We concluded that the high degree of in-firm training that was necessary during the high-growth period may have contributed to improvements in labor quality and productivity growth during the postwar period. We also stated that this practice helped create a relatively immobile labor force which contributed to Japan's so-called lifetime employment system. Unfortunately, the immobility of labor has become one of the major problems for the Japanese economy now that it is in a period of structural adjustment. For better or worse, the younger generation that has entered the labor market in the postbubble period has never experienced lifetime employment and, as a result, is far more flexible than previous generations of laborers. This leads us to be optimistic in the long term because, as the rapidly aging older portion of the labor force retires, the younger generation will be much better prepared for the mobility and flexibility that will be required in the labor market under the economic structure that will ultimately emerge.

Unfortunately, we cannot be as optimistic about Japan's financial crisis. In some sense, it is correct to speak of Japan's bank centered financial system as "unique," but, as shown above, there is little reason to conclude that it contributed in a positive way to Japan's postwar economic success. Indeed, at least during the bubble period, the dual role of banks as both monitors and creditors seems to have created a serious moral hazard problem. Capital was allocated to often dubious projects, and Japan seems to have accumulated excess capacity in a number of areas that has yet to be worked off. While this misallocation of capital will undoubtedly correct itself at some point, it is unclear whether the same can be said for the inherent moral hazard problem which created the misallocation in the first place. Most debates concerning the banking crisis center on the issue of the use of public funds to allow the banks to write off bad loans and recapitalize. If this were the case, there would be little in terms of disincentives to prevent banks from engaging in risky behavior again in the future. While prudential requirements could potentially prevent a future disaster, the recent experience with such requirements does not instill a great deal of confidence. We believe that the best chance for Japan to avoid future financial crises is if the current economic stagnation effectively renders banks irrelevant. This suggests the appearance of a situation where the bulk of future financial activity is conducted directly through equity markets and corporate debt markets. In such a case, the monitoring relationship between banks and firms would eventually erode as equity markets increasingly take on the role of monitor.

Perhaps our biggest worry is that Japan may take a long time to adjust precisely because it can afford to do so. Japan is a wealthy country with a large current account surplus and large pool of domestic savings. Unlike other nations that, when faced with similar crises, have forced their banks to write off nonperforming loans and force corporations into bankruptcy and unemployment to rise, Japan has taken a slower course. Prudential requirements on the banks have been slowly tightened, and, as some firms have tottered into insolvency, the government has injected money into the economy in order to stabilize employment. Japan has therefore managed to avoid a major social or political crisis, but this has come at the cost of an economy that remains maladjusted and stagnant.

CONCLUSION

The analyses we have provided in this book are based on the idea that there is little about Japan's political-economic system that cannot be explained using traditional social science concepts and methods. To be sure, many standard approaches have to be adapted to capture the different contextual factors that have defined postwar Japan, but the principles guiding the mainstream approaches in economics and political science are more than adequate. As a result, we have presented a picture of postwar Japan that grew rapidly during much of the postwar period because it used more inputs and because the quality of the inputs that were used improved over the same period. We also presented a picture of a Japan that practices democratic politics in a broadly similar fashion to the developed world's parliamentary systems. Finally, the understanding of Japan we developed means that all of Japan's special features, especially those that so many associated with its postwar economic success, are based on an image that was essentially "made in America."

The future will be the final arbiter of what we have done here, something that is true for our explanation of Japan's postwar political-economic trajectory as well as the perspective we offered for the path it is likely to follow in the future. While we welcome challenges, we believe that the future will be kind to our work simply because the ideas we offered in this book have avoided the problem of the Japan that never was.

NOTES

CHAPTER 1

1. See chapter 2 for a review of this scholarship.

2. With respect to the latter, the distinction exists between scholars who identify international conditions as the primary source of Japan's troubles with those who emphasize domestic factors. For the former view see, for example, Gao (2001) and, for the latter, see for example, Katz (1998).

3. See Katz (1998) for the "system that 'soured' " view. The latter quote is from Pempel (1997) who argued that Japan's current troubles are the result of a "regime shift."

4. We should note here that there are some descriptions of Japan's political-economic institutions with which we take issue. Perhaps the most notable of these concerns the assertion that its bureaucrats are powerful, making Japan the model of a country with an autonomous bureaucracy. See Johnson (1982). For a contrary view, see Ramseyer and Rosenbluth (1993).

5. It is important to note here that economic bureaucrats were left alone by the Occupation. Indeed, it was through economic and other bureaucrats who were not purged that the Occupation authorities ruled Japan for the brief time that they did.

6. In fact, the most notable adherents of Johnson's view were nonacademics.

7. As we discuss in more detail in chapter 2 below, the dominant bureaucracy idea far overstates the power of bureaucrats and unjustifiably relegates the influence of elected officials in the economic policy-making process, just like we now know that the behavior of private actors and market forces has been much more important in the process of making economic policy than originally thought.

CHAPTER 2

1. These proponents are discussed briefly below.

2. An excellent example of this would be how Gerald Curtis's 1988 book, mentioned above, updated and partially amended the views of postwar politics contained published earlier in thee postwar period. Examples include the books by Thayer (1969) and Fukui (1970).

3. The most notable example here would be former Princeton University political scientist, William Lockwood. See his essay, "Japan's New Capitalism," in Lockwood (1965).

4. See Johnson (1978).

5. See Johnson (1982).

6. The full statement of Prestowitz's views can be found in Prestowitz (1988).

7. See especially, Fallows (1989 and 1994).

8. Van Wolferen is also president of the Institute for Independent Japanese Studies and has devoted the bulk of his writing to explaining what he originally referred to in a 1986/87 *Foreign Affairs* essay as "the Japan Problem." See van Wolferen (1986/87).

9. We should also point out that there are other revisionists who helped popularize the Chalmers Johnson view of Japan. Perhaps the most notable are Micheal Crichton in his novel, *Rising Sun* (Crichton, 1992), Pat Choate in his book on how Japan's lobbyists in the United States are manipulating America's political and economic system (Choate, 1990), and Eamon Fingleton who argued in his book that Japan was on track to overtake the U.S. by the Year 2000 (Fingleton, 1995).

10. To be fair, we must point out that not all subscribers to the revisionist view would say that Japan is undemocratic. T. J. Pempel, for example, states that Japan has as free and "formally representative" a democracy "as any in the industrialized world," but he reveals his revisionist leanings when he adds that it has at the same time "forged a conservative coalition that for most of the postwar period was also invulnerable to most mass politics. See Pempel (1999), p. 166.

11. See, for example, Calder (1988), Curtis (1988 and 1999), Richardson (1997), Kohno (1997), Flanagan et al., (1991), and Ramseyer and Rosenbluth (1993).

12. This is quite an understatement because, in its first postwar election of 1946, 363 political parties put up candidates. See Scalapino and Masumi (1962), p. 33.

13. See, for example, Fukui (1970) and Thayer (1969). See also, Scalapino and Masumi (1962).

14. Chapter IV, Article 41, "The Constitution of Japan," promulgated 1947.

15. It was from the Government Section of the Allied Occupation of Japan that individuals were chosen to write Japan's postwar constitution, Baerwald included.

16. See Baerwald (1974).

17. When we say both houses, we mean Japan's upper House of Councilors and its lower House of Representatives. It should also be noted that approval of both is required except in the cases of treaties and the budget where the will of the Lower House can prevail. See Baerwald (1974), p. 124.

18. For a comprehensive examination of the Occupation's purge of wartime leaders, see Baerwald (1959).

19. For a representative example of this view, see, for example, Curtis (1988).

20. Johnson (1982), p. 40.

21. The reference here is particularly to the well-known University of Tokyo and, to a lesser extent, the University of Kyoto. The classic study of these and other aspects of Japan's bureaucracy remains Koh (1989).

22. See Johnson (1982), p. 47.

23. See especially Johnson (1995), chapter 9.

24. See, for example, Curtis (1988) and Pempel (1997).

25. See, for example, Woo-Cumings (1999).

26. On this point see Campbell (1984).

27. For an interesting discussion of this topic, as part of a broader discussion of Japanese politics, see Richardson (1997).

28. See, for example, Curtis, (1999), chapter 1, passim.

29. See, for example, Callon (1995), p. 2.

30. See Callon (1995), especially chapter 3. For an interesting discussion of interministerial squabbling in the area of Overseas Development Assistance (ODA), see Arase (1995) and Orr (1990).

31. For instance, Calder (1988) explains LDP intervention in many policy areas as a function of the party compensating support groups while, in the area of environmental policy, McKean (1981) sees LDP intervention as a necessary response to the citizen movements that sprang up around the environmental degradation that was quite prevalent earlier in the postwar period. Anderson (1993) emphasized the role played by coalitions of groups interested in expanding Japan's welfare state. On this policy area, see also Campbell (1992).

32. See Calder (1993), especially chapter 2 and Inoguchi (1983).

33. Samuels (1987).

34. Horne (1985).

35. See Calder (1993), especially chapter 2.

36. See Curtis (1999), Richardson (1997), especially chapter 5, and Sato and Matsuzaki (1987).

37. See Ramseyer and Rosenbluth (1993).

38. See the essays in Cowhey and McCubbins (1998) for applications of this kind of idea to aspects of politics and policy making not covered by Ramseyer and Rosenbluth (1993).

39. See especially Johnson and Keehn (1994), pp. 14–22, and more generally, see Reed (1993).

40. See Curtis (1999), p. 59.

41. See Green and Shapiro (1994).

42. Bates (1981) and Samuel Popkin (1979). For a discussion of rational choice work used in studies of China, see Daniel Little (1991).

43. See Ramseyer and Rosenbluth (1993), especially chapters 6 and 7.

44. What is interesting is that this role differentiation is not entirely inconsistent with the revisionist description of political power in Japan because, as Ramseyer and Rosenbluth have noted, it is the bureaucrats "who faithfully implement LDP policy preferences—who conceive, draft, and implement programs in the shadow of the Diet. See Ramseyer and Rosenbluth (1993), p. 13.

CHAPTER 3

1. There are of course exceptions. See, for example, Trezise (1976 and 1983), Schultze (1983).

2. See especially Johnson (1982).

3. See, for example, Prestowitz (1988) and Fallows (1994).

4. See Johnson (1995), Introduction.

5. The quoted phrase is from the subtitle of Fingleton's (1995) book, *Blindside,* in which he predicted that Japan would overtake the United States by the year 2000.

6. Katz (1998), p. 3. T. J. Pempel (1997) can also be classified as a similar critic who views industrial policy as having worked in the past.

7. Quoted in Okimoto and Rohlen, eds. (1988).

8. A good example of the range of facts that analysts typically cite can be found in Boltho (1985).

9. The argument in Boltho (1985) is illustrative.

10. See, for example, Allen (1980), Boltho (1985), and Katz (1998).

11. This does not mean that economists saw government policy in an entirely negative light because most viewed it as being supportive. See, for example, Patrick and Rosovsky (1976).

12. See, for example, Johnson (1982), chapter 2 and Katz (1998), part II.

13. See, for example, Boltho (1985).

14. See Saxonhouse (1983).

15. See, for example, Prestowitz (1988); Johnson, Tyson, and Zysman (1990); Thurow (1992); and Branden and Spencer (1983).

16. See Krugman (1990).

17. See, for example, Thurow (1992), Fallows (1994), Prestowitz (1988).

18. See especially Krugman (1996).

19. See, for example, Fallows (1994) and Prestowitz (1988).

20. For other studies, see Noland (1993) and Lee (1993).

21. This corresponds to the findings made by Saxonhouse (1983).

22. These are the average annual rates of growth calculated as the difference of logs of real gross output for each sector.

23. See especially Johnson (1982) and Katz (1998).

24. See Beason (1993).

25. The arguments of Prestowitz (1988) and Fallows (1994) are illustrative.

26. Readers interested in the methodology of calculating scale parameters should consult Beason and Weinstein (1996). See also Nakamura (1983).

27. On the problems associated with the concept of competitiveness, see Krugman (1996).

28. For a more detailed explanation of the specific time-series model used in this analysis, see Beason and Weinstein (1996).

29. Data on quotas were available only after 1965.

CHAPTER 4

1. Koike (1987), p. 289.

2. This dispute, however, has become more or less resolved by an emerging consensus that, while economically beneficial throughout most of the postwar period, Japan's labor market institutions have recently become liabilities, inhibiting the country's corporate and political leaders from taking Japan more quickly and effectively through its current period of structural adjustment.

3. As with other topics on the postwar Japanese political-economic system, there are exceptions to our characterization of the literature. On management in firms,

see Aoki (1984, 1987, and 1988) and, on labor relations, see Freeman and Rebick (1989).

4. For example, between 1970 and 1972, the number of workdays lost to strikes per 1000 workers was 96 while the same figures for the United States, France, and Italy were 544, 633, and 906 respectively. See Patrick and Rosovsky (1976), p. 37. We should also point out that Sweden's record was comparable with Japan's (97) while West Germany's was noticeably lower (57). Those European countries that are characterized by corporatist types of socioeconomic organization are also closer to Japan. See Katzenstein (1985) and Schmitter and Glenbruch (1979).

5. See NHK (1991) and Dore (1986), especially chapter 4.

6. The Japanese phrase for this practice is *shushin koyoh,* which translates directly into English as employment for life. For this reason, we use the phrase lifetime employment throughout this chapter.

7. The general exception to this concerns employees who are selected for upper-level management positions because such individuals naturally have a longer tenure with their respective firms.

8. For the Japan is unique view, see for example, Johnson (1982) and Reischauer and Jansen (1995).

9. Employees with lifetime employment are permanent, full-time workers as opposed to the significant number of temporary, part-time workers large firms employ.

10. See Dore (1986) chapter 4 and Reed (1993) chapter 4.

11. The level of an employee's education is not the only important factor in determining the level at which he or she enters a firm. This is also influenced by which university a potential employee attends and whether or not he or she graduates from that university's law faculty.

12. The concomitant to this is that wages for older employees tend to be higher than their productivity levels.

13. See Hattori and Maeda (2000).

14. See, for example, Reischauer and Jansen (1995), especially chapter 34, Thurow (1982) especially chapter 4, and Amsden (1990).

15. Dore (1986) p. 71.

16. See, for example, Reischauer and Jansen (1995), Thurow (1992), Fallows (1994), and Dore (1986).

17. One theme in the literature on Japanese business behavior is that the government encouraged only a certain number of producers in certain areas, leading to an appropriate amount of competition in those industries. See Johnson (1982) and Prestowitz (1988). On conflict as a theme in studies of postwar Japan, see Krauss, et al. (1984).

18. Reischauer and Jansen warn that images like Japan Inc. overstate the closeness of government and private enterprise in Japan; they nonetheless assert that "there is enough truth to the picture of government-business cooperation to form a sharp contrast with the United States, where the two have traditionally been considered to be enemies" (1995), p. 334.

19. Ronald Dore noted that Japanese firms "show a tendency for the balance between perception of competing interests and the perception of a common interest between rival producers of the same commodity to tilt further towards the latter than in most countries" (1986), p. 73.

20. Dore (1986), p. 62.

21. Kawai (1960).

22. Indeed, cynics suggest that university is a four-year party where in Japan students make up for lost time in developing social skills.

23. This corresponds roughly to the first two decades of the twentieth century. See Reed (1993) and Garon (1987).

24. See Dore (1986), p. 92.

25. See, for example, Thurow (1992).

26. Again, see, for example, Thurow (1992) and Fallows (1994).

27. See, for example, Sheard (1996) and Aoki (1988).

28. See Sheard (1996).

29. The near failure of Mazda is a case in point.

CHAPTER 5

1. See Dennison and Chung (1976 and 1977) and Patrick (1976).

2. See Patrick and Rosovsky (1976), especially the last chapter.

3. See, for example, Pempel (1997).

4. See Patrick and Rosovsky (1976), and *Japan Almanac* (1999).

5. This is discussed in Katz (1998), especially chapter 6.

6. Again, see, for example, Pempel (1997), who made Japan's economic growth rates one of the defining features of what he referred to as the Japanese "embedded" neomercantilist "regime."

7. See Okawa and Rosovsky (1973).

8. See *Japan Almanac* (1999).

9. In 1997, the contribution of agriculture to nominal GDP in select developed countries is as follows: U.S., 1.6 percent; U.K. 1.1 percent; Germany 1.1 percent; and France 1.7 percent. See Masami (1999). Japan is also like other developed nations in that the largest contribution to its GDP comes from the service sector.

10. See, for example, Johnson (1995).

11. Japan's imports of finished of finished goods in this year amounted to $60 billion.

12. See *Japan Almanac* (1999). Also, it is important to note that, if Japan imported too little of one product area, it happened to be in the area of services.

13. See, for example, Fallows (1994) and Prestowitz (1988).

14. See, for example, Romer (1986 and 1990).

15. Again, see Romer (1986 and 1990).

16. See section III.

17. This is certainly not true of all that was written on the Japanese economy later in the postwar period because some writers did see that trouble was looming. See, for example, Lincoln (1988), Emmot (1989), and Wood (1994).

18. Johnson (1995), Introduction.

19. Fallows (1994).

20. See Prestowitz (1998).

21. See Prestowitz, *Trading Places*, (1988), passim.

CHAPTER 6

1. See Lupia (2000).

2. See, for example, Dahl (1956) and Lijphart (1999), who are perhaps the most notable examples of empirical democratic theorists. On the deductive side, see in particular, Downs (1957).

3. Again, see Lijphart (1999).

4. Stating that, for a nation to be democratic, it must select the individuals who will hold its highest offices in free and fair elections follows closely the requirements set out in the literature of academic political economy. In this way, the discussion that follows relies much on the ideas contained in Schumpeter (1947) and Downs (1957).

5. We prefer the term *predominant* because it is less authoritarian in tone and less suggestive of election results that are predetermined. For a more complete discussion of this concept and its alternatives, see Sartori (1976).

6. For an interesting discussion of the negotiations that took place in the formation of the LDP and the Japan Socialist Party in 1955, see Kohno (1997).

7. The LDP lost its upper-house majority in the House of Councillors' election in the summer of 1989, and it lost its lower-house majority in the House of Representatives election of July 1993.

8. See Huntington (1991), pp. 266–267, where he proposes a two-turnover test for a democracy to be "consolidated."

9. See chapter 2 above.

10. This does not mean that there are no formal encumbrances because such things as signature requirements to be placed on a ballot and electoral thresholds for parties to be allocated seats in proportional representation districts are a normal part of democratic politics. It does mean that any restrictions must be reasonable, constitutionally sanctioned, and democratically derived.

11. See, for example, Hrebenar (1986).

12. See, for example, Prestowitz (1988) and van Wolferen (1989).

13. Again, the classic work on Japan's political culture can be found in Richardson (1974)

14. See, for example, Nestor (1989).

15. The reference here is to the three national daily newspapers, the *Mainichi Shinbun*, the *Asahi Shinbun*, and the *Yomiuri Shinbun*. To these one could also add the *Nihon Keizai Shinbun,* which would be equivalent to the *Wall Street Journal* in the United States and the *Financial Times* in the U.K.

16. See Reed (1993).

17. See Johnson and Keehn (1994) and, more generally, Green and Shapiro (1994).

18. See chapter 4 above.

19. See Kernell (1991).

20. See Kernell (1991) especially chapter 1.

21. Zoku is usually translated as a "policy tribe" and refers to groups of LDP politicians who specialize in one or more policy areas. The most thorough study of zoku can be found in Inoguchi and Iwai (1987).

22. See Calder (1988).

23. See also Richardson (1997) especially chapter 7 and Cowhey and McCubbins (1995).

24. By extension, this discussion also includes all political parties in a governing coalition.

25. We make this distinction only because not all governing parties actually control a majority of seats in their respective legislatures as has been true for fairly long periods in many Scandinavian countries and for a very short period of time in Japan in 1994. The reference here is the short-lived government of Hata Tsutomu, which lasted for two months in the spring of 1994. See, for example, Budge and Keman (1990) for a discussion of this idea of a party surviving a motion of no confidence.

26. For a further discussion of these ideas, see Budge and Farlie (1983) and Boix (1998).

27. See Curtis (1988) especially chapter 2.

28. The only exception to this concerns the entries for the 1960–1961 data point, which involves the average of only eighteen polls.

29. Small- and medium-size firms, defined as wholesalers and retailers with fewer than 100 employees, service firms with fewer than 50 employees, and all other firms with fewer than 300 employees, have an enormous presence in the Japanese economy. This definition comes from the small business chapter written by Takashi Yokokura in a volume edited by Ryutaro Komiya and others on Industrial Policy. See Komiya et al. (1984).

30. It is not true that support for protecting Japan's farmers has been universal. Since about 1980, Keidanren, or the powerful business group known as the Federation of Economic Organizations, supported opening the rice market as a gesture of cooperation with Japan's trading partners. This was naturally opposed by farmers and by the LDP.

31. We say in principle because Japan was given a six-year grace period from 1995, after which rice was put on a tariff schedule.

32. The legislative act referred to here is the 1942 Staple Food Control Act. Also, it should be pointed out that over time the LDP did eventually reduce the amount of subsidies it extended to the nation's farmers. Moreover, in 1990, the practice of trading in voluntarily marketed rice through bidding was begun. According to a new 1995 Food Law, the Japanese government became limited to purchasing 1.5 million tons of rice whereas in the past it had purchased all domestically produced rice. See, for example, Donnelley (1977).

33. In 1955, 44 percent of Japanese lived in towns and villages, 36 percent lived in cities with a populations of 300,000 or less, and 20 percent lived in cities with a population of 300,000 or more.

34. The new system for the Lower House is a parallel system where 300 seats are selected from single member districts and 200 seats are selected from eleven proportional representation districts. What is interesting is that the single-member district portion of the new system remains malapportioned. As of the summer of 1998, 74 (25%) of the system's 300 districts had more than twice the population of the third best represented district (Shimane 3), and as one would expect, the underrepresented districts were all in urban areas. See *Asahi Nenkan* (1999).

35. Perhaps the quintessential example of this is that of former LDP faction leader and Prime Minister, Tanaka Kakuei, extending a bullet train line and transferring large amounts of government largesse to his home prefecture of Niigata. See Calder (1988) chapter 6.

36. For a more detailed discussion of small business policy in Japan, see Calder (1988), chapter 7 and Patrick and Rohlen (1987).

37. Beason (2000) discusses how the bank-centeredness of Japan's financial system began to change in the 1990s.

38. The reason for the large-firm bias has to do with the fact that banks required their borrowers to maintain compensating balances for the finance they received, a requirement that most small- and medium-size firms could not adhere to. We discuss this and the government's financial institutions in more detail below. See Beason (1993) on how smaller businesses in Japan obtained easier access to private capital as banks accumulated enormous amounts of capital throughout the 1970s and 1980s.

39. Calder (1988), p. 322. This pattern was confirmed by the industrial policy analysis presented in Chapter 3 above.

40. Again see Calder (1988) p. 322. This was also confirmed by the industrial policy analysis presented in chapter 3 above.

CHAPTER 7

1. This phrase is taken from an article written by Masaru Kohno and Yoshitaka Nishizawa on Japan's electoral business cycle. See Kohno and Nishizawa (1990).

2. It is the same kind of electoral imperative that led Edward Tufte to find that certain transfer payments in the United States increased dramatically just before elections. See Tufte (1978).

3. The discussion of political change that follows is the beneficiary of ideas contained in Dalton, Flanagan, and Beck (1984).

4. For a discussion of this idea in the American party system, see Sundquist (1983).

5. See Budge and Farlie (1983), especially chapter 2.

6. For the sake of our discussion here, we are assuming that both ecological and sectoral change lead to a governing party losing support. We do note that, while it is far less common in the experience of governing parties, these two kinds of electoral change can result in a strengthened majority.

7. This is because the most easily identifiable socioeconomic groups will already be part of another party's support constituency, and unless abandoned by that party, such groups will not be available for targeting.

8. The reference here is to policies that lead to the expansion of welfare state benefits such as better health care, pensions, and the like. See Ramseyer and Rosenbluth (1993).

9. These data are from the 1976 JABISS national election survey. See also Steiner, Krauss, and Flanagan (1980), especially chapters 6–8.

10. The implication here is that, in response to electoral imperatives, members of the U.S. Senate and House of Representatives behave in the same fundamental manner, party differences notwithstanding. For a discussion of this kind of politician behavior in the United States, see Mayhew (1974).

11. When we use the phrase "fortunate geography," we are referring to the fact that all but two of Japan's major cities are on coastal plains, which allows their air to ventilate quickly and that most of Japan's rivers run fast enough to clean themselves once pollution is haltd at its source.

12. The Jiji data show that LDP support from owners of small- and medium-size firms dropped nearly fifteen percentage points between 1968 and 1974 alone.

13. The discussion that follows is based on Patterson (1994a).

14. One of the most interesting discussions of the economic role played by small firms in Japan is found in an edited volume on industrial policy. Unfortunately, the volume and the chapter on small- and medium-size businesses in Japan is in Japanese. For those with the requisite skills, see Yokokura (1984).

15. The quote is from Calder (1988), p. 343.

16. For a discussion, see Cole (1959).

17. Again, see Calder (1988).

18. Perhaps the best English language treatment of the Japanese financial system is Suzuki (1987). While dated, the book by Adachi (1983) is a good general introduction in Japanese. See also Calder (1993).

19. For a discussion of these issues, see Hamada and Horiuchi (1987) Beason (1993), and Suzuki (1980 and 1987).

20. For the calculations used to produce these data, see Beason (1993).

21. See Johnson (1978), p. 148.

22. This was the Law Concerning Special Measures for Long Term Investment of the Trust Fund Bureau Funds and Funds Accumulated from Postal Annuities and the Postal Life Insurance Annuity. See Calder (1988 and 1993).

23. What is interesting about this point is that it was made by Chalmers Johnson in his book on Japan's public policy companies. See Johnson (1978).

24. This phrase is from Suzuki (1987).

25. We excluded the Central Cooperative Bank for Commerce and Industry because the lion's share of this institution's funds have been raised through the issuance of bank debentures. Data on lending amounts for each of the above institutions was taken from *Keizai Tokei Nenpo* [Economic Statistics Annual], published by the Bank of Japan. See Nihon Ginko (various years).

26. For a more detailed discussion of this process, see Davis, Dempster, and Wildavsky (1966) and, in Japan, Campbell (1977).

27. Government borrowing amounted to 25 percent of the FILP in the 1960s but dropped to 5 percent in 1975.

28. This twenty-year span of time has been chosen for this analysis because it begins with a period when small business owners were loyal to the LDP and covers succeeding periods when these core supporters fell away from the LDP only to return several years later.

29. Time series models involve a certain set of statistical problems that, if present and left unattended, can lead to biased estimates. The estimates presented in Table 4.3 are the result of all necessary statistical tests being performed and necessary corrections being made. For a more detailed of the statistical issues associated with this model, see Patterson (1994a).

30. A rural area is defined as a regional municipality with fewer than 300,000 people.

31. See Horie and Umemura (1986), especially chapter 1.

32. The LDP's use of public goods in its electoral strategy is discussed more fully in Ramseyer and Rosenbluth (1993).

33. The classic example of a public good is national defense, which all citizens of a nation receive whether they are taxpayers or not.

34. As explained above, the LDP's majority in the Diet had declined substantially by the 1970s, which forced it to find new support. For a general discussion of the politics of welfare policy in Japan, see Anderson (1993).

35. The discussion that follows is taken from Patterson and Beason (2001).

36. There have been instances when as many a three supplementary budgets have been passed in a single calendar year. See Campbell (1977), especially chapter 8.

37. An example of this would be the supplementary budget that was enacted on September 2, 1978. See *Asahi Nenkan* (1979).

38. In 1977 and 1978, there were four supplementary budgets that were enacted to carry out economic stimulus (*keizai taisaku*) as well as other fiscal policies. However, as explained above, unlike those presented in the table, these four packages did not involve separate government announcements. We should add here that LDP General Secretary, Nonaka Hiromu, stated publicly that he wanted a fiscal stimulus packaged to be implemented just before the June 2000 election, but one was not officially announced and put together at that time.

39. While this methodology produces numbers comparable with the "consensus" understanding of the value of the economic stimulus packages, it still somewhat overstates the magnitude of many of them. Perhaps the best illustration of this is the September 1995 package. When loan allocations and previously budgeted land purchases are netted from the ¥14 trillion total, ¥9 trillion of expenditure remains. Of this amount, ¥1.1 trillion was earmarked for Uruguay Round countermeasures, but it was not made clear whether this would be allocated to expenditure or loan programs. Depending on the outcome, the calculated total of "hard" expenditure would be ¥7.9 to ¥9.0 trillion.

40. For an illustrative discussion of efforts by the Ministry of Finance to reduce budget deficits in the 1970s, see, for example, Noguchi (1987).

41. *Far Eastern Economic Review*, March 11, 1993.

42. For evidence of this view of economic stimulus policies, see Beason (2000).

43. Both lower-house (House of Representatives) and upper-house (House of Councillors) contests are included in our statistical analysis.

44. During the twenty-four-year period from 1975 to 1998 inclusive, twenty-six cabinet reshuffles occurred.

45. Jijitsushinsha (1981 and 1992). Cabinet support data collected by *Jijitsushinsha* after 1991 were provided by the Chuo Chosasha.

46. For the period under consideration, the mean value of the year-on-year changes in the production index was 2.79, while minimum and maximum values were −19.2 and 14.0 respectively.

47. There are a number of statistical issues associated with this type of analysis. For example, one important issue involves whether or not package announcements exhibit some temporal dependence. For this reason, results are presented both with and without a time dependent control to illustrate that the model is robust is both cases. If the reader is interested in an extended discussion of these and other statistical issues, see Patterson and Beason (2001).

48. See Richardson (1997), especially chapter 7.

49. Again, see Richardson (1997).

50. See Curtis (1988), Kato (1994), and Richardson (1997).

51. See Kato (1994), Kernell (1991), and Richardson (1997).

52. This is true for the 1988 upper-house election and the 1993 lower-house election.

53. This is a point discussed by Kabashima (1998), especially chapter 3.

CHAPTER 8

1. To be fair, Curtis (1988) does address this theme of underlying political change in his earlier assessment of postwar Japanese politics.

2. The term *dissolution* here does not refer to the LDP itself but rather the 1955 party system it once headed as Japan's predominant party.

3. The party returned to power in June 1994, but only as part of a coalition led by a Prime Minister from the Social Democratic Party of Japan (SDPJ). It is currently the largest member of a three-party coalition that includes the Conservative Party and the Komeito.

4. In the 1993 election, the LDP received 36.6 percent of the national vote, while, in 1996, it received 32.8 percent of the vote in the single-member districts and 38.5 percent of the vote in the nation's proportional representation (PR) districts. See Ashai Shinbun *Senkyo Honbu* (1997). In the June 2000 election, the LDP did somewhat better, receiving 41 percent of the vote in the nation's single-member districts but only 29 percent of the vote in the PR districts. See *Chunichi Shimbun,* June 26, 2000.

5. The LDP's seat bonus was particularly notable in the nation's 300 single-member districts where the party received 32.8 percent of the vote but 169 or 56 percent of the seats. In the nation's PR districts, the party received 38.5 percent of the vote but 70 or 35 percent of the seats. In the June 2000 election the LDP received 41 percent of the vote in the system's single-member districts but 59 percent of the seats and 29 percent of the vote in the PR districts but only 31 percent of the seats.

6. Many analysts of Japanese politics did not view the LDP's electoral defeat in 1989 as contrary to the party's resurgence because, being less powerful than the House of Representatives, they reasoned that what happened in the Upper House would not repeat itself in the Lower House.

7. See, for example, Curtis (1988) and Sato and Matsuzaki (1986 and 1987).

8. As one might guess, the postwar party system in Japan is known as the 1955 system.

9. In this sense, our treatment is no different, but for the most notable exceptions, see Kohno (1997), Masumi (1962), and Patterson (1994b).

10. There were lower house elections held in 1946, 1947, 1949, 1952, and 1953 during this presystem period.

11. 1980 and 1986, the LDP obtained 47.9 percent and 49.4 percent of the vote respectively but in 1979 and 1983, the party received only 44.6 percent and 45.8 percent respectively.

12. The first of the new conservative parties was the *Nihon Shinto* or Japan New Party. The other two were the *Shinseito* or New Life Party and the *Shinto Sakigake* or New Party Harbinger.

13. For a discussion of the evolution of political parties during this time, see Hrebenar (2000) and Curtis (1999).

14. For example, the well-known Japanese sociologist, Watanuki Joji referred to the period of predominance and the left-right battles that were its hallmark as Japan's "culture politics." We should add here that Revisionists, who relegate elected officials to a secondary role in the policy process, have also taken LDP predominance as a given. See Kohno (1997) especially chapters 1 and 2 for a discussion of revisionist as well as other views on party politics in postwar Japan.

15. For the genesis of this view, see Inglehart (1977), and for its application to the Japanese system, see Flanagan (1984).

16. See, for example, NHK (1991) and Sato and Matsuzaki (1986).

17. For a more detailed discussion of these reasons, see, for example, Sato and Matsuzaki (1986 and 1987) and Curtis (1988).

18. Campbell (1966), p. 44.

19. A more recent example of this is the fact that most unaffiliated electors voted for the Democratic Party of Japan in the 2000 lower-house election. As many as 37 percent voted for the DPJ while that party's vote share for all Japanese was 15 percent.

20. This argument is perhaps most developed in Richardson (1997) and in Curtis (1999).

21. See Richardson (1997) passim and Kabashima (1998).

22. While Richardson (1997) argues that candidate oriented voting choices have been important in Japanese elections, he adds that many farmer and business LDP supporters turned against the party in the watershed election of 1993 because of policies the party supported that hurt their interests. He also argues that members of Japan's urban, educated, and nationally oriented electorate turned against the LDP because of such issues as corruption and a poorly performing economy.

23. See the Classic article by one of the original members of the American Voter team, Philip Converse, "The Concept of a Normal Vote," in Converse (1966). See also Petrocik (1989).

24. For a discussion of the tenets of saliency theory as well as its application, see Budge and Farlie (1983) and Petrocik (1996).

25. See Budge and Farlie (1983), chapter 2.

26. The saliency theory framework also assumes that the electoral impacts of salient issues are static and remain consistent over long periods of time.

27. For a detailed discussion of this content analysis conducted for the postwar period, see Patterson (1994b).

28. Studies were available for the 1967, 1969, 1976, 1983, 1993, and 1996 lower-house elections. We also consulted election surveys taken by Japan's Clean Election League.

29. The one exception to this is the short-lived government led by Japan New Party leader, Hosokawa Morihiro, which proved to be competent and popular in the foreign policy area.

30. Dropping a dummy variable for one electoral period is necessary to eliminate multicolinearity among the regressors. In the model, the first electoral period dummy has been removed, which eliminates the statistical problem but also facilitates testing the hypothesis that the LDP's underlying support continued to decline throughout the postwar period.

31. The Regression F Statistic is F = 78.10 at a confidence level of Prob >F 0.0000).

32. This is obviously not the only reason the LDP endured for nearly four decades as ruling party because Opposition fragmentation was an important factor to be sure. Nonetheless, the significantly high level of underlying support the party enjoys illustrates the electoral difficulties the Opposition has faced in trying to oust the party from the governing position.

33. This is accomplished by taking each election's issue score, multiplying it by the coefficient on the "issues" variable in Table 6.3, and then either adding or subtracting that percentage from the LDP's actual vote share in each election.

CHAPTER 9

1. See Landsberg (1993), chapter 2.

2. This is obviously an oversimplified picture for the simple reason that for a short time a non-LDP ruled Japan that enacted a number of political reforms.

Moreover, even certain LDP leaders appeared to break out of their mold and enacted some kind of reform, like Hashimoto's Big Bang and Koizumi with his strong pro-reform rhetoric. These specific cases will be considered in greater detail below.

3. Nonaka Hiromu (2002), "Jakusha Kirisute Wa Seiji De Wa Nai," [Cutting Down the Weak Is Not Politics] *Chuo Koron* (April): 61–63.

4. The minor reforms referred to here involve the adding of Lower House seats to urban areas that had exploded with population growth throughout the postwar period while reducing the number of Lower House seats in some of those rural areas that had experienced a distinct decline in population.

5. See, for example, Curtis (1999).

6. The discussion that follows is from Patterson (1998 and 2003).

7. The Japanese term for this home base is *jiban*.

8. The data for this analysis came from Miyagawa (1996).

9. See *Yomiuri Nenkan* (1995) and Patterson (1994c)

10. It was also the Hosokawa administration which finally effected the replacement of Japan's old election system with a new set of rules.

11. This is also why some of the Hosokawa's legislative problems occurred in the Upper House where his coalition did not possess a majority.

12. The reference here is to the cabinets led by Obuchi Keizo and Mori Toshiro.

13. One important reason for this was that potential support for the New Frontier Party was diluted by the appearance of a new opposition party, the Democratic Party of Japan.

REFERENCES

Abegglen, James C. (1958). *The Japanese Factory: Aspects of Its Social Organization.* New York: The Free Press.

Abegglen, James C. (ed.) (1970). *Business Strategies for Japan.* Tokyo: Sophia University.

Adachi, Tetsuo (1972). *Gendai no Ginko* [Contemporary Banking]. Tokyo: Nihon Keizai Shimbunsha.

Allen, G. C. (1980). *Japan's Economic Policy.* London and Basingstoke: Macmillan Press.

Almond, Gabriel A. and Sidney Verba (1963). *The Civic Culture: Political Attitudes and Democracy in Five Nations.* Boston: Little, Brown, and Co.

Amsden, Alice (1990). "East Asia's Challenge to Standard Economics," *The American Prospect* (Summer).

Anderson, Stephen J. (1993). *Welfare Policy and Politics in Japan.* New York: Paragon Books.

Aoki, Masahiko (ed.) (1984). *The Economic Analysis of the Japanese Firm.* Amsterdam: North Holland.

Aoki, Masahiko (1987). "The Japanese Firm in Transition," in Kozo Yamamura and Yasukichi Yasuba (eds.), *The Political Economy of Japan, Volume 1: The Domestic Transformation.* Stanford: Stanford University Press.

Aoki, Masahiko (1988). *Information, Incentives, and Bargaining in the Japanese Economy.* New York: Cambridge University Press.

Aoki, Masahiko (1990). "Toward an Economic Model of the Japanese Firm," *Journal of Economic Literature* 28: 1–27.

Arase, David (1995). *Buying Power: The Political Economy of Japan's Foreign Aid.* Boulder, CO: Lynne Reinner.

Asahi Nenkan (various years). [Asahi Yearbook]. Tokyo: Asahi Shimbunsha.

Asahi Shimbun (1997). *Senkyo Honbu* [Election Compendium]. Tokyo: Asahishimbunsha.

Baerwald, Hans (1974). *Japan's Parliament: An Introduction.* New York: Cambridge University Press.

Baerwald, Hans (1959). *The Purge of Japanese Leaders Under the Occupation.* Berkeley and Los Angeles: University of California Press.

Bates, Robert (1981). *Markets and States in Tropical Africa.* Berkeley and Los Angeles: University of California Press.

199

Beason, Richard (1993). "Cost of Borrowed Funds by Firm Scale in Japan: An Empirical Study," *Economic Studies Quarterly* (March).

Beason, Richard (2000). "Separation Risk and Firm Size-Earnings Relationships in Japan and the United States," *Japan and the World Economy* 12;3: 193–209.

Beason, Dick and David Weinstein (1996). "Growth, Economies of Scale, and Targeting in Japan (1945–1990)," *Review of Economics and Statistics* 78: 286–295.

Boix, Carles (1998). *Political Parties, Growth, and Equality: Conservative and Social Democratic Economic Strategies in the World Economy*. Cambridge: Cambridge University Press.

Boltho, Andrea (1985). "Was Japan's Industrial Policy Successful," *Cambridge Journal of Economics*. 9: 187–201.

Brandon, James A. and Barbara Spencer (1983). "International R&D Rivalry and Industrial Strategy," *Review of Economic Studies* 50: 707–722.

Budge, Ian and Denis Farlie (1983). Explaining and Predicting Elections. London: Allen and Unwin.

Budge, Ian and Hans Keman (1990). *Parties and Democracy: Coalition Formation and Government Functioning in Twenty States*. Oxford: Oxford University Press.

Calder, Kent (1988). *Crisis and Compensation: Public Policy and Political Stability in Japan*. Princeton: Princeton University Press.

Calder, Kent (1993). *Strategic Capitalism: Private Business and Public Purpose in Japanese Industrial Finance*. Princeton: Princeton University Press.

Callon, Scott (1995). *Divided Sun: MITI and the Breakdown of Japanese High-Tech Industrial Policy, 1975–1993*. Stanford, CA: Stanford University Press.

Campbell, Angus et al. (1960). *The American Voter*. New York: John Wiley and Sons.

Campbell, Angus (1966). Surge and Decline: A Study of Electoral Change," in Angus Campbell et al. (eds.), *Elections and the Political Order*. New York: Wiley.

Campbell, John C. (1977). *Contemporary Japanese Budgetary Politics*. Berkeley and Los Angeles: University of California Press.

Campbell, John C. (1984). "Policy Conflict and Its Resolution Within the Governmental System," in Ellis Krauss et al. (eds.), *Conflict in Japan*. Honolulu: University of Hawaii Press.

Campbell, John C. (1992). *How Policies Change: The Japanese Government and the Aging Society*. Princeton: Princeton University Press.

Choate, Pat (1990). *Agents of Influence*. New York: Alfred Knopf.

Chunichi Shimbun (2000). [Chunichi Newspaper]. June 26.

Coburn, Judith. (1969). "Asian Scholars and Government: The Chrysanthemum on the Sword," in Edward Friedman and Mark Seldon (eds.), *America's Asia: Dissenting Essays on Asian-American Relations*. New York: Random House.

Cole, Allen R. (1959). *Political Tendencies of Japanese in Small Enterprises*. New York: Institute of Pacific Relations.

Converse, Philip (1966). "The Concept of a Normal Vote," in Angus Campbell et al. (eds.) *Elections and the Political Order*. New York: John Wiley and Sons.

Cowhey, Peter and Matthew McCubbins (1998). *Structure and Policy in Japan and the United States*. New York: Cambridge University Press.

Crichton Michael (1992). *Rising Sun*. New York: Bantam Books.

Curtis, Gerald (1988). *The Japanese Way of Politics*. New York: Columbia University Press.

Curtis, Gerald (1999). *The Logic of Japanese Politics*. New York: Columbia University Press.

Dahl, Robert (1961). *Who Governs: Democracy and Power in an American City*. New Haven: Yale University Press.

Dahl, Robert (1956). *A Preface to Democratic Theory*. Chicago: University of Chicago Press.

Dalton, Russell J., Scott C. Flanagan, and Paul Beck (1984). *Electoral Change in Advanced Industrial Democracies*. Princeton: Princeton University Press.

Davis, Otto, M. Dempster, and Aaron Wildavsky (1966). "Theories of the Budgeting Process," *American Political Science Review* 60: 529–547.

Dennison, Edward and William Chung (1976). "Economic Growth and Its Sources," in Hugh Patrick and Henry Rosovsky, (eds.) *Asia's New Giant: How the Japanese Economy Works*. Washington, D.C.: The Brookings Institution, pp. 63–162.

Dennison, Edward and William Chung (1977). *How Japan's Economy Grew So Fast*. Washington, D.C.: The Brookings Institution.

Domhoff, G. William (1978). *The Powers that Be: Processes of Ruling Class Domination in America*. New York: Random House.

Donnelley, Michael W. (1977). "Setting the Price for Rice: A Study in Political Decisionmaking," in T. J. Pempel (ed.), *Policymaking in Contemporary Japan*. Ithaca: Cornell University Press.

Dore, Ronald (1986). *Flexible Rigidities: Industrial Policy and Structural Adjustment in the Japanese Economy, 1970–80*. Stanford: Stanford University Press.

Downs, Anthony (1957). *An Economic Theory of Democracy*. New York: Harper Collins.

Emmott, Bill (1989). *The Sun Also Sets*. New York: Times Books.

Far Eastern Economic Review (1993). March 11.

Fallows, James (1989). "Containing Japan," *The Atlantic* (May).

Fallows, James (1994). *Looking at the Sun: The Rise of the New East Asian Economy and Political System*. New York: Pantheon Books.

Fingleton, Eamonn (1995). *Blindside: How Japan Is Still on Track to Overtake the U.S. by the Year 2000*. New York: Houghton Mifflin.

Flanagan, Scott C. (1984). "Electoral Change in Japan: A Study of Secular Realignment," in Russell Dalton, et al. (eds.), *Electoral Change in Advanced Industrial Democracies*. Princeton: Princeton University Press.

Flanagan, Scott C. et al. (1991). *The Japanese Voter*. New Haven, CT: Yale University Press.

Freeman, C. (1987). *Technology Policy and Economic Performance: Lessons from Japan*. New York: Pinter Publishers.

Freeman, R. B. and Marcus E. Rebick (1989). "Crumbling Pillar? Declining Union Density in Japan," *Journal of Japan and The International Economies* 3: 578–605.

Fukui, Haruhiro (1970). *Party in Power: The Japanese Liberal Democrats and Policymaking.* Berkeley and Los Angeles: University of California Press.

Gao, Bai (2001). *Japan's Economic Dilemma: The Institutional Origins of Prosperity and Stagnation.* Cambridge: Cambridge University Press.

Garon, Sheldon (1987). *The State and Labor in Modern Japan.* Berkeley and Los Angeles: University of California Press.

Garvey, Gerald T. and Peter Swan (1996). "Corporate Governance and Employment Incentives: Is the Japanese system Really Different," in Paul Sheard (ed.) *Japanese Firms, Finance, and Markets.* Melbourne: Addison-Wesley.

Green, Donald and Ian Shapiro (1994). *Pathologies of Rational Choice Theory.* New Haven: Yale University Press.

Hamada, Koichi and Akira Horiuchi (1987). "The Political Economy of the Financial Market," in Kozo Yamamura and Yasukichio Yasuba (eds.), *The Political Economy of Japan, Volume 1: The Domestic Transformation.* Standord: Stanford University Press.

Hattori, Ryota and Eiji Maeda (2000). "The Japanese Employment System (Summary)," *Bank of Japan Monthly Bulletin.* (January) (English Summary)

Horie, Fukashi and Mitsuhiro Umemura (1986). *Tohyo Kodo to Seiji Ishiki* [Voting Behavior and Political Consciousness]. Tokyo: Keio Tsushin.

Horne, James (1985). *Financial Markets: Conflict and Consensus in Policymaking.* Sydney: Allen and Unwin.

Hrebenar, Ronald J. (1986). *The Japanese Party System: From One-Party Rule to Coalition Government.* Boulder, CO: Westview Press.

Hrebenar, Ronald J. (2000). *Japan's New Party System.* Boulder, CO: Westview Press.

Huntington, Samuel (1991). *The Third Wave: Democratization in the Late Twentieth Century.* Norman, OK: University of Oklahoma Press.

Inglehart, Ronald (1977). *Silent Revolution: Changing Values and Political Styles Among Western Publics.* Ann Arbor: University of Michigan Press.

Inoguchi, Takashi (1983). *Gendai Nihon Seiji Keizai no Kozu* [The Composition of the Modern Japanese Political Economy]. Tokyo: Keizaishimposha.

Inoguchi, Takashi and Tomoaki Iwai (1987). *Zokugiin no Kenkyu: Jiminto Seiken o Gyujiru Shuyaku Tachi* [A Study of Policy Tribes: major Actors of LDP Governments]. Tokyo: Nihon Keizai Shimbunsha.

Japan Almanac (1999). Tokyo: Asahi Shimbunsha.

Jijitsushinsha (various years). *Jiji Nenkan* [Jiji Yearbook]. Tokyo: Jijitsushinsha.

Jijitsushinsha (1981 and 1992). *Sengo Nihon no Naikaku to Seito* [Postwar Japanese Parties and Cabinets]. Tokyo: Jijitsushinsha.

Johnson, Chalmers (1978). *Japan's Public Policy Companies.* Washington, D.C.: The American Enterprise Institute.

Johnson, Chalmers (1982). *MITI and the Japanese Miracle.* Stanford: Stanford University Press.

Johnson, Chalmers (1995). *Japan: Who Governs? The Rise of the Developmental State.* New York: W. W. Norton.

Johnson, Chalmers (1998). "Cold War Economics Melt Asia," *The Nation* (February 23): 16–19.

Johnson, Chalmers and E. B. Keehn (1994). "A Disaster in the Making: Rational Choice and Asian Studies," *The National Interest* (Summer): 14–22.

Johnson, Chalmers, Laura Tyson, and John Zysman (eds.), (1990). *Politics and Productivity: The Real Story of Why Japan Works*. New York: Ballinger.

Kabashima, Ikuo (1998). *Seiken Kotai to Yukensha no Taido Henyo* [Political Change and the Changing Content of Voter Attitudes]. Tokyo: Bokutakusha.

Kato, Junko (1994). *The Problem of Bureaucratic Rationality: Tax Politics in Japan*. Princeton: Princeton University Press.

Katz, Richard (1998). *Japan: The System That Soured*. Armonk, NY: M. E. Sharpe.

Katzenstein, Peter (1985). *Small States in World Markets*. Ithaca, NY: Cornell University Press.

Kawai Kazuo (1960). *Japan's American Interlude*. Chicago: University of Chicago Press.

Kernell, Samuel (ed.) (1991). *Parallel Politics: Economic Policymaking in the United States and Japan*. Washington, D.C.: The Brookings Institution.

Kinmouth, Earl H. (1986). "Engineering Education and Its Rewards in the U.S. and Japan," *Comparative Education Review* 30: 396–416.

Koh, B. C. (1989). *Japan's Administrative Elite*. Berkeley and Los Angeles: University of California Press.

Kohno, Masaru (1997). *Japan's Postwar Party Politics*. Princeton: Princeton University Press.

Kohno, Masaru and Yoshitaka Nishizawa (1990). "A Study of the Electoral Business Cycle in Japan," *Comparative Politics* 22:151–166.

Koike Kazuo (1987). "Human Resource Development and Labor-Management elations," in Kozo Yamamura and Yasukichio Yasuba (eds.), *The Political Economy of Japan, Volume 1: The Domestic Transformation*. Stanford: Stanford University Press.

Komiya, Ryutaro et al. (eds.) (1984). *Nihon no Sangyo Seisaku* [Japanese Industrial Policy]. Tokyo: Tokyo Daigaku Shuppankai.

Krauss, Ellis S., Thomas P. Bohlen, and Patricia G. Steinhoff (1984). *Conflict in Japan*. Honolulu: University of Hawaii Press.

Krugman, Paul R. (1990). *Rethinking International Trade*. Cambridge, MA: The MIT Press.

Krugman, Paul R. (1996). *Pop Internationalism*. Cambridge, MA: The MIT Press.

Landsburg, Steven E. (1993). *The American Economist: Economics and Everyday Life*. New York: The Free Press.

Lee, Hiro (1993). "General Equilibrium Evaluation of Industrial Policy in Japan," *Journal of Asian Economics* 4: 25–40.

Lijphart, Arend (1999). *Patterns of Democracy*. New Haven, CT: Yale University Press.

Lincoln, Edward J. (1988). *Japan: Facing Economic Maturity*. Washington, D.C.: Brookings Institution Press.

Little, Daniel (1991). "Rational Choice Models and Asian Studies," *The Journal of Asian Studies*. (February): 35–52.

Lockwood, William (1965). "Japan's New Capitalism," in William Lockwood (ed.), *The State and Economic Enterprise in Postwar Japan*. Princeton: Princeton University Press.

Lupia, Arthur (2000). "Evaluating Political Science Research: Information for Buyers and Sellers," *PS: Political Science and Politics* (March): 23;1: 7–13.

Masumi, Junnosuke (1962). *Parties and Politics in Contemporary Japan.* Berkeley and Los Angeles: University of California Press.

Mayhew, David (1974). *Congress: The Electoral Connection.* New Haven, CT: Yale University Press.

McKean, Margaret (1981). *Environmental Protest and Citizen Politics in Japan.* Berkeley and Los Angeles: University of California Press.

Mills C. Wright (1956). *The Power Elite.* New York: Oxford University Press.

Ministry of International Trade and Industry (1960–1990). *White Papers on Small- and Medium-Sized Firms.* Tokyo: MITI.

Miyagawa, Kogi (1996). *Shosenkyoku Handobukku.* [Small Election District Handbook]. Tokyo: Seiji Koho Senta.

Nakamura, T. (1981). *The Postwar Japanese Economy—Its Development and Structure.* Tokyo: University of Tokyo Press.

Nakamura, S. (1983). "Explaining the Japan and U.S. TFP Difference," *The Economic Studies Quarterly* 43: 326–336.

Nakasone Yasuhiro (1998). "Politicians, Bureaucrats, and Policymaking in Japan," in Frank Gibney (ed.), *Unlocking the Bureaucrat's Kingdom.* Washington, D.C.: The Brookings Institution.

Nestor, William (1989). "Japan's Mainstream Press: Freedom to Conform?" *Pacific Affairs* 62: 29–39.

Nihon Ginko (various years). *Keizai Tokei Nenpo* [Economic Statistics Annual]. Tokyo: Nihon Ginko.

NHK (1991). *Gendai Nihonjin no Ishiki Kozo, Dai San Kan* [The Structure of Modern Japanese Consciousness, 3rd Edition]. Tokyo: NHK Books.

Noguchi, Yukio (1987). "Public Finance," in Kozo Yamamura and Yasukichio Yasuba (eds.), *The Political Economy of Japan, Volume 1: The Domestic Transformation.* Stanford: Stanford University Press.

Noland, Marcus (1993). "The Impact of Industrial Policy on Japan's Trade Specialization," *Review of Economics and Statistics* (May): 241–248.

Nonaka Hiromu (2002). "Jakusha Kirisute Wa Seiji De Wa Nai" [Cutting Down the Weak Is Not Politics]. *Chuo Koron* April: 61–63.

Okimoto, Daniel (1989). *Between MITI and the Marketplace: Japanese Industrial Policy for High Technology.* Stanford: Stanford University Press.

Okimoto, Daniel and Thomas Rohlen (1988). *Inside the Japanese System: Readings on Contemporary Society and Political Economy.* Stanford: Stanford University Press.

Orr, Robert M. (1990). *The Emergence of Japan's Foreign Aid Power.* New York: Columbia University Press.

Patrick, Hugh and Henry Rosovsky (eds.) (1976). *Asia's New Giant: How the Japanese Economy Works.* Washington, D.C.: The Brookings Institution.

Patrick, Hugh and Thomas Rohlen (1987). "Small-Scale Family Enterprises," in Kozo Yamamura and Yasukichio Yasuba (eds.), *The Political Economy of Japan, Volume 1: The Domestic Transformation.* Stanford: Stanford University Press.

Patterson, Dennis P. (1994a). "Electoral Interest and Economic Policy: The Political Origins of Financial Aid to Small Business in Japan," *Comparative Political Studies* 27: 425–447.

Patterson, Dennis P. (1994b). "Issues, Agendas, and Outcomes in Postwar Japanese Politics," Ph.D. Dissertation, University of California, Los Angeles; Department of Political Science.

Patterson, Dennis P. (1994c). "The Demand for Political Reform in Japan," *The Public Perspective* (May–June).

Patterson, Dennis P. (1998). "New Rules, Old Outcomes: Explaining the Political Impact of Japan's New Election System," in Michael Donneley (ed.), *Confidence and Uncertainty in Japan: Proceedings of the Tenth Annual Conference of the Japan Studies Association of Canada.* Toronto: University of Toronto–York University Joint Center for Asia Pacific Studies.

Patterson, Dennis P. and Richard Beason (2001). "Politics, Pressure, and Economic Policy: Explaining Japan's Use of Fiscal Stimulus Policies," *World Politics* (July).

Patterson, Dennis P. (2003). "Continuity by Design: The Electoral Impacts of Japan's Double-Ballot, Parallel Election System," Texas Tech University, Photocopy.

Pempel, T. J. (ed.) (1990). *Uncommon Democracies: The One-Party Dominant Regimes.* Ithaca, NY: Cornell University Press.

Pempel, T. J. (1997). *Regime Shift: Comparative Dynamics of the Japanese Political Economy.* Ithaca, NY: Cornell University Press.

Pempel, T. J. (1998). "Japan's Search for a New Path," *Current History.* December: 431–436.

Pempel, T. J. (1999). "The Developmental Regime in a Changing World Economy," in Meredith Woo Cumings ed. *The Developmental State.* Ithaca, NY: Cornell University Press.

Petrocik, John R. (1989). "An Expected Party Vote: New Data for an Old Concept," *American Journal of Political Science* 33: 44–66.

Petrocik, John R. (1996). "Issue Ownership in Presidential Elections with a 1980 Case Study," *American Journal of Political Science* 40: 825–850.

Popkin, Samuel (1979). *The Rational Peasant.* Berkeley and Los Angeles: University of California Press.

Prestowitz, Clyde (1988). *Trading Places: How We Are Giving Our Future to Japan and How to Reclaim It.* New York: Basic Books.

Prestowitz, Clyde (1998). "If Japan Crashes, How Bad Can It Be?" *World Press Review* June: 11–13.

Ramseyer, A. Mark and Frances Rosenbluth (1993). *Japan's Political Marketplace.* Cambridge, MA: Harvard University Press.

Reed, Steven (1993). *Making Common Sense of Japan.* Pittsburgh, PA: University of Pittsburgh Press.

Reischauer, Edwin O. and Marius Jensen (1995). *The Japanese Today: Continuity and Change.* Cambridge: Belknap Press of Harvard University.

Richardson, Bradley (1974). *The Political Culture of Japan.* Berkeley and Los Angeles: University of California Press.

Richardson, Bradley (1997). *Japanese Democracy: Power, Coordination, and Distribution.* New Haven, CT: Yale University Press.

Romer, Paul (1986). "Increasing Returns and Long-Run Growth," *Journal of Political Economy* 94: 1002–1037.

Romer, Paul (1990). "Endogenous Technological Change," *Journal of Political Economy* 98: 571–602.

Said, Edward (1979). *Orientalism.* New York: Vintage Books.

Sartori, Giovanni (1976). *Parties and Party Systems: A Framework for Analysis.* New York: Cambridge University Press.

Samuels, Richard (1987). *The Business of the Japanese State: Energy Markets in Comparative and Historical Perspective.* Ithaca, NY: Cornell University Press.

Sato, Seizaburo and Tetsuhisa Matsuzaki (1986). "Jiminto Rekishiteki Shori no Kaibo" [The Anatomy of the LDP's Historic Victory]. *Chuo Koron* (October).

Sato, Seizaburo and Tetsuhisa Matsuzaki (1987) *Jiminto Seiken* [LDP Administations]. Tokyo: Chuo Koronsha.

Saxonhouse, Gary R. (1979). "Industrial Restructuring in Japan," *The Journal of Japanese Studies,* vol. 5.

Saxonhouse, Gary R. (1983). "Tampering with Comparative Advantage," *Testimony Presented Before the United States International Trade Commission Hearings on Foreign Industrial Targeting.*

Scalapino, Robert and Junnosuke Masumi (1962). *Party Politics in Contemporary Japan.* Berkeley and Los Angeles: University of California Press.

Schlessinger, Jacob (1997). *Shadow Shoguns.* New York: Simon and Schuster.

Schmitter, Philippe and Gehard Glenbruch (1979). *Trends Toward Corporatist Intermediation.* London: Sage.

Schultze, C. L. (1983). "Industrial Policy: A Dissent," *The Brookings Review* (Fall) vol. 2.

Schumpeter, Joseph (1947). *Capitalism, Socialism, and Democracy.* 2nd ed. New York: Harper and Brothers.

Sheard, Paul (ed.) (1996). *Japanese Firms, Finance, and Markets.* Melbourne: Addison-Wesley.

Solow, Robert (1956). "A Contribution to the Theory of Economic Growth," *Quarterly Journal of Economics* 70: 65–94.

Solow, Robert (1957). "Technological Progress and the Aggregate Production Function," *Review of Economics and Statistics* 39: 312–320.

Sorifu (various issues). *Yoron Gekkan* [Public Opinion Monthly]. Tokyo: Sorifu.

Steiner, Kurt, Ellis Krauss, and Scott Flanagan (eds.) (1980). *Political Opposition and Local Politics in Japan.* Princeton: Princeton University Press.

Sundquist, James L. (1983). *Dynamics of the Party System,* rev. ed. Washington, D.C.: The Brookings Institution.

Suzuki, Yoshio (1980). *Money and Banking in Contemporary Japan.* New Haven, CT: Yale University Press.

Suzuki, Yoshio (1987). *The Japanese Financial System.* Oxford: Clarendon Press of Oxford.

Taira, Koji (1970). *Economic Development and the Labor Market in Japan.* New York: Columbia University Press.

Thayer, Nathaniel (1969). *How the Conservatives Rule Japan.* Princeton: Princeton University Press.

Thurow, Lester (1992). *Head to Head: The Coming Economic Battle Among Japan, Europe and America.* New York: William Morrow and Company.

Tilton, Mark (1996). *Restrained Trade: Cartels in Japan's Basic Materials Industries.* Ithaca, NY: Cornell University Press.

Trezise, Philip (1976). "Politics, Government, and Economic Growth in Japan," in Patrick, Hugh and Henry Rosovsky (eds.). (1976). *Asia's New Giant: How the Japanese Economy Works.* Washington, D.C.: The Brookings Institution.

Trezise, Philip (1983). "Industrial Policy Is Not the Major Reason for Japan's Success," *The Brookings Review* (spring) vol. 1.

Tsebelis, George (1990). *Nested Games: Rational Choice and Comparative Politics.* Berkeley and Los Angeles: University of California Press.

Tufte, Edward R. (1978). *Political Control of the Economy.* Princeton: Princeton University Press.

van Wolferen, Karel (1986/87). "The Japan Problem," *Foreign Affairs* (Winter), pp. 288–303.

van Wolferen, Karel (1989). *The Enigma of Japanese Power.* New York: Alfred Knopf.

Vestal, James E. (1989). "Evidence on the Determinants and Factor Content Characteristics of Japanese Technology Trade, 1977–1981," *Review of Economics and Statistics.* (November): 565–571.

Wallich, Henry C. and Mable I. Wallich (1976). "Banking and Finance," in Patrick, Hugh and Henry Rosovsky (eds.). (1976). *Asia's New Giant: How the Japanese Economy Works.* Washington, D.C.: The Brookings Institution, pp. 249–316.

Watanabe, Theresa (1993). "Profile Bureaucrat Breaks Mold; Author Lambastes the Culture of Conformity in His Native Japan," *Los Angeles Times* (September 28).

Weinstein, David E. (1995). "Evaluating Administrative Guidance and Cartels in Japan," *Journal of Japanese and International Economies* 9: 200–223.

Woo-Cumings, Meredith (1999). *The Developmental State.* Ithaca, NY: Cornell University Press.

Wood, Christopher (1994). *The Bubble Economy.* New York: Atlantic Monthly Press.

Yamamura, Kozo (1982). "Success That Soured: Administrative Cartels in Japan," in Kozo Yamamura (ed.), *Policy and Trade Issues of the Japanese Economy: American and Japanese Perspectives.* Seattle: University of Washington Press.

Yokokura, Takashi (1984). "Chusho Kigyo" [Small and Medium-Sized firms] in Ryutaro Komiya et al. (eds.), *Nihon no Sangyo Seisaku* [Japanese Industrial Policy]. Tokyo: Tokyo Daigaku Shuppankai.

Yomiuri Shimbunsha (1995). *Yomiuri Nenkan* [Yomiuri Yearbook]. Tokyo: Yomiuri Shimbunsha.

INDEX